The Internet and the Madonna

RELIGION AND POSTMODERNISM

A series edited by Mark C. Taylor and Thomas A. Carlson

THE INTERNET AND THE MADONNA

Religious Visionary Experience on the Web

Paolo Apolito
Translated by Antony Shugaar

The University of Chicago Press

Chicago and London

Paolo Apolito teaches cultural anthropology at the University of Salerno and at the University of Rome (III). He is the author of several books, most recently *La religione degli italiani* (2001).

Antony Shugaar is a translator, journalist, and author who has translated more than one hundred books from Italian and French, most recently Giorgio's *Memoirs of an Italian Terrorist* (2003).

The University of Chicago Press, Chicago 60637
The University of Chicago Press, Ltd., London
© 2005 by The University of Chicago
All rights reserved. Published 2005
Printed in the United States of America

13 12 11 10 09 08 07 06 05   1 2 3 4 5
ISBN: 0-226-02150-5 (cloth)

Originally published as *Internet e la Madonna,* © Giangiacomo Feltrinelli Editore Milano 2002.

Library of Congress Cataloging-in-Publication Data

Apolito, Paolo.
    [Internet e la Madonna. English]
    The Internet and the Madonna : religious visionary experience on the Web / Paolo Apolito ; translated by Antony Shugaar.
        p.   cm. — (Religion and postmodernism)
    Includes bibliographical references and index.
    ISBN 0-226-02150-5 (cloth : alk. paper)
    1. Mary, Blessed Virgin, Saint—Apparitions and miracles.   2. Internet—Religious aspects—Christianity.   I. Title.   II. Series.
    BT650 .A6513 2004
    232.91'7'02854678—dc22   200415211

⊗ The paper used in this publication meets the minimum requirements of the American National Standard for Information Sciences—Permanence of Paper for Printed Library Materials, ANSI Z39.48-1992.

To my sister Liliana

CONTENTS

TRANSLATOR'S NOTE

As the translator of this book, I found myself facing a number of challenges. One of them was to render the complexity of Paolo Apolito's ideas in English; another was to find reliable correlatives for the language, both the terms of communitary and visionary Catholicism and the terms of the online community. At one point, for instance, Apolito notes the distinction between the English terms for Web browsing that are borrowed from the language of water sports (e.g., a Web surfer) and their Italian counterparts (*navigazione, navigatore*), and considers the slightly different nuances: a surfer stays close to shore, a navigator may well be lost at sea or shipwrecked. To render this directly in English becomes paradoxical, and can only be explained in a translator's note. Here and there, the reader will find remnants of this clash, such as "browses the open Web." Open, in the sense of "open sea."

Some of Apolito's metaphors (worshipful Web surfers, archipelagoes of online visionary Catholicism, erotic shipwrecks, and so on) stem from this clash of references. Some of the other problems have to do with matching the connotations of the various terms for visionaries (there are more than one in

Italian, and I have chosen "visionary" to represent them, rather than "seer") or miracles (we do have "prodigy" as an alternate term, but I chose to stick with "miracle" for the most part).

And, finally, the passage of time from the original Italian edition necessarily means that many of the Web sites are no longer operative. I have done my best to update the URLs, but since the Web is an ever-changing universe, I would refer readers who cannot find a given site to avail themselves of the excellent resource, www.archive.org. This site offers a snapshot of the Web dating back almost a decade.

Antony Shugaar

INTRODUCTION

Laura Zink lives in Bennington, Vermont, not far from the Canadian border. She is married; she has three grown sons; and with her husband she runs a small motel. Laura Zink is a Catholic and, since 1994, she has had a series of mystical and visionary experiences. Her first vision was of a cross emerging from the moon, growing in size until it was much larger than the moon, the moon remaining at the center of the cross, like a sort of Eucharistic Host. A few months after this first vision, Laura saw the All-Knowing Eye of God and began to hear the voices of Jesus and the Virgin Mary daily. She immediately set about recording and spreading these celestial messages through the world of Marian worship. In Laura's online auto-biography, she writes that subsequently, in December 1996, as she sat at her keyboard, Jesus dictated a message announcing to her the beginning of "His Mission" on the Internet. This mission would take the form of a Web site that Laura was expected to create, with the name of *Messages from On High*. From that day hence, anyone who wished to learn what Jesus and the Virgin Mary were saying to Laura—and through her, to humanity at large—could simply type in the following URL:

http://mfoh.com. This Web site offered not only an account of Laura Zink's mystical experiences and several special messages from Jesus, but also a complete list of all the daily messages, from the very first one (17 December 1996) to the most recent one (the message of the preceding day), all carefully dated and numbered. Just click on the day or title of each message, and on your computer screen you will see the words that Jesus or the Virgin Mary dictated to Laura, along with drawings and bits of dialogue that accompany the divine communication. For instance, "Sweet thing. (Yes, Lord?) Will you write these words for Me? (Thank you, Lord? Yes, Lord?)." Then, following a drawing of two little interlocked hearts, comes the following message: "My Little one, hear Me. I speak in general terms that will reach every heart . . ."[1]

Laura Zink is not the only visionary who uses the Internet, nor is her Web site the only one that speaks of messages and visions of the Virgin Mary and Jesus Christ. In recent years, a vast number of Web sites, Web pages, links, Web rings, electronic mailing lists, newsgroups, and chat lines has offered a staggering volume of first-person accounts, documents, testimonials, messages, miraculous photographs, videos, conversations, and debates on the subject of the Catholic visionary movement.

In the wake of the great religious decline of the sixties, which had led to premature announcements of the inevitable and unstoppable secularization of society, the Catholic visionary movement—and especially the Marian visionary movement—has grown at an astonishing rate, drawing in hundreds of new seers, thousands of eyewitnesses of wondrous and miraculous phenomena, and millions of believers. This process has profoundly altered the very perception of religion among a substantial number of Catholics, shifting the course of the post—Vatican II transformation of the Catholic Church in a completely unexpected direction. Indeed, it has recreated a pre—Vatican II atmosphere, and perhaps even a full-fledged ideology of rejection and opposition to modernity.

And yet this was no return to an archaic, premodern, peasant religious practice—and indeed such a return would have been impossible. Instead, what has developed is an inextricable blend of archaic elements with elements of late modernity, practically a Catholic postmodernism. In this connection, some have identified the Virgin Mary as a sort of patron saint of postmodernism in the Catholic Church.[2] You can hardly help but see the irony of this reference, considering the rejection by believers in Marian apparitions of the more modern and enlightened attitudes of the Second Vatican Council. At the same time, it clearly captures the pervasive eclecticism that is such a distinctive feature of the Catholic visionary culture, which blends religious visions and the Internet, weeping icons and television, stigmata oozing blood and high-tech laboratories, wheeling suns and digital video cameras, mysterious clouds and futuristic telescope-mounted cameras, divinations and faxes. In other words, a wave of neo-Baroque religious belief in miracles and wonders, simultaneously combined with a massive expansion in the use of high-tech equipment and apparatus.

This new wave of religious visions has been concentrated in the more technologically advanced nations, first and foremost the United States. And in the nineties, the United States witnessed the most extensive spread of visionary phenomena and associated forms of worship. Even though the most famous and significant case in the second half of the twentieth century occurred outside this area—at Medjugorje, in Bosnia, in the former Yugoslavia—the influence of that case would be incomprehensible without some reference to the countries that ensured its success: immediately, Western Europe, and specifically, Italy; later, and to a decisive degree, the United States. If we examine the organizations and associations specifically dedicated to this apparition, the television networks and the radio broadcasters that devoted airtime to it, the strategic role played by ecclesiastics and religious institutions in the promotion of its importance, the millions of pilgrims who have visited this small Bosnian town, and the considerable sums of money that have been donated, we will find that the Madonna of Medjugorje is also somewhat European, rather Italian, and nowadays quite American.

For that matter, the fact that the world's most advanced nation in technological and economic terms should be playing a leading role in a highly technological phenomenon ought to come as a surprise to no one. While visionary culture first took root in the United States during the eighties, today the lion's share of the world's seers, messages, and visionary announcements come from the United States. America influences the rest of the world and, especially on the Internet, occupies many of the spaces that have been established for Marian visions.

To paraphrase the well-known traveling seer Vassula Ryden, if the Virgin Mary now speaks in English, she speaks it with a decidedly American accent.

In this book, while I shall not ignore the growing phenomenon of the visionary movement in its more general terms, I shall focus primarily on the role that technology plays in that growth, and especially on the advent of the Internet on the visionary scene. These developments constitute the final culmination of a process that clearly demonstrates the capacity of a religious belief based on wonders and miracles to make use of the resources of late modernity to reinforce its own stature, a stature that is certainly imbued with traditional archaic wonders but, at the same time, rich in unprecedented technological forms of "celestial signs." For that matter if, as Paul Virilio puts it, ours is a time of "generalized visualization" or "universal voyeurism," how could a religious visionary movement, which has always favored *sight* as its primary sense, fail to be attracted by the enormous potential for propagation intrinsic in the use of technological resources that results in "the amplification of the optical density of the appearances of the real world"?[3]

It is of no little importance, for that matter, in terms of the growing technological aspect of Marian apparitions, that the ideology expressed by many protagonists and theorists of the world of electronic technology and new media tends strongly toward forms of sacralizing that, on the one hand, echo an earlier technological eschatology that harks back to Pierre Teilhard de Chardin (1881–1955),[4] and on the other hand, find expression in a recent, explicit "prophetic" and "visionary" technological dimension.[5]

In the world of Marian apparitions as conjugated through technology, the traditional tension between religious belief based on the charisma of a seer or a mystic—in other words, with those who have direct relations with the beyond—and a religion that is institutionally structured according to hierarchical authority finds a sudden and unexpected punctuation, inasmuch as a more immediate and almost natural use of technological resources on the part of the seers and mystics makes it objectively more difficult for religious authorities to control and regulate things.

Still, technology does not necessarily ensure the victory of the charismatic over the institutional, of the inspired seer over the diocese attempting to control and limit the role of that seer. Technology has its own rules, procedures, and methods of operation that, unpredictably, tend to render obsolete and irrelevant the very dialectical tension between the charismatic and the institutional. The massive utilization of technological resources to verify, document, and propagate visionary phenomena winds up endowing those very resources with many of the functions and much of the legitimacy that were once the object of contention of the two antagonists. Photographs and videos of the supernatural, laboratory experiments, and finally the Internet itself tend to incorporate religious

relations, practices, and beliefs within their own procedures and mechanisms. In the end, all intentions to the contrary aside, these technological media tend to neutralize any aspirations to transcendency, though
such aspirations would seem to be the very psychological and religious
sources of the visionary culture. When they are absorbed and processed
by the technological *form*, they remain caught within a disconcerting immanence.

The technologizing of the visionary and the wondrous, in other words,
after it has weakened the institutional, tends to marginalize the charismatic, shifting the focus as it does from the "gift" of a direct relationship
with heaven to the technical structure of the procedures of vision and contact with the beyond: films, lenses, diaphragms, chips, monitoring equipment, tests, databases, CDs, DVDs, and then modems and connections
and all the rest, in order to document, preserve, prove, test, demonstrate,
and, in the end, *produce*. Despite the profound emotions that visionary
phenomena are capable of triggering, it is inevitable that the growing
centrality of technology tends to shift to a peripheral role both believer
and seer, in other words, the human being as subject of an epiphanic
experience, since the decision to document a vision also tends to reduce
the vision in question to little more than an *object*, with a corresponding
desubjectification (and commodification) of the phenomena.

And so the age-old tension, described above, transfers itself to the relationship between human experience and technology, which is to say, the
relationship between individual experience and community experience,
on the one hand, and the sacred immanence of visions, multiplied and
propagated, on the other; while the capture of much of this personal experience in turn passes within the perimeter of technology.

You should not think that technology imposes a cold and disenchant-
ing regime, despoiling and stripping of legitimacy all aspects of the sacred. There is no opposition between the sacred and technological disenchantment. On the contrary, this technology is seen by the visionary
culture as a powerful and unique resource for a new reenchantment of
the world, which produces unprecedented practices of sacralizing in relation to places and instruments, objects and persons who would not be or
are not contemplated within the context of institutional religious sacred-
ness, and would appear to be particularly incompatible with a definition
of technology as an institutional site of disenchantment. And if this reenchantment is continually undercut by the commonplace of the technical

reproduction of the phenomena, at the same time it is capable of providing an unending array of new paths and occasions for the practice of updating the sacred.

All the same, the technological sacred cannot help but be, first and foremost, *technological*. Unquestionably, technology facilitates the visionary movement, because it attests to it, and yet at the same time it reduces it to its immanence; it democratizes it, while at the same time simplifying it to the point of making it commonplace; it broadcasts the experience of direct contact with heaven—brought down to earth—and yet it subjugates that experience to the commercial and functional network of its products. Apparitions, in the era of the triumph of technology, have become diffuse, numerous, universal and, at the same time, individual; and yet they remain within the horizontal realm of technology, to which one accedes through technical and economic—not spiritual—means. Technology, by allowing and legitimizing every form of the extraordinary, winds up imposing the wonder of itself, enclosing and delimiting every other wonder within its own on/off switches.

And yet, collective orientations seem to provide evidence of something quite different. Nowadays, there is a greater willingness to believe in miracles and wonders: according to a survey conducted by the Pew Research Center for the People and the Press (Washington, D.C.), the percentage of the American public that "completely agrees" that "even today miracles are performed by the power of God" increased by 14 percentage points from 1987 to 1997, from 47 percent to 61 percent.[6] At the same time, there is a distinct tendency to reject the avowedly skeptical attitudes espoused by such organizations as CICAP,[7] in Italy or CSICOP[8] in the United States, which systematically attempt to explain miracles and wonders in ways other than by simply declaring them to be miraculous and wondrous.

Believers in apparitions (and they are not alone in this), instead, officially ask that technology, and the science from which that technology is derived, serve only to reinforce claims of miracles, to become a faithful instrument for the proof and experimental testing of apparitions and miracles in general. In reality, technological equipment does more than simply *investigate* wonders; indeed, to a considerable degree, it *produces* them. The more an instrument of investigation appears to be neutral, the more it reveals itself to be unreliable and deceptive. It is not a proclamation of scientistic or antiscientistic ideology that will swing the scale in the struggle between science and miracle, but rather the apparent neutrality of technical and scientific procedures and their pervasive influence in the way that we think and live in the contemporary world, so that an antiscientistic and antitechnological statement is already conceived and composed within a system of thought and action defined by the growing role of technology in the world.

The relationship of visionary religion and the resources of contemporary technology is, moreover, ambiguous, since on the one hand religion allows itself to be permeated, as it were, by technology, while on the other hand visionary religion also demonizes technology. In other words, the visionary dimension which is today largely technological is also riddled with an intense fear of the very resources that contemporary technology makes available, especially the resources of both new and old media. This fear joins and amplifies the more generally apocalyptic, dramatic, and catastrophist attitude that typically informs the ideology of modern Marian apparitions, from the nineteenth century to the present day. If the development of technology has aroused two emotions in Western society over the last few decades, fear and hope,[9] the Catholic visionary movement has focused primarily on the former of the two: fear.

In the United States in particular, many of the messages attributed to the Virgin Mary and Jesus—which seers and "locutionists" (people who, like Laura Zink, claim to receive messages from an invisible celestial figure) work tirelessly to spread everywhere they are able—evoke technological threats, considered as so many doors opening on an imminent and apocalyptic future. Joyce M. Lang, for instance, attributes the following warning to the Virgin Mary: "Children,—this is your technology: it will become a sword turned against you in the hands of the spirit of deceit."[10]

John Leary ascribes the following to Jesus: "Jesus said: 'My people, now you will see how your modern technology is headed toward its ruin. . . . Your modern electronic tools will trip you up because they are imperfect. Trust only in Me and you will have everything that you need.' "[11]

This seer, who works as a chemical engineer at the Eastman Kodak Company, says that Jesus has warned him against spy satellites that monitor the movements of individuals, sensors and video cameras that track people's every move, and invasions of privacy through cell phones.[12]

Others, reading from the text of Revelation,[13] fear that a technological Antichrist will attempt to implant a tiny microchip under the skin of the hand or head—especially of children in the schools—capable of controlling the personalities of its victims.

In reality, Kevin Warwick, a professor of cybernetics at Reading University in Great Britain, had a two-centimeter chip experimentally implanted in his arm in 1998; with the chip, he was able to transmit a series of electronic impulses that activated mechanisms to open and close the door of his laboratory, turn on and off lights and equipment, and so on.[14] Two years later, the mass media announced that the experiment was being extended to attain a sort of electronic telepathy.[15]

There was an obsessive insistence in visionary circles with the "computer bug" of New Year's Day of the year 2000, the so-called Y2K, the date on which it was feared that the entire worldwide system, now entirely dependent on computers, would collapse in a catastrophic loss of order and equilibrium, marking the advent of the Apocalypse. It is precisely the fear of Y2K—not limited to the world of the Marian visionary movement, but common to most of the society of the technologically developed world—that reveals how many of these apocalyptic religious fears, tied in one way or another to the unpredictable outcome of technological progress, correspond to (and may well be a reflection of) a widespread collective feeling of misgiving, if not of full-blown fear—the diametric opposite of hope, if not of enthusiasm—in relation to the technological challenges of recent years. This feeling is to be found in every social class, and crosses the boundaries of all political groups, the scientific community, the religious community, and ordinary people everywhere. The body of media production based on the technological fears of the new millennium—one of the most popular and prolific areas of endeavor—expresses this transnational lingua franca of suspicion and alarm particularly well. One especially successful film, *The Truman Show* (directed by Peter Weir), has helped, through the immense influence and popularity of the movies, to exacerbate an already common fear.

Stefano Rodotà, privacy commissioner in the Italian government, has spent many years studying and monitoring the transformations and risks posed to privacy, social interaction, and democracy itself by new technological applications. This is how he began an essay on that movie:

> Is technology killing privacy? Every member of the audience must
> necessarily leave the theater with this question in his or her mind after
> watching the movie *The Truman Show*, which describes the intrigues
> and maneuvers of a powerful central agency of espionage in turn-of-the-
> millennium America. The question is a fair one because, aside from the
> exaggerations authorized by theatrical license, the depiction of various
> techniques for the surveillance of private citizens—satellite monitoring,
> cross-referencing of financial data—is not entirely fanciful. . . . As we

wonder about the future of privacy, we are actually wondering about the
future of democracy.[16]

Our concerns go well beyond the fiction of the mass media. In 1998,
the office of Scientific and Technological Options Assessment of the European Parliament published a report on "surveillance technology" that
described the dangers of an intrusive political surveillance of the citizenry
through the use of sophisticated technology. Three years later, a special
temporary committee of the European Parliament published a report on
Echelon, a National Security Agency program for the interception of millions of individual, business, and government messages, expressing considerable alarm.[17] The introduction of the new Intel Pentium III processor
triggered great concern, in cultural and political spheres, for the dangers
of surveillance of private citizens that it entailed.[18]

In this connection, there has been a significant shift from the great
apparitions of the nineteenth century. The Catholic visionary movement
of that period took a whole-hearted, polarized position of support for certain principles against others, choosing clearly one political and ideological front and rejecting all others. Lourdes, Rue du Bac, and La Salette[19]
all served to stoke the flames of a church polemic against the "errors of
modernity": liberalism, positivism, atheism, and so on. The visions of Fatima, in turn, took on many of the same accusations and extended them
in the twentieth century, especially with the use of her prophecies in the
decades that followed 1917, against Marxism and the Russian Revolution.

In contrast, what happens nowadays, at least in the realm of the widespread fears of the expansion of the power that technology wields over
everyday modern life, is a product of globalization and the standardization
of the problems of survival. Fear of Big Brother no longer aligns one political position against another, but is felt by one and all, in an expression of
a ubiquitous uncertainty in the face of an increasingly rapid technological
progress that is completely outpacing traditional cultural, political, and
social processes.

The point of all this, at least as far as the visionary movement is concerned, is that this fear focuses primarily on aspects of new lifestyles,
the consequences of technological progress, especially visible because featured in discussion in the mass media. This fear almost never extends to
alarm over the increasingly technological aspects of religion itself, and
especially of the visionary movement. That movement makes ample use
of technological resources, to the point of constructing a technological

devotional environment, and has thus strengthened itself to a degree un-precedented in the past, and thereby radically transforming itself. There seems to be no awareness of this process, precisely because of the depth to which it has penetrated and the "naturalness" of its use.[20] Hence the failure to perceive a contradiction between the simultaneous use and de-nunciation of technology.

Let us consider television first of all.

In the visionary world, reciprocal and concordant declarations are at-tributed to the Virgin Mary and the Devil regarding the negative effects of television and the movies in the lives of the faithful. At Medjugorje, for instance, from the very beginning, in 1981, the seers reported that the Vir-gin Mary asked the faithful not to watch television because it undermined the efficacy of prayer:[21] "Turn off your television sets, turn off your radios, and pay attention to the programs of God."[22]

The Devil himself, at Medjugorje, supposedly let it be known that he was using television, threatening the seers that he would "put films in their heads," and promising, "I will give money to the people who run the television networks in exchange for broadcasting bad movies that will lead the young people astray from prayer, I will put those bad movies in the heads of the young to lead them away from the Holy Mass."[23]

And yet television has been an exceedingly powerful instrument in publicizing the apparitions of Medjugorje, which occupy a fundamental role in the present-day visionary landscape. Information about the pil-grimage, the visions, and the messages has been propagated primarily by the hundreds of television shows about Medjugorje broadcast around the world, and by the thousand of films and videos distributed to believers.

As an aside, we should likewise note the massive use of television, as well as the harsh condemnation of the same medium, in Islamic fun-damentalism: "It is well-known that the Algerian fundamentalists have given a nickname to the satellite dishes which enable their compatriots to keep the outside world in view; they call these *antennes paraboliques* [dish antennas] "*antennes paradiaboliques*," in other words, 'devil's dishes.' But this demonization does not prevent the Islamic movements, like others, from acquiring television channels or Internet sites in order to put for-ward claims to other forms of universality."[24]

On the other hand, the simultaneous condemnation of technology and its intense utilization are generally signs of the nonarchaic nature of ide-ologies that hark back to the archaic in our postmodern world. One em-blematic instance of this is found in the Neo-Luddite movement, which "tends to consider the whole technology as an evil, and yet uses email, computers, and laser printers to spread that concept."[25]

Television has been more than a mere vehicle of visionary publicity. By altering our very perception of reality, it not only encouraged the proliferation of modern-day apparitions, but also their sequence. The fact that visionaries can see the Virgin Mary day in and day out for years, as happened at Medjugorje, is nothing other than a sign of the pervasiveness of the model of daily television watching (viz., *vision*).

Now let us examine photography. Broadcast television supplied only the habit of generalized visibility, that is, a psychological and cultural background to a familiar, multiple, daily vision. Television images of the beyond, however, are relatively rare, sometimes promised but seldom delivered. The same is not true of photographs, which have proliferated to an astonishing degree in the world of Marian believers. Photography has offered an extraordinary argument in favor of equating vision with belief: "seeing is believing," writes the Web master of the Apparition of Thiruvananthapuram, India.[26] The ancient and false model according to which we should believe always and only that which we see with our own eyes has found an unimaginable level of exaltation in the context of visionary culture thanks to photography, despite the widespread understanding of the tricks, fabrications, and montages that this medium allows. On the sites of apparitions, in magazines and newsletters for the faithful, in prayer meetings organized with a seer, and finally, on the Internet, you can find an unbelievable number of "wondrous" photographs, in which lighting effects, silhouettes, and opaque objects are interpreted variously as images of Jesus, Mary, saints, angels, mystical doves, and so on. There is also a vast repertory of "true images" of Jesus and the Virgin Mary, which have been sent by—or captured without the knowledge and permission of—the celestial figures themselves, bouncing from one corner of the planet to another, resulting in a singular effect of overlapping, mingling, and syncretism, considering the fact that they are often assembled with images from the incessantly fecund world of New Age beliefs.

Compared with television, photography has the advantage of offering an image of a nearby presence that, although invisible to human eyes, appears to have been captured by the technological eye of the lens.

The power of photography, which proves overwhelming to millions of worshipers, lies in the fact that it renders general the experience of the vision, removing it from the aristocratic solitude of the imponderable celestial selection. Photography is "democratic," it excludes nobody, it eliminates all special relationships with heaven. That which has been photographed belongs to everybody, not only to whoever takes the picture. It was also the case with the traditional "true icons," such as the Veronica in Rome, that they appeared before the eyes of everyone and not only the eyes of the chosen visionaries; all the same, in contrast with those true icons, miraculous photography is not a wonder in which the social body participates collectively and which originates and is consolidated within that social body, with the added support of the ecclesiastical institution; instead, it is a product that has been carved out and circumscribed in a private, technologically constructed space. It is an object obtained through a direct relationship with heaven, not filtered through any institutional mediation, nor any charismatic mediation, but rather through the mediation of technology. Moreover, while there is only one Veronica, there are thousands of miraculous photographs, each the unique product of an individual technological relationship between the worshiper and heaven.

In truth, in a relationship with heaven characterized by this "technological democracy," there is the hidden risk of an excessive simplification, a standardization that leads toward a general banalization. Miraculous photography reduces the spiritual complexity of the relationship with heaven to nothing more than itself, that is, to the technological and material operation of a camera obscura, a film, and a series of microchips.

Like photography, video provides an active and direct tool with which to obtain a personal (or group, or territorial) miracle. It is not an uncommon occurrence to turn on a video camera and capture a miracle, which can be viewed and reviewed at will. In particular, in the case of the so-called miracle of the sun, every worshiper—if he wishes and if he owns a video camera—can bring home his own personal miracle and show it off, trade it with others, and even collect many varied miracles, from all over the world. And moreover it is in the video itself, as we shall see, that an entirely unexpected miracle can emerge.

But, first, computer graphics, and, subsequently, virtual reality are threatening to make photography and video obsolete in their capacity to offer stimuli for the world of visionaries. They offer mechanisms for the visualization of images endowed with a degree of autonomy and with their own rules, by virtue of which the images almost become full-fledged images; moreover, virtual reality incorporates the observer within its own dimension.[27] Already for centuries similar effects have been produced in the world of pretechnological visionaries, and now that world is experiencing a new growth from these recently developed resources.

Still images, moving images, images with which it is possible to interact, object-images with which it is possible to establish a relationship as if they were image-objects: a vocabulary that can be used to talk about both religious apparitions and the old and the new media of images. If we overlay the two universes, a certain lexicon nowadays remains identical. Even the objects reference one another in turn: in Garabandal, a Spanish village where between 1961 and 1965 Marian visions took place that are extremely important in the world of contemporary visionaries, the Madonna announced to Conchita a great miracle intended to encourage humans to repent of their sins. This miracle would leave a permanent sign: "The sign that will remain," says Conchita, "will be able to be seen, photographed and televised but it will not be able to be touched."[28]

All the objects on earth that have been photographed or filmed or processed through a computer can be seen, but cannot be touched. For that matter, however, a certain corporeal quality of the Madonna, still present at Lourdes one hundred fifty years ago (the Madonna spoke in dialect so that Bernadette could understand her) or at Oliveto Citra fifteen years ago (the Madonna "got tired"), tends to be reduced or to disappear entirely in a media-driven environment that feeds on pure images. It is no accident that one of the best known and most common apparitions on the Internet is the vision of Zeitoun, Egypt, in which the Madonna appears as a pure image—photographed, filmed, broadcast—atop a bell tower, standing perfectly still for days without talking, moving, or giving any sign or indication but her own image.

In a time of visionary technology, apparitions are no longer problematic but rare events (like miracles themselves), offered as a divine gift to a single person (or a few people). It is not the multiplication of the phenomena of celestial visions as much as the degree of visual technology involved which allows an ever greater number of people—potentially all of humanity—to have a physical, concrete, visual contact with heaven.

In this way, the relationship between heaven and earth passes from the ecclesiastical dimension to the technological dimension, which becomes its site of actual experience, the measure of "truth" and the model of reference, breaking sharply away from the control of the ecclesiastical hierarchy. The scientific laboratory and the technological device become the instruments with which we ascertain the "truth" of the apparitions, replacing and implicitly rendering practically useless the theological virtue of faith and the authority of the ecclesiastical magisterium. The camera or the video camera (for the vision) and, to a lesser degree, the medical and scientific dossier (for the visionaries) play increasingly important roles in all apparition-related phenomenology, precisely because they would appear to be neutral, objective, and self-evident.

In conclusion, in the visionary context, the Catholic religion, a religion of faith and nonvision, is transformed imperceptibly—but decisively—into a religion with a "scientific" basis, technologically "tested," desubjectified and self-evident, in which in the final analysis the divine is reduced to a "verifiable" sign, which is therefore reliable. One of the central proofs of the authenticity of apparitions today is the "supernatural experiment," that is, the experimental verification of the detectable effects of the manifestations of celestial entities, which then implicitly becomes the very proof of the existence of those entities.

And in the end comes the Internet. From a dependency on television, photography, and video—reinforced during the eighties, that is, in the period of a new and vigorous phase of growth of visionary Catholicism, inaugurated at Medjugorje—the world of apparitions has transitioned over the past five or six years onto the Internet, where, as we have seen, it has encountered a technological "visionary movement"[29] that cannot help but reinforce it.

The American locutionist Laura Zink first appeared on my computer screen a few years ago, while I was looking for new reports about Marian apparitions on the Internet; with the naïveté of a neophyte, I expected that the Web was little more than a simple data bank, an easy-to-access news library. I had asked a few search engines, that is, the systems for automatic research through the data present on the Web, to provide me with the latest information on the subject by tapping in the keyword "apparitions." And I was swamped by a tidal wave of hits: one day in January 1998, Excite, one of the best-known search engines, alerted me to the presence of 83,670 Web pages; AltaVista, 48,030; Yahoo, 15,831; Virgilio, an Italian search engine, 14,110. To begin would also have meant never finishing, because it was not even possible to restrict the boundaries of this ocean of data. Already, just to orient myself, even without understanding fully the structural features, the forms of the entity, required hours and hours of work at the computer. Of course, not all the Web pages had to do with apparitions of the Virgin Mary (if I tapped in the word "Madonna," instead, I would be given mostly hits related to the rock singer, with a minority of references to the mother of Jesus Christ). A few responses had to do with art Web sites, others had to do with music groups. Moreover, a good number of these pages were repetitions; others were multiple references to the same events, since search engines do nothing more than to gather together all the occurrences of the words that are being searched. Nonetheless, the results were certainly overwhelming, when compared with other terms or topics of a certain widespread interest and curiosity.

Quite soon I realized that the Web was not simply a place to find information about Marian visions. It didn't take me very long to understand that the Internet is not an online digital map of everything that exists in the offline reality: it is also a place for the organization of Catholic visionary culture, since it offers that culture an extraordinary infrastructure, making it possible to establish relationships and multiply contacts in a way that would have been unimaginable in the past. Hundreds of Web sites, with thousands of "virtual visits" to each, factors out to numbers with five or six zeros and even more. According to the claims of the Medjugorje Web site, since 1996 it has been visited more than fifteen million times. The Internet is also a place of Marian worship, since it can be used for prayer, to visit sites in a devoted manner, and to supervise ritual practices. Lastly, for worshipers it is a place of community, where it is possible to organize devotional groups, prayer groups, and visionary correspondence groups; where objects are exchanged, as well as prayers and advice.

We may think that, unlike television, video, or photography, the Internet does not encompass active possibilities for miracles. Like the telephone, for instance, it does no more than to expand the opportunities for contact, encouraging relationships; like trains and airplanes it allows visits and views that otherwise would not be possible. In itself, however, it neither produces nor does it provide proof of a miracle, in the way that television, video, and photography do in the broadest sense. In reality, this is not the case, since for worshipers, the Internet is also a site of miracles, in which heaven can be seen directly, in which heaven speaks.

Most important of all, however, the Internet is much more than a technical instrument for contacting heaven, in the way that photography or video is. The Internet is a new reality, which exists alongside the customary reality of visionary devotion, and at times in contrast with it, and more frequently, without anyone taking much notice, replacing it entirely. Unlike photography and video, the Internet makes no reference to a baseline reality outside of itself to which anyone—a bishop or a visionary, a gullible worshiper or a skeptical one, the church or a sect—can refer, invoking its legitimate representation, in the name of which one evaluates or rejects a product of technology. The Web refers to itself; the online reality that it puts into play is self-referential; every element of it refers to something else inside the Web: once a miraculous photograph makes its way onto the Internet, for instance, it refers no longer to a possible celestial entity captured by a camera in the physical place of the apparition, as it continues to do offline, but rather to the ceaseless drifting movement of and among digital images on the Web. What is more, the fact that the Web should be for a surfer a reality that disappears and reappears whenever he sits down in front of his computer screen reduces and in a certain sense eliminates any element it may have of continuity with the world outside that screen.

In this context, we can attempt to understand why photography and television do produce celestial visions, while on the Internet, at least so far, none have been recorded. As Lellouche suggests in an essay on the subject of the "screen," the photograph is still a way of rendering visible nonvisual dimensions of reality: which is to say, for a worshiper, that which is invisible in heaven.[30] But the computer screen has no need of external reality, because it produces a new, virtual reality all its own, made up of pure image: and it is exactly this characteristic—it is an immense universe of noncorporeal images—that so uniquely qualifies the Internet as an exhaustive and self-referential location for the presence of celestial figures. In other words, the Web, unlike photography, has no need for the presence of a real world beyond, because it replaces it with its own world beyond, that is, with its own virtual world: not visions of heaven, out there, but rather visions of heaven, in there.

In the world of globalized information, an image or a message enjoys universal circulation once it enters the Web; but from that moment on it will only refer to other messages, other images; it will exist only as a step in the incessant flow, immanent actualizations of the transcendence of the virtual. In a certain sense, therefore, the delocalization that is such a distinctive characteristic of the Internet extends to heaven as well, which loses its traditional geospiritual standing, and shifts into the virtual mystery of the Web. Instead of completing the process of technological immanentization of heaven begun by photography, videos, and tests, the Web shifts the transcendence from the "external" side of heaven to the internal side of it, of its virtual order: the transcendence of heaven becomes transcendence of the Web.

And so, to a far greater degree than other technological resources, the Web could potentially bring about a radical transformation of visionary culture and, as a result, Catholicism itself.

In sociological terms, then, the Web pushes inexorably toward a redistribution of sacred power among the subjects involved in the apparitions: in the first place, to the detriment of the *auctoritas* of the hierarchy, inasmuch as the speed and the omnipresence of the Web allow personal self-legitimations on the part of the visionaries and their groups of supporters, leapfrogging past the lengthy and increasingly cautious procedures of hierarchic legitimation. All the same, in a later phase even the visionaries have their prestige considerably reduced (I am referring especially to those who are already quite well known outside the Internet), their thunder stolen by Web operators, who construct the new legitimacies, and coopted by individual surfers, who make choices.

On the other hand, the process of democratization mentioned in reference to the photography and video of the supernatural reaches its culmination with the Internet. Indeed, it is now no longer limited to a regulation of the relationship between heaven and earth, on the part of the worshiper; it also allows an individual to contact any other individual in order to share his or her own visionary experience, with no further need for the filter of a local or institutional authority, but instead directly reaching into the diffuse planetary swarm of Web surfers.

Indeed, the Web especially elevates the individual surfer, to whom it attributes a context of very broad liberty, allowing him to move without any restrictions, to accept or reject, to construct or deconstruct, to remove or to insert. To him and only to him falls the choice, the selection, and the decision concerning the inspiration of the visions and the messages, the matter of orthodoxy, the tricks and wiles, the Devil and the Holy Water, since the traditional evaluation of institutional *auctoritas* finds itself relegated to the same level of authority as anyone else in the horizontal landscape of the Web, and even the visionaries cannot attain a strong and exclusive position, since they are all kept on the same level by the electronic mechanism.

In contrast, this cybersurfer, having leapt onto the bridge and having seized the helm of online navigation, will sooner or later experience a radical loss of the center—orientations, foundations, hierarchies—which vanishes, along with the periphery, the outskirts, into nowhere, by definition. In the referenceless flow of the Web, the solitude of the surfer is a prerequisite for his orientation, which cannot exist in advance, but which should develop itself during the trip. In reality, that task is rendered difficult, if not impossible, by the absence of cardinal points of direction, by the mixture and overlapping of significances, and by the weakness of the very contrast between true and false, which is replaced by the contrast between actual and virtual.[31] On the one hand, then, the Web gives the individual pride of place, while on the other hand, the individual discovers that he is weak, disoriented, and marginal: the dynamic that overtakes him is no longer focused on him, but escapes into interconnections, swerves off into the system of continuous deviations, opening out into the exciting, but also overwhelming, endless labyrinth of links.

The Web, finally, encourages overlapping and interpenetration between the sacred and other areas of our collective life, such as love, play, irony, and even in religious territories, areas of spirituality, the imaginary worlds of the mystical, to the point of bringing about a certain envelopment of visionary Catholicism, independent of, and often directly counter to the intentions of those who experience apparitions, in the vast array of omnivorous and generic strands of media-driven religion, open to the signs and the wonders of the New Age.

The Internet is hardly transparent; it resists a quick and easy reading of its content. This poses—and it is probably best to state this immediately— new problems of comprehensibility, for worshipers, as well as for the researcher. When an anthropologist enters the Web, she loses all traditional points of reference for her research. There is no longer a space-time point of reference upon which to focus her investigation: could she perhaps work back to the individual screens, the individual Web users in their homes, offices, Internet cafes? Nor are there well-defined events, in relation to which she can be an external "observer" while also being an internal "participant." The Web is a continuum without temporal punctuation or alternation, no weekdays and weekends, special occasions and ordinary times. And the Web is devoid of predetermined social categories: classes, groups, ranking, ethnic divisions. The scholar watches as subjective and planetary singularities follow their paths in accordance with unpredictable forms and idiosyncratic characteristics. In the real world, he had worked according to certain models of cultures and systems; he would match the actions he observed to those models and interpret them accordingly, locating them in the space-time continuum of his research. As a result, the specific singularity of the actions that he was recording in his fieldwork would be absorbed, in turn, as an example, an occurrence, a confirmation in the general explanatory model, from which he had begun or which he had arrived at through successive approximations. But when the scholar finds himself working on the "actualizing" paths of the Web, he can no longer easily resolve the singularity, the individual root of each event. Any typifying, grouping, or classifying that he may do runs the risk of eliminating or discarding the very singular root of the events of "actualization" or "virtualization" that are so characteristic of the Web, and thus eradicating its basic meaning. For that matter, even though the Web is largely made up of intertwining acts of communication among individuals, whether we call them navigators or surfers, nothing can prove to us that they actually correspond to well-defined identities. "Laura Zink," "Brian Alves," "Joe," "Lou," and "Adrienne" are first and foremost functions of navigation, matrices of communicative shifts, "phantoms" that no authority certifies as representing offline identities.

The Web has no dense and stable realities with respect to which the eye can be certain of finding a minimum of independence and otherness. To a large degree, the gaze that looks at the Internet is inside the Internet, in that each surfer processes and creates the reality of which the Web is formed, because of the fact that he cannot absorb the theoretical whole of the virtualizations, but only that which he himself actualizes on the screen and therefore puts into play. In other words, if a researcher goes to Medjugorje, he will be able to look at the institutions, the choreographies, the symbolisms from an external viewpoint; on the Web that researcher is necessarily inside and therefore will inevitably organize his participatory observation on the "electronic terrain," which will certainly refer him to modalities and routes waiting to be established with a dust cloud of correspondents scattered through the global information network (the Web, in the final analysis, is the global interconnection of all its users) but which is essentially based upon the relationship with the machine that provides him with all this. Therefore, he himself becomes, quite often, the very surfer that he is discussing.

Before I enter into the actual analysis, beginning with an overview of visionary phenomena around the world (first of all, outside *[hereafter silently]* the Web), I would like to offer a warning and a grateful acknowledgment.

The warning has to do with the way I use language in this book.

An anthropologist, as I previously mentioned in my first book about Marian apparitions,[32] is not required to answer the question of whether the Madonna appeared in one place or another, nor whether it is possible for a celestial entity called the Madonna actually to appear. He is not a theologian, he is not in institutional terms a worshiper, and he is not writing in a religious context. In his own private life, he has an array of choices, but he has no right or reason to discuss those matters as an anthropologist, nor is he asked to do so as a private citizen. Indeed, an anthropologist is legitimized by the scientific community to decipher human signs, not to carry out a theological investigation of the world beyond, in connection with which he has no instruments that authorize him to express opinions. He may choose between faith and agnosticism, but, since those also belong to his personal sphere, he cannot write about them as an anthropologist. It is the signs of humanity, or perhaps we should say, the signs that are recognized as valid or invalid by worshipers that authorize him to speak, those signs that constitute the context in which those worshipers see or believe in the vision of the Madonna. It is in that fully human context, based upon information and communications about the event, on languages and institutions, that the anthropologist does his work. He writes about that context. And in relation to it (and not his own personal options), he interprets, evaluates, and draws conclusions.

And all of this has a curious effect on the language that must be used. How can we report visions, locutions, prodigies, and miracles of all sorts? Scrupulous methodology would call for the use of the conditional and the subjunctive rather than the indicative—"is said to have appeared" instead of "appeared"—and for spangling the text with a succession of "allegedly," "attributed," "so-called," and so on. In truth the desire to prevent misunderstandings—which some readers have mischievously propagated for other books written in the past on the same subjects—had initially led me to use these forms to excess, and as a result the book was dull and tiresome, even to me, the author. I was obliged to recognize that evidently I am unable to write in a way that is at once conditional yet lively, methodologically cautious while literarily engaging. And so I decided to give up and make use of direct, indicative forms, when the context required it, reserving the sharply doubtful form only for those cases in which it seemed absolutely necessary, and in which it seemed to me that the writing did not suffer too greatly as a result. And so, I rely upon my reader to refrain from extrapolating in an arbitrary manner, and to understand that the overall approach has been and is one of methodological detachment. A "view from a distance."

After this warning, an acknowledgment. This is my third book on the world of visionary Catholicism.[33] The idea developed out of my curiosity about the fusion of these two visionary fields, the Internet and the Madonna. The immediate stimulus was my preparatory work for a lecture for the San Carlo Foundation of Modena in March 1998 on the relations between visionary culture and technology. I could have stopped once I had finished the lecture: research into the field of electronics is not exactly typical fare for an anthropologist, especially in Italy. But, aside from the general pleasure of studying the subject, if I did continue, it was essentially for two reasons. First, because my students and a few colleagues to whom I had spoken of this project displayed a curiosity and an interest that pushed me to continue; secondly, and above all, because William A. Christian, Jr., to whom I am deeply indebted, was so generous in his encouragement, advice, and discussion, rendering a little less solitary my adventures as a surfer through the cyberspace of Marian visions.

Chapter 1

APPARITIONS ON AND OFF THE WEB

The Proliferation of Apparitions

Joseph Reinholtz, a retired railroad employee, lived in a suburb of Chicago, Illinois; he had suffered from serious vision
problems since 1980. In 1987 he went on a pilgrimage to Medjugorje. Here the visionary Vicka Ivankovic laid her hands
upon him, during prayer. After Joseph returned home, his
sight gradually improved. The first thing that he saw clearly
was a statuette of the Madonna that he had at home—and the
statue was weeping. Two years later, Joseph went back to Medjugorje; before he returned to Chicago, Vicka told him that,
once he was back home, he should look for a crucifix that he
would find next to a tree with three branches; he should spend
time praying near it. Back home in Chicago, Joseph Reinholtz
set out in search of a crucifix with the requisite features, and he
found it at the Queen of Heaven Cemetery, in Hillside. He began to go there every day to pray. On 15 August 1990, as he was
praying near the crucifix, Joseph Reinholtz saw the Madonna.
In November of that year, he saw her a second time: this time
the Madonna was accompanied by the Archangel Michael and

by other saints. The apparitions then began to take place daily, except for Fridays (in the meantime, the archbishop of Chicago, with whom Joseph was in contact, had asked him not to go to the cemetery on Fridays). Sometimes, Joseph would see, along with the Madonna, also Jesus, Saint Joseph, and other saints. But he was chiefly familiar with the Madonna. One day, he even took a ride in the country in a car, with her and a pair of angels. The car was driven by Pat, a woman who helps Joseph organize prayer meetings; the Madonna sat in the front seat, between Pat and Joseph. The angels sat in back. Joseph told Pat—who was excluded from the celestial perceptions—what the Madonna was saying, and together they laughed until tears came to their eyes. They thought it was hilarious that the Madonna should be so curious to ride in a car, and her naïve comments made them laugh loud and long. On the way back into town, suddenly the Madonna disappeared, though still visible were the two angels sitting on the back seat, their heads between their hands, pressed against the rear windows. Suddenly Joseph saw the Madonna descending from heaven, and she came to a halt on the hood of the car. The visionary told Pat to stop the car immediately, because he was afraid that the Madonna might come to harm in the busy traffic; he admonished the Madonna rather sternly, "Don't frighten me like that. I love you too much."[1]

The story of the visions experienced by Joseph Reinholtz, one of the 393 apparitions reported around the world between 1980 and 2000, is emblematic in more than one way. First of all, it took place in a country, the United States, where there were only 21 reports of apparitions in the thirty-five years between 1945 and 1979, while in the twenty years from 1980 to the present, there have been more than 150. Moreover, this occurrence was closely connected with Medjugorje. Lastly, on the one hand, sophisticated communications technology was crucial to the diffusion of this report; and on the other hand, it was evocative of themes and motifs of a devotional ingenuity that hint at a general reenchantment of the world, produced within the context of the "disenchantment of technology." We should give some thought to each of these aspects.

Let's take them in order, starting with the number of apparitions. There are a variety of calculations of the number of Marian apparitions in different periods of time: throughout the Christian era, over the last two centuries, in the twentieth century, in the period since World War II, in the last thirty years, and so on. The numbers generally fail to correspond from one calculation to another, even for the same periods of time. In reality, the number of alleged Marian apparitions cannot be counted with any precision. What, indeed, would we count? The number of reports of visions? If we chose that criterion, then, paradoxically, we would have to include as well the reports of people who had been diagnosed, and even treated, for mental illness, either following or simultaneous with their claims of visions. Then should we take into account only those people who have generated a following, in the hope that this would rule out cases of personal hallucinations associated with psychotic states? Perhaps, but there is no guarantee that a positive social response rules out the risk of psychosis. Should we then restrict the count to the number of visions accepted by the church? If we were to do that, then we would drop over the last two centuries to fewer than fifteen approved visions, and we would exclude such famous cases as Medjugorje and Garabandal. Should we restrict the cases to those under investigation by the ecclesiastical authorities? If we do that, of course, we would run the risk of including events under investigation not because there is a fairly plausible case, but to the contrary, because the local church is hoping to use a negative finding to eliminate the "confusion" among their worshipers in the wake of the supposed apparition. In cases of that sort, the investigation is undertaken primarily in order to produce a condemnation. We would instead exclude those cases upon which the church is maintaining "silence and reservation," even though it might consider them with a secret positive interest.

And so what should we do? Our calculation of the number of apparitions takes into account the sole criterion of the renown of the event itself. Reports of apparitions that succeed in attracting the notice of public opinion and maintaining it for some period of time can be included in the statistics. No traces remain of any others. It is inevitable that in the contemporary world this would be a result, primarily if not exclusively, of the possibility of gaining access to the mass media: the press, radio, television, and finally the Internet. A more homogeneous distribution of the mass media certainly encourages the spread of reports of apparitions, since the network that produces the facts deemed worthy of becoming news, sifting them from less noteworthy facts, is denser wherever there is a more concentrated network of newspapers and radio and television broadcasters, more diffuse and locally articulated.

There are at least three conditions required for reports of events of this sort to come to light: first of all, as we said above, an effective media network. In the second place, sufficient freedom of information for the report to be published. For instance, it is probably fair to assume that there were more actual cases of visions in Communist Eastern Europe than the statistics would suggest. We can safely assume that the news media—as well as the general state of repression—under Communist regimes offered no play to events of this sort. Third, a context that would encourage diffusion of the report. A network that selects the news reports that will be published does not determine the degree of interest or irrelevancy of a report of an apparition in a vacuum; the report is evaluated in relation to specific cultural and historic conditions. In postwar Italy, for instance—as in the rest of Europe during the cold war[2]—there was certainly a remarkable proliferation of visions. The great emphasis attributed to episodes of this sort, however, traced its basic justification to the context of the tension and conflict between political and ideological affiliations prior to and following the elections of 18 April 1948: even minor and insignificant cases were given play in the press that they would not have received ten years later or ten years earlier.

Taking these considerations into account, there have been almost seven hundred cases of Marian apparitions worldwide between 1945 and 2000.[3] Some claim that there have been a far greater number; mention is made of nine thousand cases of presences or cults springing from Marian presences around the world.[4] In reality, however, if we limit the count to the relatively famous and notable cases, that number is grossly excessive. If, on the other hand, we are referring to the visionary or paranormal experiences of worshipers, the number might be far greater, even approaching the millions. In fact, my research activity consists of a continuous sampling of a submerged continent of prodigies and reenchantments of the world, an anonymous and diffuse visionary territory, from which a few hundred especially famous cases emerge. Let us now take a closer look at the numbers.

If we put together the numbers for the developed Western world (North America, Western Europe, Australia, and New Zealand) between 1945 and 1999, out of the total of 692 cases worldwide, we find 538 come from these areas, equal to 77.7 percent. Those areas accounted in 1970 for 51 percent of the world's Catholics, while in 1987 they accounted for 40 percent,[5] and in 1997 for 37 percent.[6] We see, then, that the number of apparitions does not correspond to the worldwide distribution of Catholic population, since it is clearly linked to the strength and freedom of information about and within the Western world with respect to other areas (Eastern Europe, Asia, Central and South America, Africa, the Middle East). The information that circulates throughout the world is primarily of

Western origin, and therefore concerns primarily the West, though there are significant differences from country to country.

The sources concerning apparitions are also primarily Western. Aside from the well known publications by Billet and Laurentin,[7] and Hierzenberger and Nedomansky,[8] there are now Internet sites that present lists and compilations: *Major Apparitions of Jesus and Mary*,[9] managed by James and Rosemary Drzymala and Michaela Dasteel, from Buffalo; *Messages from Heaven—the Apparitions of the Virgin Mary*,[10] whose Web master is Bryan Walsh; *Marian Apparitions of the 20th Century*,[11] administered by the Mariological Society of America; The Marian Library/International Marian Research Institute, administered by the University of Dayton, in Ohio; *The Index of Apparitions of the Blessed Virgin Mary*,[12] managed by David C. Van Meter, a Catholic scholar in Utica, New York; and, in Italy, the List of Marian Apparitions on the Web site *Profezie per il Terzo Millennio*, whose Web master uses the pseudonym "john smith."[13]

The statistics in the chart shown below are taken from the sources mentioned above, as well as, in a few outstanding cases not considered by those sources, from my own personal archives.

I shall limit myself to a few observations.

First, the sharp decline in phenomena of this sort in the sixties and part of the seventies was, according to some, a result of the repressive attitude of Cardinal Ottaviani, the prefect of the "Holy Office."[14] In reality, however, it can be laid to complex religious and pastoral policies on the part of the mother church and the local churches, which all expressed a change in the perception of popular worship with respect to the flourishing growth of the visionary experience in the years immediately following the Second World War: As *La Civiltà Cattolica* editorialized in 1988, "Even the ecclesiastical authorities begin to manifest, toward the end of the fifties 'some degree of hesitation and concern in the face of the reemergence of certain clear-cut exaggerations in the Marian cult.' "[15]

And so, in the words of Wolfgang Beinert, "the excesses of Catholic devotion to the Virgin Mary (due in part to anti-Protestant motivations), which perhaps reached their apex during the papacy of Pius XII, gave way during the sixties to a vast silence, heavy with embarrassment."[16]

In reality in those years two processes were attaining maturation after taking root over the preceding decades, especially outside Italy: a growing "Marian minimalism"—which had however always considered its adversary, devotional maximalism, a pawn of Rome and the Vatican, which culminated in a more sober doctrinal evaluation of the Virgin Mary in the

Table 1. Alleged Marian apparitions around the world, 1945–1999

Apparitions	Total	Western world	Western Europe (excluding Italy)	Italy	USA	Canada, Australia, New Zealand	Rest of the world
1945–1999	692	538	155	166	170	47	154
(%)	(100)	(77.7)	(23.7)	(23.9)	(24.5)	(6.7)	(22.2)
1945–1979	299	242	100	109	21	12	57
(%)	(100)	(80.9)	(33.4)	(36.4)	(7)	(4)	(19)
1980–1999	393	296	55	57	149	35	97
(%)	(100)	(75.3)	(14)	(14.5)	(37.9)	(8.9)	(24.6)
1945–1949	68	58	29	27	1	1	10
(%)	(100)	(85.2)	(42.6)	(39.7)	(1.4)	(1.4)	(14.7)
1950–1959	103	89	32	49	5	3	14
(%)	(100)	(86.4)	(31)	(47.5)	(4.8)	(2.9)	(13.5)
1960–1969	52	41	15	17	4	5	11
(%)	(100)	(78.8)	(28.8)	(32.6)	(7.6)	(9.6)	(21.1)
1970–1979	76	54	24	16	11	3	22
(%)	(100)	(71)	(31.5)	(21)	(14.4)	(6.5)	(28.9)
1980–1989	200	138	38	37	49	14	62
(%)	(100)	(69)	(19)	(18.5)	(24.5)	(7)	(31)
1990–1999	193	158	17	20	100	21	35
(%)	(100)	(81.8)	(8.8)	(10.3)	(51.8)	(10.8)	(18.1)

Vatican Council II, and an urgent demand that the incipient ecumenicalism not be hindered by a form of devotion that often appeared to verge on idolatry, at least from the point of view of other Christ-centered religions.[17]

William Christian has rightly noted that, in general terms, over the past two centuries:

> Church sympathy for visions has waxed and waned. It waxed in the mid to late nineteenth century (the model was La Salette and the Lourdes), the mid-1930s (the model was Lourdes), the late 1940s (the models were Fatima and Lourdes), and the 1970s and 1980s (the models were Fatima and Medjugorje). The needs of the church periodically overcome its suspicion of lay revelation, and particular popes have been more sympathetic than others. But there also exists a cyclical dynamic of discouragement that emerges when visions threaten church authority or become commonplace.[18]

At any rate, in the eighties, the "great silence" came to an end: a period of extraordinary visionary activity began, producing four times as many apparitions as during the sixties. In order to understand this phenomenon, which cannot be attributed to a single cause, but rather develops out of the intertwining of a complex array of social and religious transformations, we must obviously keep in mind the new shifts in ecclesiastical politics, including the 1978 election as pope of a Marian, Karol Wojtyla—by no means a development of secondary importance—but also changes in religious sensibility. Enzo Pace emphasizes a "long-term tendency," originating with the Vatican Council II, leading to the rediscovery of a "community church," and above all to a new appreciation of "charisma" in terms of the institution as a new foundation of faith.[19]

There is a general picture, which we might term "epochal," in the context of which these changes should be placed. The collapse of the ideologies of progress which, despite all their limitations, ensured a conceivable future; the overwhelming saturation of information—the unforeseen consequence of the proliferation of the instruments of communication and information networks; a generalized disorientation due to the absence of the cardinal axes of development and progress on account of the increasing complexity and fragmentation of social, economic, and scientific structures; the rapidity and unpredictability of change, and, in general, the crisis of the concept of "modernity," have all resulted in the weakening of the very idea of the future and a reduction of the vista to the present. The great diffusion in the Christian world of Pentecostalism, "une culture religieuse du présent,"[20] is in religious terrain a signal of the centrality of the "present" in the sensibility of the contemporary collective.

In the Catholic sense of the sacred there has been an orientation of the religious sensibility toward the immediate, toward the existential quest for a sacred that could be experienced immediately, in the present and no longer in waiting, no longer postponed to indecipherable future scenarios. In visionary Catholicism, this sensibility has found expression in the spread of mystical and visionary ways of life, perceived as no longer exceptional but simply as normal relationships with a heaven that is no longer distant and impenetrable in its mysterious transcendence, but instead immanent, present in myriad signs and experiences; it has also found expression in the expectation of an imminent end of the world, in new and ancient beliefs and ways of thought, which all have to do with the crisis in the conception of the future, taken as a plan. Apparitions, therefore, have become a valuable tool for the actualization of the sacred.

In this, oddly enough, they were well ahead of the more recent interplay, on religious ground, of virtualization and actualization, so characteristic of the "virtual," which we shall consider, with Pierre Lévy, below.

Moreover, in the profound uncertainty of contemporary life—ancient certainties dissolving suddenly, with no new clearly configured certainties to replace them; an enormous expansion of knowledge that has removed more certainties than it has created; a hypercomplex and fragmentary world, split up among the hundreds of possible "descriptions," whether scientific, political, or religious; an exponential and cacophonic prolifer-ation of "instructions for use"; handbooks, encyclopedias distributed in supplements, guides on "everything you need to know to . . ."—a loqua-cious Madonna, who speaks every day, more than once daily, in hundreds of places, referring to herself from one place to another around the world, even though she contradicts herself from time to time, has offered a hope for a larger protective scheme, a protective scheme that indicates to wor-shipers a line, a direction, an orientation, outside the slower, traditional, abstract pastoral orientations and in the exciting context of miraculous events, with "undeniable" cosmic signs, prophecies, healings, and mira-cles of all sorts.

The proliferation of Marian manifestations, in conclusion, wound up creating a mechanism of reciprocal confirmation, since if on the one hand visionary epidemics were once—and for the most part, still are today—discouraged by the church, currently every new phenomenon establishes itself precisely in virtue of having been a reprise of so many other reprises currently underway, that is, a new case of a form of proliferation that is reminiscent of the iterative models of advertising, in contrast with the relative exceptionality of the old-time apparitions.

In the background, moreover, is the phenomenon that Pace identifies in the spread of post—Vatican Council II Catholic movements, especially the charismatic movement, and that is, the reinforcement of individual-ism in the Catholic religion. Indeed, these movements have appealed to the widespread individual desire for a religious experience that constitutes a personal contact with the divine. As a historian of Protestant Pentecostal movements in Latin America puts it, nowadays "the worshiper and the pastor speak with God, not about God."[21] Contemporary apparitions show, in their "democratic" and mass proliferation and diffusion, a demand for individual experience of the divine and the sacred epiphany. And there-fore it is no accident that a noteworthy role in this process of actualization of the sacred should have been played precisely by the process of "Pente-

costalization" of large sections of the Catholic world, "placing in a central
position the individual and his possibility of experiencing the sacred."[22]

As is well known, the Pentecostalization of Catholicism began in the
United States as early as the sixties, and spread almost immediately to
Europe.[23]

> The most evident formal characteristic consists of a specific style
> of prayer, to a large degree borrowed from classical Pentecostalism,
> admittedly with some differences in emphasis. The charismatics tend
> to address the Holy Ghost, by whom they wish to be possessed in
> order to obtain their gifts, their "charisms," such as that of speaking
> in unknown tongues. In their meetings they address one another with
> their baptismal names, they embrace, they kiss one another, they sing
> and play musical instruments.[24]

The most distinctive characteristic of the neo-Pentecostals is the
"charism" of healing. In the United States there are exceedingly famous
neo-Pentecostal healers, who also work via television. In 1973, at Notre
Dame Saint Mary, in Indiana, the Dominican friar Francis McNutt established a full-fledged operation, the Healing Service.[25] In Italy, there are
well known charismatic priests of the Rinnovamento dello Spirito, such
as Father Emiliano Tardif, who recently died, or Father Betancourt; they
are (or were) able to attract tens of thousands of people to their meetings,
eager to receive cures themselves or to witness the healing of others.

It is interesting to note that, within and behind the best known Marian
apparitions of the present day, we will often find charismatics. Especially
in the United States, many of the contemporary visionaries are members
of charismatic groups or have participated in healing masses, such as
those held by Tardif and Betancourt. In the final analysis it is not surprising that, in the context of charisms, it is possible to move from speaking
in unknown tongues or the healing of incurable diseases to seeing the
world beyond.

Concerning the relationship between charismatics and apparitions,
the little-known prehistory of Medjugorje is emblematic. In May 1981
there was a meeting in Rome of Rinnovamento dello Spirito. Among the
participants was Father Tomislav Vlasic, who shortly thereafter was to become the parish priest of Medjugorje. Father Vlasic, during a ceremony,
asked that a prayer be said with laying on of hands upon him for the "healing of the church," because he felt that he was growing increasingly pes-

simistic about the future of his own parish ministry. During the prayer, Sister Briege McKenna, who had the gift of "a healing ministry," mystically saw him seated as an officiant in a church, surrounded by a vast crowd of people. Behind his seat, in her vision, there was a stream of water pouring out of the altar. At the same time, Father Tardif heard a voice meant for Vlasic: "Do not fear. I am sending you my Mother." The apparitions began a few weeks later, in June.[26] The career of many contemporary visionaries passes through the charismatics and through Medjugorje. For instance, Agnès-Marie, in France, entered the charismatic world in 1988, and in 1998 she went to Medjugorje, becoming a visionary in 1999.

A second interesting element emerges from the general data: between 1945 and 1979 there have been 299 cases of apparitions, 80.9 percent of which were in the Western world. We can note that this percentage is greater than it was for the same area throughout the entire period from 1945 to 1999 (77.7 percent). This is a statistic that, in keeping with the hypothesis of the positive relationship between the number of apparitions and the degree of development of the media network, can be explained with an increasingly homogeneous distribution of news from the rest of the world as we move forward to the present time, in correspondence with a steady improvement in the world communications systems. In other words, in the fifties, sixties, and seventies, there would have been more apparitions in the Western world only because the reports of apparitions coming from the rest of the world were spottier than they became in the decades that follow. And in fact the numbers for the seventies confirm this trend: only 71 percent of the apparitions (that is: of the reports of those apparitions) come from the Western world, as opposed to the 79 percent and the 86 percent of the previous decades. And in the eighties, the decline in the Western world's share continued, dropping to 69 percent.

But in the nineties, the Western share suddenly shot up to 82 percent of the total, with a thirteen-point increase, and in that increased share no less than 63.2 percent involved cases that had taken place in the United States: a hundred episodes, more than half of the cases in the whole world, to which we must add a countless assortment of cases insufficiently famous to make their way into the statistics, but important enough to be mentioned in the mailing lists.

In reality the aggregate Western statistic for the nineties is partly misleading: in that decade, in Europe and in Italy, as well as the non-Western world, the phenomena declined drastically from the previous decade; in Canada, Australia, and New Zealand they increased by a third, but the boom, more than doubling in number, is found in the American phenomena, which rose from the forty-nine of the eighties—four times as many as in the previous decade—to a hundred in the nineties. How can we interpret these numbers? The improved and more homogeneous worldwide distribution of news mentioned above was expected to consolidate the previous trend of a decline in Western numbers over the course of the years, as information systems progressively improved around the world—if you will, taking into account also the percentage decline of Western Catholics in the context of the world as a whole. For that matter, if we observe the percentage progressions for Europe and Italy, we see a steady decline, even when, in the eighties and nineties, there are absolute increases over previous decades. Let us compare, in particular, the statistical progressions of America and Italy—Italy being one of the largest Catholic countries.

How then can we explain this growth in American cases, both in terms of percentage and in absolute numbers (I am not considering in this context the data for Canada and for Australia and New Zealand), of a phenomenon that seems to have reached its peak in the exceptional decade of the eighties?

Let us begin by noting that many American visionary phenomena develop in the context of communities with long-standing Catholic cultures, such as Arab Christian communities or Latin American immigrant communities. But it would be wrong to circumscribe the expansion of the phenomenon to these communities, because the most famous American cases do not come from those communities. Moreover, if the phenomena in question were merely expressions of marginal ethnic groups who discussed them in their exclusive isolation, the media would not have given them the remarkable treatment that in fact they have, causing dozens of television and radio broadcasters, and hundreds of print journalists, to attend the announced apparition in the sky over Lubbock, Texas, in 1988, or, before a crowd of many tens of thousands of people, the latest supposed message of the Madonna to Nancy Fowler in Conyers, Georgia, in 1998. Or the appearance of the Madonna on the covers of *Time* and *Newsweek*, and on the front pages of the *New York Times*, the *Los Angeles Times*, *USA Today*, and so on.

"The Virgin Mary's influence has spread well beyond the bounds of Catholicism," claimed Elaine Gale of the *Los Angeles Times*, in late 1998, and "a growing number of Americans of all Christian denominations is turning to the Virgin Mary as a comforting spiritual guide and a symbol of peace in turbulent times."[27]

Table 2. Alleged Marian apparitions in Italy and the
United States, 1945–1999

Apparitions	Italy	USA
1945–1949	27	1
(%)	(39.7)	(1.4)
1950–1959	49	5
(%)	(47.5)	(4.8)
1960–1969	17	4
(%)	(32.6)	(7.6)
1970–1979	16	11
(%)	(21)	(14.4)
1980–1989	37	49
(%)	(18.5)	(24.5)
1990–1999	20	100
(%)	(10.3)	(51.8)

And so the interpretation that traces these phenomena back to marginal groups gives little or no explanation of this enormous growth.

We can certainly state that it was not so much an increase in the actual number of phenomena, as an increase in the space accorded to them by the media. Many will remember that the nineties began with *Time Magazine* devoting its front cover to the subject of Marian apparitions. That, however, is just another way of posing the same question. In fact, why should the media have devoted so much space to these phenomena, if not because they expressed a new collective sensibility, in the West but especially in the United States, with a rising temperature marked by the interest from marketing? In fact, given the growing popularity of the Virgin Mary, Gale told us, her image was commercialized in many ways: reproduced on purses and bags, surfboards, T-shirts, shower curtains, lawn ornaments, bumper stickers bearing the legend "Eat, Drink, and See Mary," and more.

But even if we identify the mass media and marketing as two fundamental engines driving the process of epidemic diffusion, expressing and reinforcing a widespread sensibility in a circular manner, like all social phenomena of a mimetic nature, still we cannot overlook the fact that the growing popularity of the Virgin Mary is one of the most significant signals of a number of far-ranging cultural and political transformations.

In the United States, the decade of the eighties began with an extraordinary organizational and political growth of fundamentalist religious forces, which gave rise to the New Religious-Political Right (NRPR), a coalition of all American conservative forces of the Christian religion, which favored the election of President Ronald Reagan.[28] The religious spirit has always been important in the history of the United States. But in the eighties, taking full advantage of the crisis of the progressive ideologies of the previous decades and the spread of electronic technologies, the fundamentalist and conservative component of the American religious world took on new visibility and power in the civil and political life of the nation. This was the decade in which the disconcerting phenomenon of televangelists, who had created immense fortunes by exploiting the trust and expectations of miracles on the part of millions of television worshipers, reached the height of its development, under the protective wing of President Reagan.

This fundamentalist movement had come into existence and had slowly consolidated in the seventies:

> The great political and religious movement that began in those years has
> proven increasingly capable of linking the activity of thousands of small
> churches, certain congregations that were even liberal at one point, and
> open to cultural secularization, the charismatics of all confessions, and
> the grassroots political structures of the conservative right. Its most
> powerful weapon was the electronic technology through which it was
> possible to create an enormous marketing structure linked to a diverse
> array of economic interests, lobbies, and sources of political power.
> Its strength lay in its strategic ability to join together heterogeneous
> and even contradictory groups and currents, into a single cohesive
> force, present and militant in a myriad array of specific interventions,
> committed to creating a new cultural landscape, the mass hegemony
> over the religious imagination.[29]

In that period, then, a cultural landscape was established within which phenomena that were considered miraculous and which were associated with religion were no longer thought of as relics of the past or irrational ravings. To the contrary, this invigorated form of fundamentalism, aside from its demands that the Bible be interpreted literally and be considered infallible, was quite open to miracles and wonders. Many televangelists were—and are—believed to be capable of healing, from nearby and from a great distance; to be continually in contact with God and with his representatives; to foretell apocalyptic events through prophecies or interpretations of the Bible. In Roberto Giammanco's words, the fact that fundamentalist ideology, beliefs, and precepts should circulate extensively "on television in all possible formats, appearing in an avalanche of promotional publications solidly established on the market, in thousands of sermons and in the speeches of politicians, is an indication that in the past decade [the eighties], the components of the ruling model of the American imagination have undergone a major reformulation."[30]

Relations between Protestants and Catholics have never been particularly good in the United States, and therefore we should not imagine an automatic expansion of the fundamentalist Protestant religious framework to Catholicism. It is true, all the same, that the first steps of American Catholic neo-Pentecostalism, between 1966 and 1967, took place precisely in meetings with American Protestant neo-Pentecostals, and that, aside from the religious and organizational structure of the two movements, the encounter was also encouraged by the shared idea of the imminent return of Christ, that is, the millenarianist Second Coming,[31] which in the Catholic world found its greatest resonance in the apparitions of Garabandal, Spain, not coincidentally in the sixties. In any case, if there were sharp divisions on the theological and doctrinal plane, and the divisions were unquestionably stark—suffice it to consider the role of the Madonna, for instance—in terms of conservative political benefits, there were numerous reasons to work together, culminating in April 1994 in a document, *Evangelicals & Catholics Together: The Christian Mission in the Third Millennium*, which gathered the more conservative sectors of both religious camps.[32] Aside from any tactical coordination, then, the favorable ideological terrain that had developed in America favored all antimodern religious revivals.

It is therefore understandable that in the Catholic world as well such a cultural shift should have found a response in the more conservative sectors and should have translated into a new sensibility, which in turn found its most distinctive expression in an intense flourishing of the visionary movement. For that matter, over the last two centuries, the visionary movement has almost always gone hand in hand with an intransigent religious and political conservatism.

What was needed, however, was an occasion and an instrument to catalyze this new sensibility. And that was provided by Medjugorje, the village in Bosnia which was the site of the most famous Marian apparition of the

second half of the twentieth century, thanks to a powerful publicity campaign that, after it won over the devotional public in Europe, and especially
in Italy, took the United States by storm.

Medjugorje

Every case of apparition that has attained a certain level of renown has
soon produced a sort of visionary "epidemic" in the surrounding territory.
It happened in the past at Lourdes, it happened at Fatima, and it happened
in Belgium following the apparitions of Beauraing and Banneux, in the
years 1932 and 1933, which in the year 1933 alone produced twelve phenomena of imitative visions.[33] In the case that I studied in considerable
depth, at Oliveto Citra, a small town in the Salerno area, I was able to
observe that, following the phenomena that occurred there, there were
imitative events in nine other towns in the surrounding area[34] (none of
which, however, is counted in the statistics presented above, due to their
brief duration and the scant attention they were given on a national Italian
scale). In general, precisely this sort of epidemic phenomena provokes the
"skepticism" and "perplexity" of the most critical Catholic observers.[35]

In the case of Medjugorje, however, we are in the presence of a more
complex phenomenon. Here the epidemic effects have gone well beyond
the territory of the country of Bosnia, though they were powerful there as
well.

Unquestionably, the growing importance of the mass media played a
part. By turning the world into a "global village," the mass media were
able to shift the epidemic echo effect of Medjugorje not merely beyond
the local context, but even outside the national boundaries. This Bosnian
village was the first site of visionary Catholicism to make significant use of
the effects of globalized information and communications: once the first
news reports began to spread, this new dimension of communications
immensely enlarged the scale of the events' renown, grafting in highly
effective publicity mechanisms. With Medjugorje, we are dealing with
one of the most powerful publicity campaigns ever conducted around a
religious phenomenon, as was noted from the very beginning, and from
the interior of the ecclesiastic world, when *La Civiltà Cattolica* remarked,
diplomatically, on the "impression" that there might be "a publicity campaign, very well organized on a grassroots basis."[36] In the few years that
followed, with the coordination of the Franciscan Center in Steubenville,
Ohio,[37] a veritable flood of books, articles, videocassettes, film clips, radio

and television programs, and even educational pamphlets about how to found prayer groups based on the apparitions, poured first into the European countries that are traditionally most open to these phenomena, such as Italy, France, Germany, Spain, and Ireland, and then on to the rest of the world. In Italy especially promotional committees and prayer groups sprang up everywhere. In Gera Lario, Radio Maria, a Catholic radio network with over eighty stations broadcasting throughout Italy, specialized in the propagation of messages about the apparition and in the production of news reports. There was a general proliferation of "Medjugorje" newsletters, some of which were simply mimeographed; others, properly published. The Italian periodical *Eco di Maria*, which is now published in fifteen different languages and has a print run of 800,000 copies, was the first. A broad-based and amazingly rapid diffusion of reports about Medjugorje was undertaken in many parishes, in prayer groups, in religious sites. It became possible to receive the latest daily message of the Madonna, translated into your own language, a day or two after it was announced in Medjugorje. Paid advertising even began to appear.[38]

Over the course of the years, as the number of pilgrims ballooned frantically, the impact of the propaganda grew as well. Not only did it make use of an increasingly sophisticated and efficient structure, but it also relied upon the millions of pilgrims who, once they returned home, worked in what seems to have been a largely spontaneous manner to spread the word, founding new prayer groups and local newsletters, at times—especially in the beginning—making use of the worldwide organizational network of the Franciscan order.

There developed a thriving market for more or less official travel agencies that even today work almost exclusively on trips to Medjugorje, providing all-inclusive package tours for individuals or groups, for brief visits or extended stays. Many of these agencies offer private audiences with the visionaries or with Father Jozo Zovko, one of the monks who have been most active in supporting the apparitions (and in producing nationalist Croatian propaganda during the war in Bosnia), and who—despite the fact that he has been suspended *a divinis* and expelled from the order—continues to play a fairly prominent official role, sanctioned by the sanctuary of the Queen of Peace,[39] as well as to travel around the world in support of the apparitions.[40]

The statistics concerning the arrival of masses of pilgrims verge on the unbelievable, like all the statistics concerning this remarkable mass phenomenon. The most conservative number for the first ten years, which is to say up to 1991, when war broke out in Bosnia, ventures no higher than ten million, but some speak of seventeen million[41] while others declare there were nineteen million.[42] Although there were far fewer pilgrims during the fighting, the flow continued and resumed with renewed energy after the peace treaty. According to the *Medjugorje Press Bulletin*, which every fifteen days supplies on the Internet the number of pilgrims, we know that in the first few months of 1998 there were 303,500 communions, and in the month of May alone, 107,000 communions, with 3,248 officiating priests. In the entire year of 1997 there were 1,020,000 communions with 25,762 priests. Even though Father Ivan Landeka, the former parish priest of Medjugorje, emphasized in the *Bulletin* that "what we do not need on these occasions are spectacle and numbers,"[43] there seems to be a sort of obsession with counting and statistics. We are informed that there were 29.31 percent more pilgrims in 1997 than in 1996 and that there was a further increase in 1998. Father Landeka himself hoped that the numbers could regain the level of 1990, a good year from before the war. In reality, this obsession with numbers seems to be common to all sites of apparitions or prodigies, since the ecclesiastical approach that is adopted in the face of all claims of miracles is a reference to the evangelical tree that can be recognized by its fruit. This is how Cardinal Ratzinger, prefect of Congregatio Pro Doctrina Fidei (Congregation for the Doctrine of the Faith), responded to a question from Vittorio Messori on these issues:

> One of the criteria we have adopted has been to separate the aspect of a genuine or alleged "supernatural" quality of the apparition from the aspect of its spiritual fruit. The pilgrimages of ancient Christianity were directed toward sites about which our modern critical approach might be somewhat perplexed in terms of the "scientific authenticity" of the tradition that attaches to it. This does not mean that those pilgrimages were not fruitful, beneficial, and important to the life of the Christian people. The problem is not so much a matter of modern hypercriticality (which, among other things, can turn into a new form of credulity) but rather a question of the evaluation of the vitality and the orthodoxy of the religious life that has developed around those sites.[44]

An evident example of this ecclesiastical logic can be found in the well-known Roman case of Our Lady of Tre Fontane. In 1947 Bruno Cornacchiola, a former Adventist, claimed that he had seen the Madonna. His declaration became the basis of a cult. The apparitions were never recognized by the church; as for the cult, however,

> when the cardinal vicar of Rome (whose office it is to perform episcopal functions in the name of the pope, representing him officially) said Mass in the spring of 1987 at Tre Fontane, he never said a word about the apparition, which is not officially recognized at all. There is an official recognition of the cult, but not of the supernatural character of the apparition. We need to keep these nuances in mind if we are to appreciate the generous liberty which the church advocates in the area of apparitions.[45]

The same kind of "generous liberty" was at work in the imprimatur with which the bishop of Cochabamba, Bolivia, authorized the circulation of the books of Catalina Rivas, a visionary who had received stigmata, and who published the messages that the Virgin Mary and Jesus had supposedly entrusted to her to tell the rest of the world. In the text of the imprimatur, there is a reference to the seriousness and orthodoxy of the books, their clear intention to lead the faithful toward an authentic spirituality, and a recommendation of the books "como textos de meditación y orientación espiritual," but there is not the slightest reference to Rivas's claims that they are a collection of authentic celestial messages.[46]

One important instrument of propaganda for Medjugorje consists of the trips that the visionaries and priests of the organization make around the world. A single example of an extremely crowded calendar, which includes the seers, the priests who work with them, the theologians, and all the other supporters who—under whatever heading—have been transformed into propagandists for Medjugorje: the visionary Ivan Dragicevic, who now spends six months a year in the United States, in October 1997 began a trip that ended in late January 1998, which took him to Indiana, California, Washington state, Colorado, Oklahoma, Texas, Illinois, New Jersey, Oregon, New Mexico, Florida, Ohio, Minnesota, Delaware, and Maryland. Two months after his return from the United States, Ivan flew to Ireland, as well. We should keep in mind that during these meetings the Bosnian visionary continued to have his visions, which therefore took place in the presence of tens of thousands of people who had gathered to see him. Here is what a Vietnamese worshiper wrote about another trip that Ivan made to the United States: "I had the greatest joy and privilege to be there, when Our Lady visited Ivan Dragicevic in the Seattle Center in March 1999. I want to consecrate the rest of my life to the propagation of Our Mother's messages and God's Love to the Vietnamese Community."[47]

On other occasions, it was visionaries inspired by Medjugorje who had their own visions in Ivan's presence: at Marmora, in Ontario, on 27 September 1992, Véronique Demers was the fourth person to see the Madonna in that site since multiple visions had begun on 27 July. Her vision took place during a lecture that Ivan delivered to an audience of twenty thousand.[48]

Aside from the travel around the world of visionaries and monks from Medjugorje, voyages by bishops and cardinals to the Bosnian sanctuary played an important role. Again, from the *Press Bulletin* we learn that between 1997 and 1998 Medjugorje was visited by numerous high-ranking ecclesiastics from Canada, New Zealand, Australia, the United States, Brazil, Mexico, and Ireland.

That there was also a noteworthy presence in the mass media is demonstrated by the fact that major publications, such as *Newsweek* and *Life*, devoted their covers to the phenomenon of apparitions; Western television networks broadcast documentaries and interviews; popular programs in the United States such as *Unsolved Mysteries* and *Inside Edition* continue to investigate the supposedly inexplicable phenomena; a movie was even made on the Medjugorje story, called *Gospa*, with Martin Sheen and Michael York; the *Compton's Interactive Encyclopedia* in CD-ROM wrote about it in the new 1998 edition.

Now let's look at the Internet. If as of this writing we look for mentions of Medjugorje on the Internet, the search engines provide staggering numbers of relevant pages: Google, 40,100; Lycos, 27,723; HotBot, 15,000. Clearly, Web sites about Medjugorje are numerous and popular. One of the most important sites, Medjugorje Web, according to Van Meter, has received since 1996 more than fifteen million hits.[49] The list is lengthy, and includes various languages: French, German, Polish, Portuguese, Korean, Hebrew, and, the largest in absolute numbers, Italian and English (from both the United States and United Kingdom). And it is impossible to calculate the number of Medjugorje links, which is to say, the connections to other Web pages present in the Web sites of the world devoted to the Madonna and her apparitions or even in other types of Catholic Web pages. If we consider that throughout the world, but especially in the United States, there are now thousands of personal Web pages put together by Catholic devotees of the Madonna, and that each of those Web pages unfailingly has a link to some Medjugorje Web site, then you can guess, however vaguely, at the circulation of this information on the Web. By means of these links and their echoes in various discussion groups, mailing lists, newsgroups, and chat groups, the monthly messages of the Madonna are diffused in at least thirty languages. The phenomena of this small Bosnian town can also be found as links in Web pages devoted to the paranormal, the occult, all sorts of mysticism, interreligious prophecy, and religious syncretism.

Last, we should keep in mind that often it has been precisely at Medjugorje that, for the first time, miraculous manifestations were either announced or legitimized that subsequently spread around the world on the sites of apparitions, clearly modeled on those of Medjugorje: from crosses of light to sun miracles, from miraculous photographs to inexplicable healings, from perfumes and voices to transformations of rosaries made of various materials into gold. And, also at Medjugorje, in an epidemic outbreak whose numbers are once again astonishing, hundreds and perhaps thousands of nuns, priests, monks, and simple worshipers had their first mystical experiences of small or large visions, locutions, or minor perceptions, inaugurating their visionary careers, once they returned home.

Medjugorje has been and continues to be the target of ferocious attacks, on the Web as well. It has generated far more conflict and tension, some of it internal to the Catholic world, than Lourdes or Fatima. Medjugorje has regularly laid itself open to doubts, criticism, and denunciations in the midst of the violent disagreements that arose almost immediately between the visionaries and monks and the episcopal see of Mostar (which issued more than one condemnation of the apparitions, later reiterated by the Yugoslav Episcopal Conference, culminating in 1996 with the armed kidnaping of Bishop Ratko Peric, who remained for about fifteen days a hostage of the monks of Medjugorje).[50] An embarrassing Croatian nationalistic characterization that attached to the conflict emerged primarily during the war, producing an ambiguous overlapping of the flows of money for the civilian population from worshipers and international assistance, with the flows of money for the Croatian military and paramilitary groups.[51] All the same, Medjugorje's continuous presence in the international media, be that only as the target of criticism and attacks, has helped to increase its fame, confirming in the eyes of the worshipers the authenticity of the apparitions, which has been reinforced rather than diminished by the debates (triggered, in their view—in a cosmic and historical vision of events—by the Devil and his followers).

In conclusion, the "territory" of Medjugorje upon which its epidemic impact acted and continues to act is in fact the entire Catholic world, as well as parts of the Protestant, Orthodox, and New Age worlds.

In the decade of the seventies, which is to say, before Medjugorje (whose phenomena began in 1981), there were 76 cases of apparition throughout the world: 11 in the United States, 40 in Europe (16 of which were Italian), and 25 in the rest of the world. If we move up to the eighties, the number of cases leaps to 200, 75 of which are European (37.5 percent)—37 of which were Italian (representing 49.3 percent of the European cases)—while there were 49 cases in the United States (24.5 percent), 14 in Canada, Australia, and New Zealand (English-speaking countries in the developed world), and 62 in the rest of the world (31 percent). There was an increase everywhere, but among the Western nations, the most substantial increase was in the United States, followed by Canada and Australia. Among the European nations, the sharpest increase was in Italian cases, from 40 to 49 percent of all cases on the continent, followed by Ireland, Spain, and Germany.[52] It is well known that Medjugorje had immediate and powerful penetration in Italy in particular; I have already noted that the *Eco di Maria*, the first newsletter, was Italian. In 1984 in Milan, the Comitato Medjugorje was founded and began publishing the newsletter of the same name. It was quickly followed by other similar committees in numerous cities in Italy, with other newsletters. Communities and prayer groups sprang up, engendering all sorts of experiences and activities. I shall not list the dozens of local and national television programs, the articles in newsweeklies and daily newspapers, the radio broadcasts. Among the Italian apparitions influenced by Medjugorje, I shall limit myself to mentioning the apparition of Pescara (1988), where the visionary Maria Fioritti and her spiritual advisor, Don Vincenzo Diodati, announced astounding celestial signs on 28 February; despite the prohibition of the local bishop, a huge crowd assembled, only to be disappointed when no supernatural phenomenon materialized. The case, which was reported in the most important Italian dailies,[53] developed out of a large parish pilgrimage to Medjugorje, with the participation of seven hundred worshipers.[54]

But if there was growth in America in the eighties, there was an explosion in the nineties. In confirmation of the general declining trend in the West, over the last decade there have been only 37 cases in Europe (19.1

percent), with 20 cases in Italy (and of those, however, 12 were linked to an "epidemic" of weeping images), 21 in Canada, Australia, and New Zealand, 35 in the rest of the world (18.1 percent), while in the United States there were 100, equal to almost 52 percent of the cases in the world.

Medjugorje had by this point landed once and for all in the United States, and the effects were immediately visible. At the end of the eighties and in the early nineties, numerous associations and organizations were founded in order to spread the messages of Medjugorje: for instance, Caritas of Birmingham, an organization that two or three times a year distributes a magazine with the monthly messages of Medjugorje (220,000 copies); or Come Alive Communications, founded in 1988 in Linwood, Pennsylvania, which distributes "miraculous" photographs of Medjugorje; or Gospa Missions, founded in 1990 in Evans City, Pennsylvania, with twenty-two regional offices in the United States and other offices in Croatia and Africa. Many of these organizations were founded by someone who had made a pilgrimage to Medjugorje. That was the case with the Queen of Peace Ministry, established in 1988 in California, which organizes an average of fifty pilgrimages a year to Medjugorje and distributes *Echo of Mary Queen of Peace*; or the Behold Thy Mother Prayer Center, founded in 1992 in Austin, Texas, by Tom Collins, a Protestant lawyer who converted to Catholicism after a trip to Medjugorje.

A research project by the Marian Library/International Marian Research Institute on Marian organizations in America[55] was based on a list of eighty-one Marian associations, which replied to a questionnaire. Of those eighty-one, no fewer than forty-six were directly oriented toward apparitions and twenty-three were oriented principally to the apparitions of Medjugorje.

As of this writing, nearly all these organizations have Internet sites, such as Medjugorje in America, developed in Massachusetts to "promote the important messages of Medjugorje which are an extension of the messages of Fatima," and which has two Web sites[56]; or Bright Light, Inc., founded in Michigan, "and inspired, and called to service, by the messages of the Blessed Virgin Mary."[57]

As informative as the numbers may be, it is worth exploring the stories that underlie many of these American cases.

Joseph Reinholtz, the visionary in Chicago described at the beginning of this chapter, is not alone in having had a vision linked to Medjugorje. An American worshiper, John Spink, warned a number of correspondents of a mailing list who were critical of Medjugorje that questioning the authenticity of that phenomenon could produce a "domino effect": "If Medjugorje is of the devil, then that means, (following this same logic) that all the other visionaries who began receiving private revelations immediately following their pilgrimages to Medjugorje are of the devil as well; Nancy Fowler, John Leary, Carol Ameche, Estella Ruiz, Gianna Talone . . . throw them all out!"[58]

And indeed:

1986. Veronica García was a young drug addict in trouble. While still in this condition, she decided to make a "skeptical pilgrimage to Medjugorje." And it was there that she began to receive messages from heaven. After she returned home to Denver, she had more visions in the sanctuary of Mother Cabrini, where another woman, Theresa, also a visionary after a pilgrimage to Medjugorje, witnessed visions and received messages.

1987. Brother David, a thirty-five-year-old Franciscan, came to Medjugorje from Weslaco, a small town in Texas; he received from the Madonna a message concerning an imminent divine warning: the famous three days of absolute darkness on earth, with catastrophes to punish the sins of humans. At first, Brother David was unwilling to spread the message, but following new apparitions in San Antonio, Texas, in which the Madonna admonished him and gave him unquestionable signs of her will, Brother David began to spread the word.

Also in 1987, Father Spaulding, from Scottsdale, a suburb of Phoenix, Arizona, led a group of young people on a pilgrimage to Medjugorje. A few months after they came home, nine of them, along with Father Spaulding himself, began to receive messages from the Virgin Mary. A prayer group was organized, meeting weekly and receiving messages from the Madonna and from Jesus, who appeared to provide "lesson[s] on . . . subject[s], like humility, compassion, pity, and greed."[59]

A few years later, in 1993, a visionary from the group, Gianna Talone, moved with her new husband, Michael Sullivan, to Emmitsburg, Maryland. The move had been requested by the Madonna herself, who continued to appear and to give messages to Gianna in her new location; there the visionary founded a prayer group and senior citizen assistance organization called the Mission of Mercy.

1988. From Phoenix, a man went on a pilgrimage to the Bosnian village. His wife, Estela Ruiz, mother of seven, decided not to go with him because—to use her own words—she was more "interested in beginning a career after raising seven children." But the Madonna visited her in that very period, while her husband was away at Medjugorje. At first, she was only a voice that said to her "Good morning, daughter," but after her husband returned home, the voice was transformed into a presence and the Madonna appeared to her, along with Jesus.[60]

Again, in 1988, from Lubbock, Texas, a pilgrimage organized by a priest, Father Joseph James, set out for Medjugorje. Three of his parishioners, a few weeks later, began to receive messages and to have visions. On 15 August of the same year, roughly twenty thousand people gathered before the church of Saint John Neumann, in Lubbock, awaiting a sign that was to arrive from heaven. Many would later testify that they had seen signs in the sun and other celestial signals.

It is still 1988. Lena Shipley was at Medjugorje, in the church of Saint John, on 18 August, when she received her first message from Jesus. She went home to Waterloo, New York, where she began to receive regular messages from Jesus and then, beginning in 1991, from the Madonna as well.

We move on to 1989. Alfredo Raimondo, in Tickfaw, Louisiana, receives an apparition of the Madonna, who asks him to gather the faithful to say Mass in honor of Saint Joseph. Roughly ten thousand people assemble, and many of them declare that they have seen prodigious signs in the sun, while others say that they saw Jesus, the Virgin Mary, and Saint Joseph; a few claim to have received messages from them. Raimondo explains that these miraculous events are the result of the fact that the Madonna was contented that so many people from that area had gone on pilgrimages to Medjugorje.

This testimonial dates back to 1989 as well: the daughter of a California woman, Patricia Soto, was in the hospital; inspired by a book on Medjugorje, Soto asked for help from a prayer group that had formed around the apparitions of the Queen of Peace. Two weeks later her daughter, fully recovered, went to Medjugorje and, since she had "never had the opportunity to go to Medjugorje," it was "Our Lady [who] brought Medjugorje to me." When her daughter returned from Bosnia, Patricia began to receive messages from Jesus and the Madonna.

Let us stop here, at the dawn of the explosive nineties.

At first, the visionaries of Medjugorje had reported a message from the Madonna according to which the apparitions that they had received would be her last appearances on the earth.[61] Those years are now in the distant past. Nowadays, the visionaries instead seem to stimulate new cases of apparitions or to legitimize with their presence new events in places that had previously been sites of visions. After the example of Ivan, which we mentioned above, here are some others: in Belo Horizonte, Brazil, the Madonna appeared to Raymundo Lopes for the first time in 1992; but when he saw her again, in February 1993, the seer Marija Pavlovic from Medjugorje was present to offer her support.[62] Then, the following month, in New Zealand, in the Medjugorje Peace Center in Auckland, while another visionary from Medjugorje was speaking to thousands of worshipers, miraculous phenomena were seen in the sky: effects of the light of the sun—spinning and leaping—once uncommon but now quite usual, apparitions of colors, and finally the manifestation of the Madonna herself.[63]

Aside from the vast mass of information that I have only partly reproduced here, it is my belief that Medjugorje provided, through its visibility and legitimizing effect, a horizon of possibility for a certain kind of visionary and mystical religious sensibility that began to take shape between the end of the seventies and the beginning of the eighties and, as we have seen in the United States, not only in Catholic communities. The unexpected power and impact of the publicity, the decisive role played by the media, who institutionalize everything that they cover, the expansion of consensus to include even respected ecclesiastical figures and theologists familiar to the mass market of press and television—all these factors progressively imposed upon the general public the unquestionable existence of a landscape of "facts" that were considered to be prodigious and were presented without subtlety or caution, suggesting in an increasingly emphatic manner the idea that these things could recur anywhere. The enormous numbers that revolve around the event, the pilgrims and the gadgets, the communions and the videos, the miraculous events and the package tours have created over the course of a few years "a shared understanding" of a reality that merged in a nonchalant manner technologies and visions, cell phones and conversations with the other world, intercontinental travel and travel on the astral plane, increasingly accurate weather reports and increasingly spectacular miracles of the sun. And all this, by now, everywhere: on the far side of the video screen or on the far side of the ocean, or on this side of ocean or screen, in one's own home or at the neighbors'; in books written by or about great mystics of past or present and in one's own diary, letters, or videotapes. And so, after the passage of just a few years, the worlds of the here and now and the world beyond have changed radically, are no longer so sharply separated, but are much more interactive, superimposed, and confused.

In a period when the Madonna did not appear very often—say the sixties—visionaries who attempted to share their own experiences would be eyed with anything but devout curiosity, or even shunned or intimidated. Only those willing to brave a collective skepticism would publicly admit having had visionary experiences. And it was unlikely that anyone would interpret certain confused or unclear perceptual phenomena in visionary terms. But when those experiences became "normal," common, and in some case authoritatively confirmed—and I am speaking of the eighties—then plausibly the number of people would grow who were willing to report their own visionary experiences, as would the number of people who interpreted their own confused perceptions by making use of the well organized vocabulary of the "signs from heaven."

Scott O'Grady was an American fighter pilot who, on 2 June 1995, parachuted from his airplane, shot down over Bosnia during the NATO intervention there. For six days he remained in hiding, until he could be rescued by his fellow soldiers. He returned home and was welcomed by President Clinton as a war hero; his adventure was widely covered by the world press. There were immediate reports of a mystical experience that he underwent during his days in hiding, though there was some embarrassment and reticence in the coverage of this story. He had had a vision of the Madonna of Medjugorje, as the pilot openly stated in an interview that he gave to Anne Ryder, of *Medjugorje Magazine*. O'Grady had heard of Medjugorje before shipping out for Bosnia, from a friend of his mother who had gone there twice on pilgrimages. Then, his airplane was actually shot down very close to there:

> I prayed to Mary, Our Mother, on the first day I prayed to all the saints,
> even to my grandparents and to my aunt. I said to them: "If you are
> in touch with the Lord Our Father up there, get me out of here." But
> I also prayed to Mary, My Mother, and she appeared as [at this point,
> he pauses] . . . it's something else and I don't know how to explain it
> in words. It was not as if I was seeing someone walking in the forest,
> but as I was praying I saw Our Lady of Medjugorje. I don't know how
> to explain it. It wasn't my imagination, I don't know how to explain it.
> It was as if I could see her, but I saw her through my emotions, I don't
> know how to explain, it was a feeling of goodness and peace like nothing
> I had ever felt before. The whole time I perceived a positive vision as if
> she had actually been present.[64]

In conclusion, to put it in simple terms, or even to put it simplistically, it is not in a Buddhist's cultural and psychological baggage to describe having seen the Madonna; it may be tucked away somewhere in the baggage of a Catholic of the seventies, but on the whole, it is not something that that particular Catholic would be likely to do; a Catholic of the eighties would have an ample array of baggage and even the predisposition to express his or her confused impressions and sensations with the clearly defined vocabulary of visions. This baggage and these customs became disproportionately widespread in the United States in the nineties.

But I would be missing a central point if I overlooked the fact that this new sensibility, predisposed toward visions and miracles, has been given an exceptional boost by the possibility that it could provide a setting for suffering, an expression of grief, that is usually limited in contemporary societies.[65] Many visionaries and worshipers have entered this new world through the path of personal grief or the grief of their relatives, a grief that would have remained mute and undeciphered in hospitals, hostels, in the places of contemporary suffering, in the home, among the ordinary people caught in the vice grip of the pain of living. Instead, in these new settings, grief and pain are talkative, they are communicated and heard. Pain becomes an experience, which is of course still coded but no longer indecipherable, thanks to the categories of meaning that the visionary culture offers. Without necessarily offering a long list of cases of visionaries who began their charismatic careers in the wake of serious personal illnesses or the illnesses of family members, or the even more numerous cases of worshipers who turned to the world of the visionary movement in hopes of obtaining healing for themselves or for others, this section can conclude with a single emblematic experience: that of Audrey Santo, or perhaps we should say, the experience of her mother, Linda Santo, from Worcester, Massachusetts.

Audrey Santo, who is now twenty years old, has been in a coma since she was three, after she hit her head in a fall at the edge of her family's backyard swimming pool in 1987. But to her family and to a growing number of worshipers, Audrey is a "victim soul," which is to say, a soul that has taken upon itself the sufferings of others, who ask her to intercede with the Madonna and God for mercy: "Many miraculous things have happened around her . . . bleeding hosts (there are 4 in the Santos' home, in a tabernacle in Audrey's bedroom), weeping statues, pictures, images that weep oil and/or blood, healings (both physical and spiritual) . . . it really is incredible! Dorothy."[66]

The visionary history of Audrey began when her mother, Linda, took her, already in a coma, to Medjugorje, to beg for her recovery. There was no miracle, but Linda continued to hope. In the theater of devotion of Medjugorje she reinterpreted the absence of recovery, producing an original account. It was not that there had been no miracle cure; instead, the miracle had been much greater than a simple recovery: at Medjugorje, Audrey had communicated directly with the Madonna and had taken on the role of "victim soul" for the physical and spiritual sufferings of others.[67] Since then, Audrey, whose story appeared in 1998 on the front page of the *New York Times,* gradually grew to become the center of a spectacular cult organized by her mother, who involved thousands of worshipers from around the world, beginning from the suffering of a little girl and a mother and transforming itself into a place for the expression of the suffering of thousands of people.

The New Visions

Thanks to Medjugorje, then, it became possible and in a certain sense easy to believe collectively that this or that story, this or that circumstance, this or that piece of "proof"—and even this or that confused personal perception—were celestial signs. What had been hidden away, abolished, opposed in the sixties, had become normal and was taken for granted in the eighties and nineties; the kind of normality that is considered typical of unusual times. And the exceptionality of the times was proved, in a circular manner, by the normality of the apparitions, according to a widespread belief. Mike wrote to his correspondents of the *Marian Discussion* group, "There have never been times like this before in the history of man. . . . With the exception of when Christ himself walked our earth, there has [sic] never been the manifestations in healings, conversions, natural manifestations, supernatural manifestations."[68]

The same thought is expressed by Bryan Walsh, one of the best known Marian Web masters on the Internet: "To make her messages heard, God has permitted an unprecedented display of her presence. With spinning suns, televised appearances, thousands of healings, millions with renewed faith and other phenomenal signs, Mary wishes everyone on earth to know and acknowledge the message she brings."[69]

A particular form of knowledge has developed, based on a readiness to interpret phenomena that are not commonplace, but at times can be quite ordinary, as signs—and in some cases fairly straightforward, uncoded

signs—from heaven. In the area of visions, especially, the ability to interpret in a celestial sense perceptions of all sorts becomes crucial. From this
has emerged a hermeneutics of the perception of the supernatural, which
needs to be learned, exercised, and explored. Leaving aside the question of
visions as a gift that the world beyond chooses to endow upon a human being, selected for unknowable reasons—Bernadette or Maximin, Jacinta or
Lucia—there is the development of another type of perceptual experience
as an activity that one learns to perform in the context of the devotional
social group, which does not strictly coincide with the "strong" vision of
the Madonna proper to the best-known visionaries, but which has more
to do with perceptions that may even be weak, indirect, ambiguous, and
in some cases questionable.

It should be pointed out immediately that in this "weak" experience,
the vision or the perception is increasingly independent of the recognition of a celestial subjectivity that freely chooses, since it is based on "objectively" perceptible things and signs, in a world in which the divine is
experienced in immanent terms, although within the context of signs of
an increasingly technological nature.

A reenchantment of the world, then: once we accept the idea of the
daily presence of the Madonna and, along with her, the presence of an array of other celestial and infernal figures, who reveal themselves through a
variety of channels, it becomes an equally daily experience—and not only
for visionaries, but for all worshipers—to identify otherworldly presences,
manifesting themselves in countless forms. To see and to speak with the
Madonna, as the "strong" visionaries do, is the highest degree of the reenchanted world. But it is also possible to have only an interior locution or to
hear voices, see images, have dreams of celestial figures, take miraculous
photographs, smell aromas, hear sounds, glimpse shadows, have premo-
nitions, or take many other steps along a descending array of miraculous
experiences which are also, generally speaking, decreasingly dependent
on the instruments of technology. Visual contacts with the Madonna or
Jesus can be of various kinds: "in person" or in an image, or through shadows, silhouettes, lights, or backlighting. In contrast with tradition, there is
not therefore a church, a grotto, a mountain, a sky, or a tree where they appear. Instead there are windows, doors, chimneys, sidewalks, floors, walls,
pieces of furniture, plates, glasses, bathrooms, parlors, bedrooms, hospitals, shops, garages, soccer fields, streetlights, car dashboards, puddles,
or even, still quite untraditional, plates of spaghetti, tortillas, buns, cakes,
pastries, pizzas, pieces of fruit, and, quite frequently, rose petals, Band-

Aids, and finally television screens, videotapes, and an indescribable array of photographs, obtained in every imaginable manner.

Even the techniques of the visions are manifold and often unprecedented for the visionary movement. For instance, in Quincy, Illinois, there is a tree in the Calvary Roman Catholic Cemetery, upon which two to three thousand visitors a day, according to the Web site that reports on it, have been converging since spring of 1988 in order to exercise their ability to glimpse a hidden image inside a clearly visible image. This technique is closely reminiscent of the one that is used to look at three-dimensional posters. The difference is that in Quincy, it is necessary to learn to perceive it upon a tree, instead of in a drawing. Once you are well trained, you will see an image of Jesus carrying a baby lamb in his arms: "It takes a few minutes for some people to see the image, but for others the image is apparent immediately."[70]

Those who cannot see, as we have mentioned, can often hear celestial voices that are physically separate, like Georgette Faniel of Montreal, who hears and can distinguish the voices of the Holy Trinity;[71] or like Father Gobbi or Laura Zink, voices that are heard with all the clarity of "a radio," or a "tape recorder," or with the brusque authority of "dictation." And these voices flow, almost as if to continue the miracle, onto the keyboard of a computer and then online onto the Web.

The traditional scents of roses, violets, celestial essences have not entirely vanished from the areas around the sacred places, or from the visionaries themselves, the charismatics. Nor have the stenches, signals of the presence of the devil, which are sometimes detected in places of visionary ferment.

But what should be emphasized is that, in comparison with a few years ago, this reenchantment of the world is not based primarily or solely upon the exceptional powers of the charismatics or the visionaries, but more and more upon the wide-scale use of technological instruments: "In this re-enchanted world, divine messages by fax can be dialed by 800 numbers, and followed on cable channels. Polaroid instamatic pictures and videotapes capture luminous signs in the sky," says William Christian, Jr.[72]

The reenchantment, then, was directed toward technological resources, investing them and being invested by them. A distanced universe of archaic beliefs, implications of religious symbolisms, surfacing once again in the visionary world, has acquired a common-sense credibility through a technological restructuring, and it has established itself in this historic phase of extreme complexity of systems of life and knowledge as a response to the widespread demand for simplification. It is as if, in the face of the obscurity of the world, the transparency of technological procedures, enlivened by archaic symbolisms, transformed and readapted, provided a new and powerful panorama of significance, offering an explanation for things and a general sense of reassurance. The reenchanted world no longer allows any unknown spaces, no unexplored territories, since it lends itself entirely to a system of interpretation of phenomena in terms of a technological recognition of celestial signs and an equally technological practice of actualization of the sacred. Everything is envisioned in a mixed worldview of archaic beliefs and technological common sense: no new discovery, no event can ever hope to challenge the solidity of the technological and mystical interpretation.

Technology is based on automatic processes and necessary results. Everyday life is carried on to a great degree amid the use of this or that technological device, and we are thus accustomed to mechanical and mindless relationships with things and with people. And so there is a transition, notable but not overwhelming given the multiplying array of technological, mechanical, and mindless habits, from the technological control of our relations with the things and the people of this world to the technological control of our relations with the world beyond: photographs, videos, laboratory tests of the afterlife, and finally the Web, which in turn stands ready and willing to envelop the world beyond within its precincts.

The vocabulary of apparitions makes increasing use of technological and media-related references, metaphors, and terms. Television, as we shall see, more than any other technological medium, is central to the accounts that seers and visionaries offer of their claimed contacts with the world beyond. The "interior locutions," after all, can be listened to "like a radio," for Laura Zink;[73] the noise that heralded the vision of Bruno Arditi, near Pescara, was that of "a jet plane," and the vision slowly took shape like "a computerized image."[74]

As for the world of the imagination, it would be impossible not to see a powerful link with the imaginary world of the media, which is made use of in contemporary life frequently, casually, and repetitively. And this is evident even to the more critically minded worshipers themselves. For instance, it was clear to Bernadette, who—in the mailing list *Messages from Heaven*—put forth some reservations, and some self-criticism, toward the generalized visionary fervor of 13 October 1998 in Conyers, Georgia, when thousands of people saw lights, the sun spinning, and other miraculous astronomical phenomena: "We are indeed weak in our faith and looking

[in the appointments that Maria offers us] for a 'Hollywood' type of production," declared one Web-site message[75]

Or to Michael Coppi, a generous promoter via Internet of messages
from numerous visionaries, who makes the following comment upon a
passage from a message by Joseph Reyes: "He tells of the Warning, the
Antichrist, and Signs. But at times he seems to go off on a tangent speaking of how the Ark of the Covenant artifact will be found and brought to
a specific Church he goes to in Virginia (hmmmmm, maybe too many
Indiana Jones movies)."[76]

For that matter, the imaginary world of the media in turn makes such
frequent use of religious themes—suffice it to think of the proliferation
of movies in which there is an apparition of Jesus[77] or the Madonna,[78] but
especially films with apocalyptic themes—that the exchange and overlapping of images and symbols from one area to the other are quite customary and reciprocal. We should emphasize that the two imaginary worlds,
especially where the apocalyptic theme is concerned, may be interconnected but at times they are ideologically different: one, the religious
world, is more oriented toward an idea of the end of the world that arrives fatalistically by cosmic decree; the other, the media world, is more
based on an apocalypse triggered by human error and therefore avoidable,
through scientific skill and personal heroism: the umpteenth reformulation of the American myth of the frontier hero.[79] But this difference of
ideological landscape, while it may not be total, nor devoid of contradictory areas of overlap, does not limit the exchange, the mutual references,
and the mingling of imaginary worlds.

Finally there is a correlation between that which has always been considered theoretically possible in Christian cultures, that is, a direct and
even physical contact with celestial figures, and that which in the media-
oriented technologies is possible day after day, that is, a direct contact,
at a distance, that is vocal, auditory, via images, and virtual, with people
at greater or lesser distances and with events that are more or less real:
it is the same cultural and psychological environment that legitimizes
and practices, on the one hand, interhuman contact through the media
and, on the other, contact with the Madonna. It is hardly surprising then
that the two types of contact, in a strongly technologized environment,
should wind up becoming merged and confused in the unreflective practice of many worshipers, and that the latter of the two should be validated
by its recent technological "possibilities," thanks to which the terrain of
the contact with heaven has even expanded, no longer limited to specific

persons—saints, charismatics, "strong" visionaries—but now available to
everyone who uses technology.

And it is precisely here that we find the source of the extraordinary
power of the technological media: in the expansion of their range of communication with heaven, in conveying the age-old contact between heaven
and earth within their own jurisdiction.

In a context in which the power of the technology of audiovisual documentation and worldwide interconnection allows everyone to appropriate equally celestial images and sounds, it becomes less and less important whether those images and sounds and documentation are obtained
through one's own resources or through the intermediation of others. Obviously, it is the Internet that has most helped to eliminate once and for
all the differences, to iron out the variations: I myself may have taken a
miraculous photograph upon the hillside of Podbrdo at Medjugorje, but
if that is not the case, I can have that photograph appear on the screen of
my personal computer with the click of a finger. In general, what the Web
allows to the worshipful surfer is an immersion in an audiovisual environment where he can perceive the world beyond, from angelic voices to
the voice of Padre Pio, from Marian images to the images of Jesus in the
galaxy, from prophetic messages to the messages of the visionaries. Knowing the source of such events and portents is not particularly important: on
the Web what counts is that the surfer stops, captures ("actualizes," as we
shall see) a moment of the flow, appropriates that moment, and makes use
of it. Where it comes from is much less important, especially since that
appropriation appears to be very easy and at the same time miraculous.

The confirmation, then, of visionary experiences is no longer limited
to the context of those experiences themselves and of the visionary culture that feeds them, but it finds a powerful ally that supports and reinforces them in the new media. They constitute a background of shared
understanding, habits, physicality, and trained perceptions, a legitimation to think and believe over which loom the visionary phenomena.
Each of these, once they have been reported and discussed, constitutes an
"emergence" that hooks up with other emergences—other astonishing
phenomena—and altogether they form the network of the phenomena
that are "evident" and acknowledged of the presence of heaven on the
earth, which support and are supported by the enormous anonymous
visionary world of the new technological devotion. The experience of contact with the world beyond—which, though it was neither rare nor unique
in the past, is still considered an emblem of the exceptional—nowadays

tends to be fairly normal for those who live in the context of technological
and visionary references: millions of "miraculous" snapshots, thousands
of recorded "voices," and an incalculable increase in the number of video-
recorded miracles of the sun:

> Dorothy, you should have come yesterday! BEAUTIFUL July 13th cel-
> ebration (anniversary of 3rd apparition at Fatima). Many priests,
> beautiful mass, Eucharistic procession, Rosary procession, etc. Try to
> come for August 13th. (Although the best is May or better yet, October
> 13th.—I missed last year and shouldn't have. My mother and sister and
> thousands of others saw the 'Miracle of the Sun'!) Terry.[80]

The mailing lists provide a representation of a surprising frequency
and normality of locutions, apparitions, messages, various miraculous
occurrences. A great many of the correspondents tell of inner locutions,
messages received through various channels, daily encounters with Jesus,
the Virgin Mary, and their personal guardian angel. No one seems to be
shy about discussing these things, which are at times treated as if they
were chatting with a neighbor. For example, Christopher, from California,
commenting upon an apocalyptic message from the seer Joseph Reyes,
does not seem to consider Reyes's contact with the world beyond a particularly singular or exceptional experience. Indeed, Christopher at a certain
point writes: "Last night, I spoke with my Angel regarding this matter.
Here is what I have learned . . ."[81]

Nor were his correspondents particularly surprised by the story. Here,
chosen from among many, is an exchange of correspondence from *Marian Discussion*, between 28 and 30 July 1998. Mark described how he
"heard a voice within my head" while he was reciting the third mystery of
the rosary, a voice that told him that if he could only refrain from sinning
for a short time, he would finally have the child that he and his wife so
desired. "Has Mary ever talked to you?" Mark went on to ask his correspondents. Cindy answered immediately: "Yes, someone has spoken to
me, maybe it wasn't Mary, but God himself; when I asked the reason for
the death of my little boy, he replied: 'Because I love his soul.'" Then Julie
answered: she described how, many months before, "He" had spoken to
her heart, asking her to offer him everything, all the pain and joy of her
life. Next it was Terry's turn, who had a very special experience she wanted
to share. She told about a nightmare she had had, in which her son died,
and in which she had immediately begun to recite a rosary to ward off

the fear that had enveloped her. And as she did so, with her eyes closed, she suddenly saw the Madonna, smiling, with her son in her arms. Mark in the meanwhile sent a new message, in which he described another visionary experience. He had developed a custom of reciting the rosary before going to sleep, and every morning at 2 a.m. he would wake up and would see someone kneeling in prayer at the foot of his bed. In order to determine whether this was simply the product of his imagination, he decided to stop saying his evening rosary. And the figure disappeared. He began to recite the rosary again. The figure reappeared. Surely, he concluded, this must be his guardian angel. What did the others think of that? According to Terry, it might not be his guardian angel, but a soul from purgatory. At this point, Ken wrote a message, telling his own miraculous story: during a religious ceremony in church, he felt ill and was obliged to leave the building. And as he prayed, with his eyes closed, he saw a white and luminous cross and, immediately thereafter, the Madonna, smiling, her arms open wide. His pain disappeared, and Ken was able to return to the church. Then it was Jacci's turn; she confided that she had never experienced any physical images of the Madonna like the others, though she had recently received a mercy from the Madonna, that is, the salvation of her husband following a heart attack that the doctors had diagnosed as certainly fatal. The doctors were mystified by his survival. Marking the end, at least temporarily, of this exchange of messages, was one from Laura Zink, who wrote to Jacci: even if she had not seen miraculous images, what is important is to live your faith, "for if images are given to us, it is to teach us how to live."

In this example of an exchange, we find a shared "territory" that includes, not always with clear distinctions, inner locutions, dreams, and visions; a territory that is both mystical and oneiric, but also, let it be clear, distinguished by pure individual imagination. Indeed, it is the result of an interwoven fabric of collective practices and beliefs, culturally constructed, technologically sustained, and socially experienced.

Here, among the countless "wonderful" stories that have taken form in the belly of Marian devotion and the world of contemporary visionaries, is an exemplary story narrated on the Internet by Diane, in which there is a blend of archaic symbolism, uses of technology, and social practices of sharing:

On about Oct. 1st, a picture of Mary with St. Ann was discovered in the home of Raymond and Nancy Skop to be crying tears of oil. On the back of this picture, on going, oil drawn pictures are being formed in the shape of a Christ Head, Mary's face, the Nativity scene and many more. The Skop's have been photographing the changes. There is also a cross hanging on the wall with a rosary bead wrapped around it and this is dripping oil. They have attached a small cup at the end to catch the oil and this seems to fill up at varied lengths of time. The cup can fill up in 60 seconds or overnight. The oil flows at different rates depending. . . . On the dresser of Nancy Skop is a mirrored tray and on that tray is 4 different statues of Mary and Jesus. These statues have been crying tears of blood and also dripping oil. The Skop's also report the statues to move. On Dec. 24th, an approximate 6 to 8 ft. painting in "olive oil" of the Nativity appeared on a white wall in the hallway of their home which leads to the master bedroom where the miracles are occurring. The Nativity drawing was seen until late on the 25th of December where it began to fade away. On December 24th, eve, approximately 11:35, Raymond Skop felt Holy Mary's presence in the home where he followed her down the stairs in his finished basement, through a hall to a bathroom. In the bathroom, she appeared to him and gave him a message on why he was chosen and how to pray. He asked the Mother to reveal herself to his wife who was standing there and Holy Mary told Ray to hold his wife's hand, at that moment, oil spewed from Ray's hands onto Nancy's then onto the floor. The apparition ended approximately at midnight. Raymond has been receiving messages in dreams for the past few months, but the apparition on Christmas Eve was his first. Nancy has videotaped Ray speaking in his sleep and has also attempted to scribe Holy Mary's message to Ray in a notebook. At the outside of Raymond and Nancy's home, on Christmas day, the most beautiful red rose was freshly bloomed. There have been many reporting of healings. The Skop's have a photograph of the trees in front of their house where you can see clouds in the shape of angels above them. Fr. John Corbin from Jersey City brought his personal statue to the site and within 5 minutes it started to cry tears of oil. He brought it home and it continued to cry for several days. I would like to inform you that I have witnessed several miracles in my life. I have been to Conyers GA, in 1966, where I have felt a statue of May's heart beating. I have also seen an icon of St. Irene crying in a Greek church in Queens NY in 1991.[82]

There is an enormous energy of social contagion in these stories of miracles, which begin as the experience of a single person, and are then

transmitted to others, originating in one place and then shifting elsewhere: statues that come to life, paintings that weep, consecrated hosts
that bleed, and each of these events are photographed and filmed, each
copy of the picture or the movie then being able to produce new miraculous occurrences for others, and so on for the copies of the copies; miraculous healings that trigger other healings in other worshipers, visions
that herald yet other visions, in an unstoppable epidemic of miracles,
which takes countless forms and which has become so openly acknowledged that at times it is taken as a basic test of faith, viz., "I think the
reason is that very few people saw the miracle of the sun and most didn't
because maybe it was a TEST OF FAITH. John Paul."[83]

But the "few" have by this point become hundreds of thousands if
not millions around the world, and those who are temporarily excluded
from their ranks will be able to see the miracles through video recordings
and photographs. Indeed these miraculous occurrences are no longer dependent upon faith alone, upon a belief built around a narration and a
traditional holy image. Thanks to the technologies of reproduction, now
"objective evidence" is available, and now people can take direct control
and possession of the phenomena, keep them at home, look at them frequently, and show them to friends.

And these phenomena can be tracked day by day, "live," "in real time,"
and most important of all, they can be documented. One woman, a devotee of Garabandal from Catskill, New York, informed her correspondents
in the *Yellowstone Forum* that she was a member of a list of 320 people who
would be immediately alerted to the announcement that the Madonna was
going to make to the visionary Conchita eight days prior to the "miracle"
expected in Garabandal, so that they could all fly together to the Spanish
village on a charter flight, specially arranged for the occasion. Even more
interesting than that was the fact that, according to her, along with these
privileged few, a television crew would be alerted from EWTN, the powerful American Catholic television network, so as to be in time to document
the miracle.[84]

We cannot consider this section on new visions complete without
pointing out that behind many of these phenomena, especially the most
startling and famous ones, there are enormous investments of money and
huge organizations, essential to creating worldwide interest in a visionary
event. Obviously this is never mentioned in the declarations of support
for an ongoing case of a vision. On the contrary, Jesus or the Madonna are

allowed to speak directly, and they themselves ask that books, pamphlets, and newsletters be written, that films be made and photographs be taken, that Web sites be opened, that all the various documents be placed on-line, and that they be recommended to the attention of cybernauts from around the world. We shall offer just one specific example to represent this new scenario, which replaces the old-fashioned messages that the Madonna would send by means of a visionary to a parish priest, or to the villagers or to the bishop. According to the association the Shepherds of Christ Ministries, the Madonna herself, on 6 October 1998, extended the following invitation:

> Please tape all messages I have given in Florida and make the tapes readily available to spread to all souls of the earth. Please publish the books of messages immediately, the time is urgent. Please do not tarry. I give you these daily messages on the Internet, please act as an apostle and circulate them to all your friends by mail, e-mail, any way possible in near and far countries. Please have a stockpile of tapes available at my Florida site for immediate distribution, and encourage those coming to Florida to circulate the tapes. Please circulate in abundance the Mary Image card and the postcard of the Good Shepherd and the Prayer Manuals.[85]

Following this heartfelt appeal, which clearly demonstrates the importance of the local and planetary diffusion of visionary texts, comes another one which calls for the divulging of those same texts among the opinion leaders of the ecclesiastical establishment, priests and bishops. In fact, the message continues as follows:

> The main purpose of the Shepherds of Christ Movement is to reach the priests with the priestly newsletter. This is written by Father Edward . Carter, a Jesuit theologian with a Doctor's degree in Theology, and chosen by my Son to write this newsletter centered in consecration for the priests. My children, it is reaching many bishops and their priests in about 90 countries this day. . . . The newsletter now goes to 70,000 priests in the world in English and Spanish. . . . Oh children, please help me to distribute this priestly newsletter in anyway possible. All this is done on a donation basis. The newsletter is being sent all over the world.[86]

Lastly, alongside and behind the devotion there is commercialization. It would be shortsighted to reduce all this explosion of visionary experience to skillful commercial manipulation, accepting as wry humor the lampooning of the Madonna of Medjugorje as the "Madonna of Tourism," or the Madonna of Clearwater as the "Madonna of Finance," as do so many critics, speaking with relatively venomous irony when discussing these phenomena. But admittedly, for the most recent years—from the contacts for my initial research via Internet in the years 1997–98 to the present day—there has been a significant shift of numerous Marian Web sites toward e-commerce. Three years ago, only a few offered for sale at the foot of the page photographs, rosaries, and gadgets; nowadays, almost all of them, from *Medjugorje Web* to the most minor site featuring relatively obscure apparitions, propose all sorts of gadgets online, either directly or through affiliated companies.

The New Visionaries

Even though visions are now a mass phenomenon, and even though thousands of pilgrims claim that they see relatively clearly defined celestial images on the sites of apparitions, however much technology democratizes those visions, the most important visionaries still remain irreplaceable: what would Medjugorje have been without the six children; what would Betania have been without Maria Esperanza de Bianchini, or Conyers without Nancy Fowler and Cojutepeque without Nelly Hurtado? Certainly, the transition online of the apparitions produced a certain degree of depersonalization, as we shall see, but offline, in the visionary world, Ivan, Maria, Nancy, and Nelly—like Bernadette, Mélanie, and Jacinta before them—continue to play a crucial role.

All the same, there are a number of radical new developments which have to 'o with the internationalization, centralization, and emancipation of th. visionaries.

When at Fatima the child visionaries were prohibited by the police to go to the site of the apparitions for the appointment of 13 August, the Madonna did not then appear to them in the police station where they were being held, but only two days later, in the usual site, Cova da Iria, when they returned there. The apparition was identified with the place as much as with any person. And indeed, when, after awhile the visionaries were marginalized, the sites of the apparition preserved all their centrality, indeed all the more so. Bernadette and Lucia withdrew to a convent, Francisco and Jacinta died young, but Lourdes and Fatima remained behind and grew up. It is no accident that Mélanie of La Salette, who refused to allow herself to be shunted aside, began to travel, presenting herself but at the same time compromising the symbolic power of the apparition.

As usual, Medjugorje was exemplary in the transformation of the models of recognized nineteenth- and twentieth-century apparitions. The hill of Podbrdo, where the first apparitions took place, was central only in the early phases. On 30 June 1981, a few days after the first vision, the children were taken away in a car by two social workers, who kept them far away from the visionary appointment; but along the route, the hill remained visible, though from a distance, and at a certain point the children asked that the car be stopped and that they be allowed to get out, and at the appointed hour they saw the image from afar.[87] Then the apparitions moved from the hill to the rectory: in this phase the location still remained decisive, though not as important as the persons of the visionaries themselves. Referring to that period, Mostar's former bishop Zanic wrote polemically in 1987:

> The Madonna, they say, started to appear on the Podbrdo of the
> Mountain Crnica, but when the militia forbade going there, she came
> into houses, into forests, fields, vineyards, and tobacco fields; she
> appeared in the church, on the altar, in the sacristy, in the choir loft, on
> the roof, on the church steeple, on the roads, on the way to Cerno, in a
> car, on busses, in classrooms, in several places in Mostar and Sarajevo,
> in monasteries in Zagreb, Varazdin, Switzerland, and Italy, once again
> on the Podbrdo, atop Krizevac, in the parish, in the rectory, etc. It is
> certain that not even half of the places where the alleged apparitions
> have taken place have been mentioned.[88]

Later, over the course of the years, the Bosnian visionaries began to travel around the world and to have visions wherever they might be, in America and in Asia, in Australia and in Europe. The apparitions were no longer inextricably bound up with a given place and, underlying that place, a culture, an affiliation. Rather, it was a quality of the visionary, an attribute, a prerequisite of the relationship between him or her and the world beyond, which for that matter he was able to actualize with great ease. As Peric, the new bishop of Mostar, put it with some irony, "the 'Madonna' appears at the 'fiat' (let her come!) of the 'visionaries.' "[89] In the past as well, mystics had experienced miraculous phenomena wherever they happened to be, but generally speaking, their significance had been entirely private and individual, and only rarely universal, as is instead the case with the visionaries of Medjugorje. It is not that the delocalization of the apparitions has stripped sacred places of all importance. Medjugorje is in fact a great Marian sanctuary, one of the most popular in the world. But the apparitions no longer coincide strictly with the site of the sanctuary—as is perfectly understood by the travel agencies that promise in their Medjugorje programs the inevitable meeting with some visionary or other—because they belong, first and foremost, to the persons of the visionaries, who travel, go from place to place, and carry the visions with themselves.

The dozens of visionaries who nowadays report apparitions travel around the world, and once they have become well known, they do not withdraw into the shadows, but rather establish, with their own presence, the value of the manifestation, as if they themselves were identifying with the apparition that they have announced, weakening or leaving entirely overshadowed the localization of the epiphany in question. The Web sites of these visionaries present the travel schedule of the upcoming weeks and months, the locations, the addresses, and the exact times of the meetings that they will hold with the faithful; you will also find an address, a telephone number, or an e-mail address to contact if you wish to welcome the visionary in question in your own city or community. This is the case with Vassula Ryden, a very controversial visionary to whom we shall return below.[90] As Father Guido Sommavilla, a follower, points out, Vassula "goes around the world a lot because she receives invitations to go. She does not go so as to place herself on show. It must be said that she does not like being the centre of attention. . . . Vassula does it because it is her duty, because it is Jesus Who wants."[91] It is true as well of Kasimir Domanski, a Polish visionary, who travels around the world at the behest of the Madonna herself.[92] Or even of "Mother Teresa," a New York–born visionary, who has not only traveled throughout the United States, but has also been in Mexico, China, Tibet, Bosnia, the Philippines, and Canada.[93] Paola Albertini, an Italian visionary who was virtually unknown until she was credited for the celestial mediation in the healing of Mother Angelica, the powerful founder of EWTN, informs the world that "Our Lady wants to be known all over the world and following her request Paola is always available to speak to your group if you wish to contact her."[94] The identification is explicit. There is no point in continuing with an endless list of examples.

Quite often these visionaries boast of a spiritual guidance provided by priests, theologians, or even the support of bishops and cardinals. Louise Lahola, from California, whose messages from Jesus, published in the book *Lessons from Jesus,* predict impending punishment because "the world must be purified," is "under the spiritual direction of a priest who is experienced and knowledgeable in mystical theology." Maureen Sweeney relies upon the spiritual guidance of Father Frank Kenney, who holds a "doctorate in Marian theology." Californian visionary Patricia Soto has been receiving locutions from Jesus since 1986, but only in the past few years has she begun to publicize them, at the behest of Jesus himself. The list of her spiritual guides and advisors is almost intimidating: Father Sean Cronin, a professor of philosophy and religious studies at Marymount College in Rancho Palos Verde, California, and formerly a professor at the National University of Ireland, at the Pontifical University of Saint Thomas Aquinas in Rome, at Oxford University in England, and at the University of California at Los Angeles (UCLA), formerly the spiritual advisor of Mother Teresa of Calcutta; as well as Father Richard Hoynes, Father John Neiman, Father Paul M. Caporali, and Father James L. Swensen, who are all parish priests or assistant parish priests in California and Nevada. On the Web page of Carlos Lopez and Jorge Zavala, visionaries from San Bruno, California, it is stated that if anyone wishes to question them about the orthodoxy of their relationship with the church, they should contact directly Father Walsh of Saint Mary's Cathedral in San Francisco, with whom the two visionaries "meet regularly." In addition to Father Walsh, the visionaries have two spiritual advisors, Father Joyce and Father Hughes.[95]

At times, moreover, the visionaries are accorded an almost official position in ecclesiastical ceremonies, during which they tell of their experiences or even receive visions. For instance, the diocese of Chicago allowed Reinholtz to participate, in 1994, in a healing mass, during the course of which he was allowed to recount his experiences as a visionary.[96] In San Bruno, Carlos Lopez received Marian messages during the third decade of the rosary during a meeting of a prayer group that was held on Wednesdays in Saint Bruno's church.[97] In Emmitsburg, Maryland, beginning in 1993 Gianna Talone would receive a weekly vision with a message during the course of the ceremonies of the prayer group at Saint Joseph's church.[98] It was not until September 2000, in the wake of an apocalyptic prophecy by the seer, that the practice was interrupted at the order of Cardinal Keeler, and the supernatural nature of her experience was later denied.[99]

Obviously, the ignorance, verging on barbarity, of the visionaries of Lourdes and Fatima would not be sufficient for these visionaries. The globe-trotting visionaries are well educated, they write books, and they are often members of the middle- and upper-middle class. They know how to speak to the crowds of worshipers who come to listen. Sometimes they hold important offices in the church hierarchy. Father Edward Carter is a professor of theology at Xavier University in Cincinnati. He has a long list of publications, and he also works as a consultant identifying other visionaries. Carol Ameche has been a Eucharistic minister in her parish church of Saint Maria Goretti in Scottsdale, Arizona; Harriet Hammons is a parish director for catechism; Ameche and Hammons together wrote a book that, by celestial inspiration, tells of their experiences and contains messages attributed to Jesus and the Virgin Mary: *Do Whatever Love Requires*. John Leary, a chemical engineer, has written seventeen books; Catalina Rivas has written eight. Vassula Ryden has been "an acclaimed artist, skilled tennis player and the wife of a Swedish international development expert."[100] Gianna Talone, who has written four books, is a pharmacist, and was the chief of the pharmaceutical division of a hospital in Phoenix. Estela Ruiz is a teacher; Rita Ring taught mathematics at the university level. Mary Jane Even was a university professor before becoming a visionary, and was capable of refuting, personally, point by point, the objections raised by a theologian from the diocese of Lincoln, Nebraska, with genuine theological essays. Father Spaulding and Brother David are priests, and we should not overlook Father Gobbi, who founded the Marian Movement of Priests in response to his own visions and locutions.[101]

In social and even matrimonial terms, moreover, often these visionaries are fairly liberated. We are a long way from the convent in which Bernadette and Lucia shut themselves up. At Oliveto Citra, the fact that the most respected visionary should have chosen marriage over the convent was one of the reasons for her progressive marginalization.[102] In contrast, Al Scott, an American visionary whose wife died in 1989, remarried in 1992 at the age of seventy-one, and until he died six years later, he lived nine months a year in Florida and three months in Michigan, in the home of his second wife.[103] Catalina Rivas has been married three times.[104] Vassula Ryden, Greek Orthodox by religion, was divorced and then she remarried in a civil ceremony, followed by a religious, Greek Orthodox wedding ceremony.[105] Gianna Talone ended her first marriage with a divorce, followed by an annulment issued by the ecclesiastical authorities—one of the 40,000 annual annulments in the United States, according to Father René

Laurentin[106]—and then she was married a second time, to Michael Sullivan. In some cases, however, these successive marriages are announced or recommended by heaven. It was the Madonna who announced to Gianna her second marriage. In Laurentin's account,[107] which seems to echo the astonishment of the Virgin Mary at the Annunciation, this is how the Madonna informed her: " 'I am about to introduce you to your future husband.' Gianna was astonished, and could not imagine how this could be possible."

Joan, Al Scott's second wife, was sent directly by the Holy Ghost.[108] Marija, too, the seer of Medjugorje, married at the behest of the Madonna.[109] And if we are to believe the words of the author of *The Medjugorje Deception*, Michael Jones, Theresa Lopez, a visionary from Denver who was influenced by Medjugorje, abandoned her husband Jeff to become "a full-time seer."[110]

The central role of the seer or the charismatic is also expressed in the aura that surrounds his or her possessions. For instance, it is not just any image that drips oil by celestial command at the home of Nasreen, in California, but a gift that was given by the well-known visionary Myrna Nazzour, of Damascus: a copy of the image, which also exuded oil, owned by the latter, whose mystical, miraculous properties were transmitted as well in the copies of her own devotional objects.

Another effect of the central role sought out and obtained by the visionaries is the strong degree of narcissism that often seems to characterize them.

The visionaries of Medjugorje soon felt that they had been entrusted with a world-wide mission whose purpose was the salvation of humanity at large. One of the visionaries states that "the future of the world depends somehow on what happens at Medjugorje."[111] And the Devil is so keenly aware of this that he offers to exchange the rest of the world for Medjugorje.[112] At Olawa, in Poland, the Madonna informs the visionary Domanski that she wants a chapel built in that town, "upon which the peace of the world will depend."[113] In New York, a message from the Madonna to "Mother Teresa" on 18 May 1987, which the "Ambassadors of God" post on the Internet, proclaims that "this, my children, is a very important apparition site. It will be the link that unites all apparition sites." In Rome, the Madonna communicates to Marisa Rossi that the apparitions she is receiving are the "most important ones," although they are also "the most difficult and strongly opposed, especially by the Clergy," and Jesus adds that the apparitions which are taking place around Marisa are "the greatest

Eucharistic miracles in the history of the Church."[114] Marisa Rossi's spiritual director, Don Claudio Gatti, suspended *a divinis* by Cardinal Ruini on 1 April 1988, sent a letter a month later to the cardinals, bishops, and priests of the church, beginning with these words: "I write you respectfully and affectionately to ask you to read this letter carefully; the contents of this letter are so important that it will go down in History, and so sayeth the Lord."[115]

No less positive that he was at the heart of history and at the center of divine redemption was Father Stefano Gobbi, founder of the Movimento Sacerdotale Mariano, or Marian Movement of Priests, through whom the Madonna conveyed the following message, on 31 December 1997, in the last of the thousands of messages sent to him over the previous twenty-five years:

> All has been revealed to you: my plan has been prophetically announced to you at Fatima and, during these years, I have been carrying it out through my Marian Movement of Priests. . . . I have now been guiding you for twenty-five years, with the words which I have spoken to the heart of this, my little son, whom I have chosen as an instrument for the realization of my maternal plan. During these years I myself have carried him several times to every part of the world, and he has allowed himself to be led with docility, small and fearful but totally abandoned to me, like a little baby in the arms of his Mother. As of now, all that I had to say to you has been said, because all has been revealed to you. Therefore, on this night, there come to an end the public messages which I have been giving you for twenty-five years; . . . From now on, I will manifest myself through the word, the person and the actions of this, my little son, whom I have chosen to be your guide and whom I am now leading to the painful summit of his mission.[116]

What this one example, chosen from many similar ones, shows is that implicitly and, in the final analysis, understandably, each and every visionary feels that he or she is at the center of the history of redemption from sin, divine plans, and fundamental choices concerning humanity. For that very same reason, each and every visionary tends to consider all the other visionaries, with the partial exception of the ones from Medjugorje, as inferior, less important, and secondary to the mission entrusted to him or her. And this view of things, in forms that are to a greater or lesser degree attenuated or amplified by the various devotional organizations, which are limited or stimulated by the religious orders or hierarchies that may be acting behind the scenes, winds up reaching the faithful, who at times debate, argue, and clash over which apparition is the most important or, in some cases, actually claim that a certain apparition is the only one.

The Network of Visionaries

All things considered, however, the conflicts tend to be rather marginal. More often, the new visionaries work with one another; they refer to each other's visions, they quote each other, they write books together, they take part in the same meetings. Some visit the Web sites of the apparitions of others, or they link to each other's sites. According to William Christian, the exchanges and the visits among visionaries are also motivated by a desire to understand what is happening to them by comparing their experiences with those of others.[117] Aside from that factor, we should keep in mind the internationalization of visionary culture, which began as early as the nineteenth century and has been reinforced over recent years due to the broadening array of technical possibilities for contact and worldwide communications. The great popularity of Lourdes would not have been possible without the railroads that were spreading across France in the late nineteenth century, as across the rest of Catholic Europe. The spread of radio and literacy were not secondary factors in the spread of the worship of Fatima. Medjugorje could never have become a destination for millions of pilgrims from all over the planet had it not been for television and civilian air travel. But the international dimension of visionary culture was encouraged by the church, at least as it was nourished by the growing integration of world culture by networks of mass communications. As early as the nineteenth century, the church identified the great apparitions as essential instruments for a restructuring of the ranks of the faithful in the face of the risks of secularization brought about by the new industrial society. It is important to our understanding of the popularity of Lourdes to point out that the little French village was a bastion in the struggle against the "modern errors" being waged in the second half of the nineteenth century: liberalism, Marxism, and positivism.[118] And how could we overlook the part that Fatima played in the Vatican's fight against communism?[119] Lourdes and Fatima were powerful instruments of the pastoral politics of the church, aimed not at this nation or that country, but at all the Catholic faithful on earth. And so on the one hand the processes of visionary expansion, diffusion, and dynamics were made possible by technological instruments; on the other hand they were encouraged, though only partly controlled, by the church. I am here not only talking about the recognition or rejection of the supernatural aspects of an epiphanous event; I am also referring to the perimeter of definition of a possible symbolic construction. However heterodox it may be, a case of apparitions does not violate the boundaries laid down by the general symbolic compatibility of official Catholicism. It is the devotional books, the little parish-church newsletters, the homilies, the accounts of other visionary phenomena, the semiofficial and official accounts that all contribute to the construction of the symbolic network within the context of which each new case of apparitions emerges, and the development of each of those cases relies in large part upon the symbolic materials taken from this landscape. Minor local visionary phenomena, the product of contagion from the famous cases—or at least of the cultural background that accommodates the possibility of celestial visions—crop up here and there in the Catholic territories, previously organized according to that which is possible and that which is not, and in any case their final destination lies entirely within the context of the legitimacy that the local or central ecclesiastical institution will either accord them or deny them.

In recent years, the growing impact of technology and the "democratic" possibilities that it allows, along with the greater role of the individual as the central actor in religious choice, and no longer as the passive recipient of an institutional offering, have all worked together to reduce the possibilities of a hierarchic control of the visionary movement. The radio messages of Pius XII were markers of an era in which the use of technology was entirely asymmetrical, and the people of God were basically faithful, passive recipients of the message. Today the camera and the computer signal a possibility on the part of the believer to gain access to an individual relationship with the world beyond, and moreover a freely chosen relationship, not imposed by the ecclesiastical institution as a devotional duty.

It is no accident that today the greatest force on earth for the legitimation of apparitions—in devotional, not institutional terms, of course—is Medjugorje, and not the Vatican: that is to say, a visionary structure of extraordinary importance (developed in part despite the Vatican, and in part with its tolerance), and antiinstitutional in its very founding impulse, on account of the violent opposition to the diocese of Mostar that characterized its establishment. And indeed, given the central role of Medjugorje, one of the goals pursued by visionaries from all over the world in order to attain recognition is some connection to the Bosnian town, through messages that make reference to it, voyages of initiation, or visits from the visionaries or priests of the town. The dense calendar of appointments, visits, trips, interviews, messages, sermons by Bosnian Franciscans, testimonials by globe-trotting visionaries constitutes a framework within which new cases of apparitions are periodically presented and later confirmed.

With the Internet, finally, the simultaneous presentation of all the cases produces a spectacular effect of visionary affirmation. Whether small or large, obscure or well known, ethnic or cosmopolitan, each new case of apparition takes its place in confirming the World Wide Web and at the same time derives confirmation from it.

The virtual network has offered a great opportunity to reinforce the global network of visionaries, with meshes both tight and loose, complex and centralized nodes, and other, outlying, less relevant nodes, all however contained within a unified fabric.

Here and there, local or institutional structures have been reinforced, in some cases through entirely fortuitous circumstances, and in other cases through affiliation with religious orders, associations, prayer groups, and publishing houses. Louise Lahola, a mysterious woman known as "The Scribe," and another mysterious "Irish priest," are linked by the fact that their celestial messages are all published by "MMR Publishing."[120] The books of the messages of Rita Ring, Edward Carter, and Miriam Grosjean, visionaries from Ohio, are all published by the Shepherds of Christ Ministries and publicized in that organization's Web site.[121] In Italy the publishing house Il Segno, in Padua, on the one hand, and the numerous newsletters dedicated to Medjugorje or other apparitions on the other, are important structures linking various experiences.

Of course, given the planetary scale of the communication, the lingua franca of contemporary visions is English, which must be used directly or indirectly by all the visionaries and, especially, in the messages that they diffuse. In Italy, the busy Web masters of the Italian sites *Profezie On Line* and *Profezie per il Terzo Millennio* translate hundreds of messages from English, the language used by many of the visionaries and their renowned messages, and they request help from their English-speaking correspondents. To use the words of Vassula Ryden, born in Egypt to Greek parents, Swiss by adoption, and separated from her Swedish husband, "The divine spoke . . . in English."[122]

Many visionaries who have established relationships of exchange and friendship, often wreathed in mystical overtones, have established personal micronetworks. Patricia Soto, from California, tells us in her Web page that "Mama Mary" requested an image of her son Jesus painted by Josyp Terelya, a Ukrainian visionary who has moved to Canada.[123] He in turn provided the illustrations for the book by the visionary John Leary, *Prepare for the Great Tribulation and the Era of Peace,* and he portrays in one painting Denise Curtin and Joseph Della Puca, visionaries from Connecticut, along with their guardian angels John and Rachel. Then the trio had a picture taken together, with the canvas in the foreground, as a documentation of their friendship.[124] Carol Ameche and Harriet Hammons, as we have seen, wrote a book together that described their shared visions.[125] Jack Smith, a visionary from Wilkes-Barre, Pennsylvania, chose for the cover of his book about his own visions, *Now Is the Time,* a "miraculous" photograph that he took during a pilgrimage to Conyers, Georgia. Mary Ellen Lucas, a visionary who has had stigmata, reached out to Jack Smith by praying to the Madonna for her intentions.[126] The apparitions of Catalina Rivas in Bolivia have long been linked to and dependent upon those of Nancy Fowler in Conyers, at least until Fowler broke off her ties with the association Our Loving Mother's Children, which administered the devotional logistics and served to link the two. Connections between visionaries are so common and accepted that a visionary who does not interact with others is described as "independent": that is the case, for instance, with Joseph Reyes.[127]

These micronetworks offer the advantage, for the visionaries, of a reciprocal reference that self-reinforces all those who take part in it. An example: Georgette Faniel, a little known Canadian visionary, stigmatized as early as the end of the fifties, declared in the eighties that God in person had asked her to emerge from anonymity, to testify to the validity of the apparitions of Medjugorje. In order to verify the celestial foundations of her experiences, two priests who had been investigating the case of Georgette since 1985 suggested to Marija, a visionary of Medjugorje, that she ask the Madonna whether the testimonials of Georgette in favor of the validity of the apparitions of Medjugorje actually came from God. The response was affirmative, and the two priests returned to Canada with renewed faith.[128] Thus we see that Georgette Faniel attested to the validity of the apparitions of the visionaries of Medjugorje, who in turn attested to the validity of the conversations of Georgette Faniel with the Holy Trinity and the Madonna. This circular attribution of authenticity has the advantage of providing the worshipers with an orientation—however unintentionally ironic inasmuch as it is circular and reversible, that is to say, in the final analysis, disoriented—in the general chaos of visionary offerings.

An important role, moreover, is played by a number of ecclesiastics of international fame, who constitute an essential form of support for the international network of the new visionaries: they too travel around the world to support the apparitions, write books that become best sellers, appear on television broadcasts, defend the visionaries from attacks by critics, and finally expand the influence of the visionary world in the offices and halls of the Vatican. Among them, we should mention Father René Laurentin (perhaps the most renowned of these supporters and promoters of the apparitions, the author of an immense number of hagiographic publications on the subject, with seventeen devoted to Medjugorje alone); Father Sommavilla; Father Gabriele Amorth, who is also a famous exorcist; Frane Franic, the archbishop emeritus of Split-Makarska; and in the United States, Wayne Weible, a former Protestant who converted to Catholicism after a visit to Medjugorje and the author of best sellers that are present in the houses of every American worshiper.

In such a welter of relationships, the institutional authorities often wind up playing a role that they neither desire nor control, inasmuch as they are portrayed with clashing standpoints and views. We should keep in mind that in the context of apparitions there are radically divided orientations within the context of the ecclesiastical hierarchy itself, where often diametrically opposed positions are taken. The case of Medjugorje provides a perfect example: the favorable views of many bishops have long been cited by the worshipers, in contrast with the very critical positions taken by the successive bishops who have occupied the see of Mostar, which has jurisdiction. In this conflict, which can only serve to increase the confusion of the worshipers, the Vatican has played its own very specific and highly ambiguous role. The position of the bishop of Mostar (who stated in 1997 in very explicit language that not only did Medjugorje "non constat de supernalitate" (not establish proof of its supernatural nature) as the document issued by the Yugoslavian bishops in 1991 limited itself to saying, but on the contrary "constat de non supernalitate" (established Medjugorje's nonsupernatural nature).) This opinion was echoed in 1998, in the letter that Tarcisio Cardinal Bertone, deputy to Cardinal Ratzinger, wrote to Gilbert Audry, bishop of Saint-Denis de la Réunion, who had requested enlightenment. In this letter, Bertone emphasized that the statement of the bishop of Mostar was legitimate inasmuch as he was the

bishop with jurisdiction, but added that "it should be considered the expression of the personal conviction of the bishop of Mostar."[129] Still more
ambiguously, Cardinal Navarro-Valls, spokesman for the Vatican, stated,
according to a French Web site that supports Medjugorje, that "we cannot
tell people that they cannot go to Medjugorje unless the apparitions are
proven to be fakes. And this has not been stated, therefore, anyone can go
there if they like."[130]

An endless list of semiofficial statements, incomplete sentences,
things said and then retracted, attributed by some—and denied by
others—to the pope, to Ratzinger, to this or that high prelate, circulates
among the worshipers on the subject of Medjugorje. No official document, of course, rejects the two formal statements of the Episcopal Conference of the former Yugoslavia, and the declarations of the two succeed-
ing bishops of Mostar, all negative and in some cases, strongly negative,
statements; but all these confused and contradictory discourses, all this
interpretation and reinterpretation renders far less clear-cut the official
stances and positions.

This ecclesiastical ambiguity has not always met with passive acceptance on the part of the faithful. Commenting on the concluding sentence
of the letter from Bertone concerning pilgrimages, which are permitted
"on condition that they are not regarded as an authentification of events
still taking place and which still call for an examination by the Church,"[131]
Doug Delorge wrote in an e-mail, "How can one of today's pilgrims make
a pilgrimage that isn't an acknowledgement of things taking place? Does
this mean that most pilgrims are going against the Church's teaching? All
of my two pilgrimages have been acknowledgements."

On the subject of Medjugorje the Vatican is clearly uncertain how to
proceed. Certainly, the file that the episcopal see of Mostar has been com-
piling for years, questioning the reliability of the visionaries and listing
an array of doctrinal errors, false statements, institutional abuses, folk-
loric ingenuity, and nationalistic (and even militaristic) manipulations of
the visionaries and their supporters, has grown to a daunting size. But
a clear declaration of intent, clearly the right thing to do in institutional
terms, supporting the bishop who has geographic jurisdiction, would only
serve to throw a vast number of worshipers, both lay and ecclesiastic—
potentially tens of millions—into a state of truly dangerous disarray, if
not full-blown panic, as well as causing considerable damage to a network of economic, political, and religious relationships that has come to
be intricate and substantial, linking the Bosnian sanctuary with much of

the contemporary Catholic world. That the Vatican is caught in a stalling position is evident, and perhaps this keeps it from establishing centralized supervision of its approach to the control of visionary phenomena from around the world—the kind of supervision that instead, during the papacy of Karol Wojtyla and under the leadership of Ratzinger's Congregatio Pro Doctrina Fidei, it has applied to so many other aspects of doctrine, ethics, and its pastoral duties.

The Visionaries on the Web

If the divine speaks English, and no longer the dialect of Lourdes, it is also because the Internet speaks for the most part in English. The growth of the visionary movement in the United States follows considerations specific to that nation, as we have seen. But the fact that the American visionary movement should have established itself throughout the rest of the world is largely due to the Web. In fact, the Web was created in the United States, which still boasts the greatest number of Web users on earth.[132] The relationship of American visionaries and their supporters with the Web is familiar, everyday, and taken for granted in way that is found in no other country. That is why when non-American worshipful surfers browse the Web out of faith-related curiosity, they already find it filled with American sites and visionaries. Moreover, when new visionaries find spaces of their own on the Web, quite often it is because they take advantage of relationships with American associations or centers, or directly with the American Web masters of apparitions pages.

With the Internet the international network of visionaries has been globalized to a degree previously unimaginable, but at the same time it has taken on a strong American connotation. It has also lost all reference to an exclusive hierarchic center. The first victim of the Internet is precisely the traditional institutional control: we no longer see the people of God who stood in a disciplined manner behind the Lourdes and the Fatimas of the Vatican, because control can no longer be easily exercised.

The Church, in part, seemed to have become more aware of the challenge arising from the Internet and in general, from the new media. A conference held in Denver in 1998, titled "The New Technologies and the Human Person: Communicating the Faith in the New Millennium," concluded its proceedings with the idea that "the Internet is a 'gift from God': if the Catholic Church does not learn to study it, accept it, and use it, it will be overwhelmed by it."[133]

On the other hand, however, it seems that the response to the challenge is limited to a multiplication of Web sites, as well as a generic ad-
monishment to exercise "discernment," as if the question were—not unlike the state of things offline—a matter of occupying spaces, which if left
vacant would simply fall prey to others. But in a delocalized reality, the
question is not whether or not you have a window, a kiosk, a location.
For an institution based on leadership, management, and rules, like the
church, the liberty to surf, to navigate, is a much more serious threat than
a relative shortfall of proprietary Web sites—which, once they are created,
occupy the same level playing field as all the others.

After ecclesiastical authority, the second set of victims of the Internet
are the strong visionaries. At first, as we have seen, technology seemed to
favor visionaries over the institution that ostensibly was meant to control
them, conferring upon them a visibility, a central role, and an unprecedented personal sacred aura. But that is only a first impression. Sooner or
later, technology demands that the powerful seers move aside and make
room for it in the production of miracles. The Internet especially seems to
limit drastically the personal space of the visionaries—but without restor-
ing the traditional power of the institution—by depersonalizing them.
The Web is unable to make use of fully three-dimensional personalities,
inasmuch as it is a place of an incessant flow of messages, on the Web
the message itself is the subject, not the source of that message, since the
source is a stable entity apart from the message, while on the Web every
subjective entity exists as a message; it is a shifting representation that
slips into the system of continuous drift. And so the visionary, too, loses
his or her substance, becoming generic, the mirror image of another visionary, or a reference to his or her message. Even a famous visionary
sees his or her individual substance dissolve. Proliferating through various diverse Web sites, visionaries become icons of themselves, devoid
of subjectivity and capacity to act, other than merely representing "the
one who sees the Madonna." Or they become fragmented, contradictory,
faded, because of the various faces with which the various sites present
them.

Quite often, moreover, the visionary is anonymous, someone who saw
something, sometime and somewhere, and all that is known for certain is
what he saw and the message that was transmitted. "The Scribe," "Maria-
mante," "S," "anonymus [sic] seer," "american woman," "servant son," "un
prete irlandese," "una veggente italiana," "lo Strumento," "la Conchiglia,"
"Gabriella," and "Maria" are all busily establishing themselves as anony-

mous names, in reference to stories of visions which, as soon as they are told, lose for good their human protagonist (already anonymous, for that matter), obscured by the messages that have been generated by those events. It is remarkable that a great number of those cases have to do with locutionists, or people who claim to receive celestial messages within themselves. Their biographical, personal, and geographic exterior vanishes, while their "interior" is transferred directly onto the Web.

Moreover, it is becoming increasingly common on the Web to transmit to users celestial messages of completely unknown provenance, which often open with laconic phrases: "Jesus says . . . ," "The Virgin Mary says . . ." To whom and where Jesus said what he said is information that is simply absent. In this case, not only has the local and community dimension disappeared, but the personal dimension has vanished as well, both replaced by the organization of media-driven communications, outside of which the event does not exist. For that matter, the system of search engines accentuates this phenomenon. Indeed, it is fairly frequent to find on the screen a page that tells of apparitions and messages without indicating to whom, where, and when they were given. In these cases, it would be necessary to work back from the individual page to the home page of the Web site, but that is not always possible, nor is it ever necessary in order to read the page that is present on the screen.

The depersonalization of the Internet is reminiscent of the marginalization of the visionaries in the past, implemented by the ecclesiastical authorities in cases of recognized apparitions: Lourdes, Rue du Bac, and Fatima. There are however substantial differences. Indeed, in this case the depersonalization does not redound to the benefit of a renewed central role for the ecclesiastical authorities; rather, it is simply the product of the standardized flow of digital communication, which prevents a personalization of the broadcaster.

In reality, we can distinguish three phases in the relationship between visionaries and apparitions, the second and third of which, although incompatible in logical terms, coexist in practice, at least for now.

A first phase, the standard one, involves an ecclesiastical intervention that pushed aside the person of the visionary, whether the vision had been accepted or rejected, in the latter case through operations of pejorative characterizations of the personality of the visionary in question.

A second phase was that of the 1970s and 1980s, in which the globalization of communications, along with the personalization and delocalization of worship, have made it possible for the new visionaries to escape the suffocating control of local religious authorities, giving them a worldwide stage that they have managed to win through the more or less effective communications practices that they have employed. (This is the phase that I described above in reference to the central role of the new visionaries in contrast with the location and the vision itself.) In these practices, what counts above all is the charismatic dimension of the visionary herself, as she travels, speaks, prays, prophesies, and occupies center stage in the attention of the crowds of worshipers who recognize her. This phase, which has not ended but indeed has in certain ways become increasingly important, develops not only through the power of global communications, but also through those new forms of religious practice, charismatic and community-oriented, described above, which took form following the Vatican Council II.

Finally, the third phase is the very recent case, made possible by the Internet, in which the person of the visionary cannot occupy a space which, on the Web, exists for no one. What counts by now is the flow of movements on the Web, not the subjective existence of the broadcaster, which at the very most can aspire to being just one node in the general flow.

How can we reconcile the characteristics of centrality of the new visionaries with the equally new depersonalization of those same visionaries? In fact, both characteristics coexist and serve different functions in different conditions of deployment.

Offline, the physical presence of the strong visionary allows for an epidemiology of weak visionaries, that is, more attenuated forms of contact with heaven, which extends potentially to all worshipers. The fact that in a visionary site there should be a strong visionary is decisive in making the weak phenomena propagate and spread: the extraordinary nature of the vision of the strong visionary legitimizes an attenuated proliferation, a contagion through concentric circles. Moreover, the extreme facilitation of communications and the accentuation of their charismatic aspects are capable of liberating the strong visionary from the limitations of location, rendering him capable of producing visionary epidemics everywhere that he is accepted.

Online, in contrast, the strong visionary no longer has any possibility of influencing directly the vision of others: empathy, evocative power, context of relationship, cultural models, direct communicative actions, all this has vanished, or it practically has. Now the context of relationships around the visionary has radically changed: there is no longer a collective focalization upon the visionary's charisma; instead surfers or Web masters either do or do not come into electronic contact with him or her, potentially with dozens of visionaries like him or her. And he, like the others, if he is able, must find in the virtualizing and actualizing wefts of the Web the capacity to reproduce the miracle. And so the miracle no longer emerges from the epidemiological conditions of the physical location; if it does emerge, it emerges from the Web, that is, from the growth of a virtual context of apparitions and miracles. If contagion occurs, it emerges from the power of the Web itself.

In the second half of the nineties, there was a significant drop in the new cases of visions, which fell from 23, 26, and 27 cases in 1992, 1993, and 1994, respectively, to 14, 8, and 7 cases in 1997, 1998, and 1999.[134] The visionary phenomenon seems to be reinforced around previously attested visions and seers. An intriguing theory, which we shall be able to test over the coming years, states that, in the wake of the boom in the decade and a half spanning the eighties and the nineties, the depersonalizing power of the Web came increasingly into play, reducing the opportunities for new visionaries, and encouraging a shift from persons to information, from experience to digital.

If this proved to be true, then we should expect in the coming years to see not so much a new array of offline apparitions as the perfection of a mechanism for the democratization of charisma, conferred less by heaven than by the increasing diffusion of virtual reality, faster connections, and improvements in digital codes. Certainly, this would constitute a radical revolution in visionary culture, which up till now has been based chiefly upon the proliferation of seers.

On the other hand, it is difficult to imagine that the Web will entirely replace offline apparitions. There is in fact something that till now has remained absent from the Web, a fundamental resource that is extremely powerful and abundant outside the Web, in the territory of visions: the Internet does not cure physical ills; the virtual pilgrim, at least so far, has not obtained any miracle cures. The symbolic efficacy so far remains confined to the physical sites of the apparitions, within the charismatic communities: that efficacy would seem to be still restricted to the presence of a community, where only the presence of a collective allows the production of miracles upon individual bodies. And it is precisely this lack that helps us to glimpse the present weakness of the solitary Web surfer: the promise and the expectation are that she will be an absolute individual in her browsing, with no other restrictions than herself and the machine that sits before her—that promethean marriage of human and tool that she was told could serve as the foundation upon which to build a new world. But without those social and symbolic ties that all the same constitute her essence and which in a religious community would have appeared to her as the possibility of miracles, she finds that she is incomplete.

All the same, it will be necessary to determine whether the fundamental isolation of the Web surfer will always remain a hindrance to the possibilities of symbolic efficacy of the Web or whether, to the contrary, the development of virtual reality in conjunction with the Web, by expanding the array of possibilities for the perception of digital environments and offering a context that is more real than reality, a hyperreality, instead culminates in attributing phantasmatically a new symbolic effectiveness to the electronic contact of everyone with everyone else.

Chapter 2

THE END TIMES

Revelation is one of the books of the canon of sacred scripture and therefore the apocalyptic prospect, which emerges from the idea of the cosmic struggle between good and evil, is not heterodox. To the contrary, it is one of the crucial elements of the Catholic religious spirit.

A central document of the Vatican Council II, *Gaudium et spes,* reiterates this point: "For a monumental struggle against the powers of darkness pervades the whole history of man. The battle was joined from the very origins of the world and will continue until the last day, as the Lord has attested"[1] (Cf. Matt. 24:13; 13:24–30 and 36–43). But the religious language is ambiguous, manifold in its meanings.[2] There are metaphorical and allegorical interpretations and there are literal and direct interpretations. That which is written in official texts or stated with all the authority of the ecclesiastical magisterium does not also correspond to what is found to be the religious practice of the faithful: at times it varies considerably. In particular, on the very divisive subject of the end of the world, the division between the allegorical interpretation of the official doctrine inaugurated by Saint Augustine, and the literal interpretation of Revelation and the Apocalypse can grow into an abyss. And so there is a transcendental Revelation, read symbolically as an expression of the "precarious state of the world" and of the "sovereign power of Christ, in whose hands the fate of mankind is placed"[3] and there is an immanent Revelation, a detailed chronicle of the events to come, or even now occurring.

Visionary Catholicism places itself in the second camp: "Since 1830 . . . there has been a marked increase in reports of Marian apparitions, increasingly associated with warnings of dire calamities to be visited on mankind if it does not repent and mend its ways—a kind of Catholic millenarianism."[4]

In this century, Fatima (after the already apocalyptic nineteenth-century visions of the Rue du Bac, La Salette, and Pellevoisin) has been characterized by an apocalyptic dimension that has grown over the decades, through the long and nerve-wracking wait for the publication of the third secret, which was finally revealed in the year 2000.

Immediately after Fatima, we have Garabandal, the previously mentioned Spanish village, where a group of girls claimed to have seen the Madonna in the sixties. Repeatedly condemned by the local bishop, and even discounted by some of the visionaries themselves, in particular Conchita (who retracted, however, her own retraction), the case of Garabandal continues to nourish the contemporary Catholic visionary imagination. This was the source of the most famous message attributed to the Madonna on the warning that God was supposedly about to send to the world, through the intercession of the Madonna, in order to prevent the Punishment.

In the eighties, Medjugorje found its way into this current. The climate of end times became very vivid very quickly in this small town in Bosnia. For instance, one of the most common accounts of the visionaries had to do with Satan, who had appeared before God insinuating that the faith of believers was only for the "good times" and that "as soon as the situation takes a turn for the worse," people would stop believing in him: "And so God decided to give the Devil permission to hold sway over the entire world for a full century."[5]

It is said that Father Tomislav Vlasic, of the parish of Medjugorje, went to speak—according to another version he sent a letter—to no less a personage than Pope John Paul II about this handover of the entire twentieth century to the Devil.[6] The reference, on the verge of plagiarism, to Revelation is quite clear. This Devil who twists and turns furiously, aware that there is little time left, as the visionaries add, is very similar to the Devil in the book from the New Testament: "The devil is come down unto you, having great wrath, because he knoweth that he hath but a short time" (Rev. 12:12). And moreover, while Revelation mentions the destruction of one-third of humanity in the general punishment, Medjugorje echoes that prophecy with two-thirds of humanity destroyed. And that is not all.

The New Testament itself is obviously a primary source for the apocalyptic messages of contemporary apparitions. But another source is constituted by the messages themselves, which refer to one another reciprocally, influencing one another, and providing shared material for a surprising remythologizing of Christianity. One common text model was an imitation of an apocryphal third secret of Fatima, widely present in the devotional press, and only recently proven false: "Fire and smoke will fall from heaven, and the waters of the ocean will turn to steam, throwing their foam to the very sky. Whatever is standing will be overturned. Millions of people will die. Those surviving will envy the dead. Distress, misery and desolation will be found around the world."[7]

Here, for instance, is how the text was echoed in a message of the apparitions which took place at Akita, Japan, in 1973, and were recognized by the local bishop: "If men refuse to convert, Our Father will allow a great chastisement to fall on the entire human race. Fire will fall from the sky. Because of this chastisement most of humanity will be annihilated."[8]

Over recent years, the apocalyptic impulse has grown, both because of the very number of alleged apparitions that reinforce it, and because of the diffuse and spreading feeling of collective uncertainty, which often finds expression specifically in apocalyptic beliefs or attitudes, not only religious but also secular, and linked to fears of natural and ecological disasters.[9] Added to these factors is the globalization of the media, offering the entire world images, as it were, on a single screen with reports on catastrophic events, whatever corner of the planet they might happen to occur. This continual media-driven "staging" reinforces the apocalyptic trend, which provides a meaningful context within which to place the events. Moreover, it interacts with fiction, exchanging contexts, perceptions, and imaginary worlds. The apocalyptic current that has become popular in the mass media—movies, television, comics, and so on—the sign and the engine of these sensibilities, has nowadays attained vast scale. If you consider how many movies, television shows, best-selling books, comic strips, and features in the daily press and the Sunday supplements were dedicated to the fears of the year 2000, there is no doubt that at the root of it all was the marketing which encouraged the spread of those concerns. But then again, marketing is hardly a pure and decontextualized invention. Its effectiveness is bound up with the expectations, curiosities, and interests of the public, which may not be the product of a genuine and deep-seated fear, but which are also not simply a matter of entertainment and idle interest.

In comparison with the model of Fatima, the Apocalypse in contemporary Catholic apparitions has been enriched with new connotations derived from the media-driven imagination, which in the United States, in its turn, is influenced by and influences an extremely rich millenarian current of Protestant origin.

Apocalyptic beliefs are quite deep-rooted in the United States, and date back to the very origins of the country.[10] During the Reagan years, they found an advocate of enormous authority in the president himself and in his close associates. Ronald Reagan believed in an imminent Apocalypse, the final battle of Armageddon, and the interpretation that held that this battle would take actual form in a nuclear war with the Soviet Union. "For the first time ever, everything is in place for the battle of Armageddon and the Second Coming of Christ,"[11] he stated as early as 1971. And in 1983, as Giammanco recalls, he "invited Jerry Falwell, the televangelist and founder of the Moral Majority in person, to attend meetings of the National Security Council (NSC) in order 'discuss with the highest military authorities plans for the nuclear annihilation of the Soviet Union.'"[12]

Reagan's Secretary of Defense, Caspar Weinberger, stated in 1982: "I have read the Book of Revelation and yes, I believe the world is going to end—by an act of God, I hope—but every day I think time is running out."[13]

That this position was not exclusive to politicians was revealed by a survey conducted in 1984 for the Public Agenda Foundation, according to which 39 percent of the national American sampling believed that the Biblical prophecy "according to which the planet will be destroyed by fire tells us that nuclear war is inevitable."[14] And even today, according to a recent survey done by *U.S. News & World Report*,[15] 66 percent of all Americans believe in the Second Coming of Christ, a classic apocalyptic millenarian Protestant belief, common also, through Garabandal, to visionary Catholicism.

The power of the panorama of apocalyptic religious fears, moreover, has increased because it has converged with the panorama of technological fears. The prospect of the end of the world—no longer populated exclusively with figures from a religious context, such as Satan or Saint Michael, but brought up to date with the appearance of historical actors such as the Soviet Union, in the recent past, and such as Islam and the United States today—is viewed as a substantially plausible event because of the risks entailed by increasingly sophisticated weapons of mass destruction and the technological transformation of existence (incarnated by symbols such as microchips inserted under the skin and the supercomputers of the World Bank). In other words, the narrative of the end of the world is no longer entrusted solely to the metaphorical language of the Revelation according to Saint John, but also, and primarily, to the literal language of modern-day journalists, politicians, and scientists.

According to Michael Cuneo, in America, apocalyptic Catholic culture has undergone a strong Protestant influence, primarily through the filter of the evangelical media, television preachers, radio shows, and such best sellers as Hal Lindsey's book, *The Late Great Planet Earth*, published in 1970. To that, Cuneo continues, we should add a certain influence of the conspiracy mindset common to the American extreme right wing. [16]

The media-driven Apocalypse has expanded beyond the bounds of what could be imagined as pure entertainment, itself becoming a referential model for the activities of groups of religious apocalyptics. From time to time events dramatically portray this phenomenon in terms that can be described as pathological; exceptional though they may be, they clearly delineate the normality of the daily interchange between the media and the Apocalypse, and in more general terms, the overlapping of media and everyday life. [17] A dramatic example, for instance, is that of the two young girls in Cologne, Germany, who hanged themselves in February 1996 in order to reach the "fifth dimension," in imitation of the heroes of Star Trek, an exceedingly popular television series that has been a source of inspiration for many of those working in cyberspace: [18] "Don't cry for us. We are not dying in vain. We want to go to the Fifth Dimension. And there we will continue to live and we will always be with you." [19]

A recent current of the mass media is added, of course, in the general array of influences upon Catholic apocalyptic beliefs, to the more traditional school of prophetic and millenarian models that have been present for centuries in the Catholic world, resurfacing in more recent years in the texts of such mystics and visionaries as Padre Pio, Therese Neumann, Anna Katarina Emmerick, Maria Valtorta, and others. But new attitudes and concerns are emerging, in contrast with these figures.

Let us examine, for instance, one of the most widespread traditional apocalyptic beliefs, that of the three days of darkness that will envelop the earth.

> I need to explain that the words . . . are the exact words of the message given to me by the Virgin. . . . In those days, the ones who are not in the state of grace are going to die of fright because of the horrible demons that they will see. The Virgin told me to close all the doors and windows and not to respond to anyone who calls from the outside. The biggest temptation we will have is that the devil is going to imitate the voices of our loved ones. She told me, "Please do not pay attention because those are not your loved ones; those are demons trying to lure you out of the house." . . . She insists that we pray to the Lord that those days will not come in the winter and that there are not pregnant women about to give birth; because if they come in winter, the cold will be intense, there won't be any artificial heat, and the women about to give birth won't have any medical assistance. . . . She told me that the hours of darkness will be exactly 72, and the only way to count them is with mechanical clocks, because there won't be any electricity.[20]

Brother David, the Franciscan brother whom we have already met, tells in the *Medjugorje Newsletter* of August 1992 how he received this terrible and naïve message right in the Bosnian village. It is impossible to overlook in this modern-day rewriting of traditional prophecies a clear dimension of self-centered petit bourgeois selfishness.

The advice attributed to Jesus or the Madonna, and found in many apocalyptic messages, is to stay indoors, shut oneself up in one's home, when the three days of darkness or some other punishment begins; not to open the door to anyone, not to be deceived by the apparently friendly voices or faces of those who knock at the door, since it will be the Devil disguised as a friend. This fear of strangers runs constantly through messages, even those that are not apocalyptic. For instance, the seer Rita Ring informs us that Jesus allegedly told her:

> You need to be alone with your children. You must have time alone with them. This intimacy is what gives you all strength and direction in Me. When others penetrate this wall too much and you lack this closeness, your wall is weaker and Satan comes in. . . . This is the strength you need in this world: prayer in the family. Be alone with your children. It

builds a strong, holy wall around you. You need a united front against this world. This time is essential every day, time alone as a family. If others infiltrate this time, even on the phone, your united front becomes very weak. Playing games, praying, crafts, and music. TV in a sense weakens this wall because it is bringing in so much from the outside.[21]

Messages that encourage a hostile rejection of the world at large, to a greater or lesser degree than this one, are very frequent and express and foster a fear of others, of strangers, and often even of neighbors— a fear that finds confirmation, as well, in many currents of the media-driven imagination, constructing and articulating in many popular films a disquieting image of the outsider, the stranger, the alien.

Even the apparitions themselves have frequently moved away from outdoor locations, public places, social meeting places, to interior sites, private places, intimate spaces. The Madonna appears in the garage, in the living room, in the bedroom, even in the bathroom, or she speaks directly to the visionary's heart or finally—with remarkable timing—she speaks directly on the screen of one's computer.

It is noteworthy that these feelings of social hostility and mutual suspicion, a generalized fear of others, should have found a religious form precisely in the ancient apocalyptic belief in the millennium of peace and prosperity that the Second Coming of Christ supposedly will establish, prior to the decisive battle against evil, at the end of those thousand years of peace. Thanks to this belief, those feelings are allowed to hold out a hope for an immanent solution, historical and attainable, to the discomfort of a mutual fear and suspicion, inasmuch as the promised resolution and salvation belongs not to the world beyond, but to a purified earth: "After the three days of chastisement are over, there will be no ungodly persons left, the godless will be annihilated. Seventy-five percent of humanity will be destroyed, more men than women. Everyone left on earth will believe in God with all their hearts. The devastation will be astonishingly great, but the earth will be purified."[22]

In this scenario—in which the evil people will finally die and the good people will rule the earth, in which the Apocalypse is muddled with a spirit of revenge that has renounced all hopes of transcendence, collapsing into a selfish and bloody-minded immanence—not all fear the hour of punishment. Indeed many, swinging from a generalized terror to the eschatological hope allowed by the Apocalypse, cannot wait for that day to dawn, and they speak of it with a "sense of impatience":

Hi Phil: . . . I too have the same sense of impatience. . . . each day
that passes by is one less day of tribulation and one day closer to the
Triumph. Whenever I am feeling down I remind myself that after this
year there is only one year left and then "by the great jubilee of the year
two thousand, there will take place the triumph of my Immaculate
Heart of which I foretold you at Fatima, and this will come to pass with
the return of Jesus in glory, to establish his Reign in the world. Thus you
will at last be able to see with your own eyes the new heavens and the
new earth" . . . Peace, Ken.[23]

Hi Pat, I read your message regarding your anxious anticipation of
the promises our Lady made to Fr. Gobbi. I can so much relate to your
feelings. I too await the Second Coming with excited anticipation.
Ann.[24]

Some of the prophecies in circulation, including this one about the
three days of darkness, are not limited to spiritual recommendations, but
include as well practical advice on "physical preparation." If purification
is going to sweep the earth clean of the wicked and leave only the good—
except for the martyrs—then the good will need to prepare if they are
going to survive. There thus emerges a "survivalist" mindset, and even
the messages from heaven offer appropriate indications on the subject.
For instance, Louise Starr Tomkiel, one of the most catastrophe-minded
visionaries, distributed on 3 October 1998 a lengthy apocalyptic message
that she attributed to Jesus, forecasting earthquakes, wars, and varied
types of destruction; the only ones who would survive would be those
who have consecrated themselves and their property to Jesus and to the
Virgin Mary, and who have obtained adequate stocks of "necessities for
housing and food and water." Her message is echoed by another celestial
message: "Physical Preparation is also necessary, but not as pressing [as
spiritual preparation]. If possible, store away some food, water, rosaries,
scapulars, blankets, winter clothes, blessed candles/matches, devotional
material (Bible, prayer books, etc.), and the like. When the time comes,
though, our guardian angels will appear to us and guide us to safety."[25] A
twenty-five-year-old American Marine stationed in Iwakuni, Japan, posted
these suggestions on a Web site entirely dedicated to the imminent end
of the world. But the advice can be even more detailed. For instance, one
might suggest a list of provisions necessary for a family of four for seven
weeks:

In order to survive the tribulation by logic we should have in storage for several families for 3.5 years a warehouse like Costco/Sams Club etc. But, since we rely on God and the Blessed Virgin Mary, all Our Lord would like to see us do is at least try to store food for these end times. Most of us, especially along the coastal areas, will have to move anyways, so store as much as you can but be ready to leave and take what you can when it is time. Our Lord and the Blessed Virgin Mary tell us that the ones who say the rosary, try to live as we should and who do have faith, will be taken care of. Also, please read the expiration dates and rotate food accordingly. However, during the tribulations, we must be charitable and yet prudent. Discernment on who we are charitable to, is also necessary. Heaven says that your food supply will be replenished. Please be prudent and secrecy is somewhat important as the military will confiscate your goods. The following is only a guide. You may substitute for food of equal value. The brand names are not important! It is important to have supplies high in food value and that do not have to be cooked. Food may be warmed on top of your kerosene heater or wood stove. Remember, there will be NO gas, electricity or water. This food list is based on the needs of FOUR persons for seven weeks.[26]

There follow very detailed recommendations about meat, fish, vegetables, fruit, dairy products, soups, salt, animal feed if necessary, nonfood products, "an adequate supply of all necessary medicines," and personal hygiene products. This message from Father Andrew, known as "The Trumpeter," represents one of the extreme cases I have found. On the site there is a list of calamities, each with suggestions of how to avoid them and how to survive: wars, revolutions, diseases, earthquakes, epidemics, nuclear leaks. Moreover, Father Andrew, whose photograph together with Pope John Paul II holds pride of place on every page in the Web site, offers a long list of devotional objects that may be helpful in warding off danger. They range from the incense of Saint Michael Archangel against demons to the herbs of the Madonna, from the miraculous grapes of Saint Damian to the holy oil of Saint Charbel, from the holy water of Saint Joseph to a long series of miraculous medallions and crosses. The site also offers information about the Catholic communities that will be designated as shelters in the days of chastisement. Two are located in Canada, one of which will house the pope after he flees the Vatican; four are in the United States; and others are in Mexico, Asia, and Europe.

It is difficult to evaluate cases of this sort objectively. We are in the presence of an extreme version of apocalyptic ideology, on the verge of caricature. It is no accident that on an Internet site with the eloquent name of *Campaign for Net Frivolity*,[27] among the sites that are ridiculed is the Web site of the "Trumpeter," and there is a special emphasis on the inevitable presence of the "angel of commerce": "the world is ending—major credit cards accepted."

I cannot evaluate the depth and power of the impact of Father Andrew's messages. But it would be wrong to focus on the issue of how marginal these ideas may be with respect to the more orthodox and official acceptance of the expectations of the Apocalypse in Catholicism. Inside the Internet the central and the marginal do not follow the same geography as is the case outside the Internet. The extremely horizontal orientation of relations and exchanges between sites, and therefore the absence of the institutional hierarchies that apply in "real" life, make it much more problematic to rely upon the categories of the central and the marginal.

Another distinctive element of the contemporary prophetic scenarios is the concern with the safety of private property, a concern which holds steady in the end times. There are numerous messages on the Internet about the three days of darkness in which it is said that "God will preserve the property of the chosen" and that it is important to consecrate property and person in order to survive the battle between God and Satan. To preserve the safety of your family and property, some believe that we should not hesitate to engage in violence. In fact, in order to keep out of your own house those who will come knocking on your door during the Warning, you may need to do more than simply not open that door. To offer an example, let us peruse the list of links found on the Web page of an Internet source that is above suspicion: Mission Net's Catholic Resource Mall—one of the five hundred Catholic sites recommended by the book *Catholicism on the Web*, by Thomas C. Fox, editor of the periodical *National Catholic Reporter*. There we will find, among other sites, *Frugal Squirrel's Homepage for Patriots, Survivalists, and Gun Owners*,[28] which provides information about survival techniques for "patriots" and "survivalists"— in the "authentic traditional American spirit"—for handgun owners and knife fans. Among other things, it claims that every thirteen seconds an armed American uses a handgun to defend himself or herself against a criminal attack, and that between January and August of 2000 in the United States, 1,575,086 criminal assaults were prevented by the use of handguns on the part of the potential victims. It is not hard to guess what industrial lobby is behind a Web site of this sort. On the other hand, there was an implicit convergence of groups of visionary Catholics and Protestant fundamentalists with groups of "patriots" and "survivalists" around the apocalyptic expectations of Y2K (see the Introduction) in the conservative American political landscape.[29]

Apocalyptic beliefs, whether they are religious or secular, can be broken down—Daniel Wojcik suggests—into two groups, the fatalistic and the nonfatalistic.[30] The first set clearly subscribes to the idea that the impending catastrophic events are inevitable, and therefore any initiatives on the part of humans would be totally useless; people can only pray and trust in the final victory. According to the second group of beliefs, on the other hand, it is still possible to intervene in order to modify the course of events, so that the catastrophe can be averted. Generally speaking, Catholic apocalyptic beliefs tend to fall into the second camp, rejecting the ineluctability of the punishment: from Rue du Bac on, along with the invitation to pray, there has also been an invocation of repentance; prayer and repentance have been considered effective means for warding off punishment. The same Warning that was discussed at Garabandal underlines, precisely, the possibility of avoiding the Punishment and often, when an apocalyptic prophecy proved to be unfounded, worshipers would attribute the fact to the efficacy of prayer and repentance. But a few recent examples of American Catholic prophecies, borrowing from Protestant models, slip toward a fatalistic belief in the imminent inexorability of a violent end.

The apocalyptic spirit linked to the Marian apparitions develops essentially out of apparitions that were not approved by the church. After Fatima, the apocalyptic matrix recognized among the most important apparitions of the twentieth century, many apparitions were not officially approved. The most frequently cited in absolute terms, Medjugorje and Garabandal, not only did not receive ecclesiastical approval, but were severely criticized. Among contemporary apocalyptic sites, only Betania in Venezuela, Akita in Japan, and Kibeho in Rwanda have been recognized; all the others were condemned, tolerated, or ignored. But the worshipers are not particularly worried about this aspect. In a message like the following, it is possible to sense the tacit criticism of the filter imposed by the ecclesiastical magisterium:

> However, if someone said a hurricane was coming, would you just sit there and read only approved books of the Church? Fatima took 30 years for approval, so should you have ignored those messages for 30

years? . . . What would be better is to COMPARE the current prophecies to
the Church teachings to discern instead of ignoring them. If you don't
think a Divine hurricane is coming, so be it. Bruce.[31]

In effect, the apocalyptic ethos, with the loss of all connection to a hierarchy of doctrinal and institutional references, has become a sort of useful
horizon to rely upon for interpretation and description of weird weather,
the risk of nuclear attack, economic recessions, social breakdown, political
corruption, the dangers of biotechnology, and even collective psychological problems.

> One would have to be blind, deaf and dumb not to see the signs as we
> see steadily head towards total societal chaos. I am a Mental Health
> Crisis Consultant, and I can tell you that in the two-county, rural area
> where I live and work, conditions have drastically worsened with regard
> to suicides and homicides with adults and teens as well. What we have,
> as a nation, accepted to be appropriate and acceptable behavior, never
> ceases to amaze me, and has certainly been foretold to us by our Lady.
> I will continue to prepare myself and my family spiritually for the
> inevitable events Mary has foretold us about.[32]

This horizon is now almost entirely independent of the official religious "system"—institutions, rules, hierarchies—within which beliefs
and practices should theoretically fit. The Church by this point is practically relegated to the background. Joseph Hunt, the "Internet Advocate
for Roman Catholic Visionaries," states that God "gave us scripture and
the Church for the 'How to . . .' of our faith, but he also gives us private
revelation for the 'When to . . .' of our faith in certain times of history.
And we are in a very grave historical period right now."[33]

For believers, this horizon of description and interpretation cannot
be left open to discussion, it is simply a matter of common sense—"you
would have to be blind, deaf and dumb"—indeed, it is obvious that it gives
rise to a quest for an appropriate plan of action:

> Question to anyone who read Carol's latest drastic message. Exactly what
> should we pack to take along with us when we need to leave our homes?
> Any advice as to how I pack for a family with 4 kids? Also, where are
> we supposed to go to avoid nuclear fallout here in California? There are
> no bombshelters or basements where I live. I'm not in a panic, but I do

want to be prepared. Any advice would be appreciated. Christ's peace
and love to you all. Jan.[34]

Jan was referring, in an exchange of e-mails in a devotional mailing
list, to a very stark and dramatic message that Carol Ameche, a visionary
from Scottsdale, was diffusing about nuclear war, environmental disasters, and calamities of all sorts that were about to strike the planet, and
about what could be done to protect oneself. In response to Jan's e-mail,
the moderator of the mailing list, Raissa Light, admonished all the members of the list, reminding them of the rule against discussing any apparitions except those that had either been approved or were under investigation, which was not the case of Ameche's apparitions. But at least one
member objected:

> I do not know what the message refers to, I did not read it. . . . I
> responded only to Jan on the basis of any disaster that could, or might
> befall us. I live in Florida and we have had a terrible winter of rain
> and flooding, then to go into summer with drought and fires and now
> hurricane season is upon us. I told her what I was doing to prepare my
> family for any kind of disaster. Which is the smart thing to do when you
> are responsible for children, their welfare and lives . . . Theresa.[35]

Immediately afterward, another letter:

> Theresa . . . I do think you are right in preparing yourself and children
> for the chastisement as Mary has told us to do through her messages to
> Fr. Gobbi. As well, as you have so correctly stated, the weather has been
> so bizarre and dangerous, that one must today prepare for the worst.
> We have been given precious gifts in our children and we, as parents,
> are expected to plan for their safety. We know from what Fr. Gobbi
> has shared with us, times will get worse (we are seeing this daily), and
> those of us who are willing to take heed of Mary's messages, will armor
> ourselves spiritually and yes, materially for what lays ahead in the near
> future. . . . Ann.[36]

What was being urged was to call for a specific course of action sufficient to ward off any individual feelings of fear—"I am not in panic,"
wrote Jan—and to act in a reasonable and cautious manner, since, as everyone assured each other, the world is proceeding and will proceed in

accordance with Marian prophecies (which, for that matter, with a circular confirmation, correspond precisely to the things that anyone can see in
daily life). And so the apocalyptic view, paradoxically, becomes a rational
way to control one's life and the lives of one's near and dear:

> After all, Mary isn't warning us of these events, just to keep us company.
> She has been sent on a mission by her Son with the hope that all His
> children will listen and benefit from His mother's words of warning,
> love and hope of salvation for all those who are willing to listen and react
> to her messages.[37]

In effect, the apocalyptic ethos is a basic prerequisite—a founding
paradigm—confirmed by the beliefs and by events interpreted in such
a way as to confirm, recursively, those same beliefs, which—once it has
been chosen—allows one to derive rationally, deductively, a form of behavior. What might seem to some to be entirely irrational behavior is simply
what reason dictates to the eyes of the apocalyptics. Faith is merely an initial presupposition, then reason does the rest. That the central instrument
of control is a form of rationality becomes evident precisely when conflicts
of interpretation or contradictions among the various messages arise:

> I must admit I am confused about what is to come. Very much so I
> want to believe in the Warning and other events which are prophesied.
> Part of the problem is one person says Mary states this and another
> states something else. Maybe someone out there can help me with my
> confusion. If Mary is appearing all over the world why do the messages
> seem singular to each case and not coordinated? Pat.[38]

Fifteen days later, the same person, after an exchange of ideas with the
various correspondents, had resolved her doubts, suggesting a comparison of the various sources rather than a total faith in any given visionary,
calling for a thoughtful distance and detachment rather than blind acceptance:

> I think we should be listening to all the messages by Mary as long
> as they do not go against the laws of The Church. Mary is telling us
> in many places around to be prepared for something. . . . personally
> we should be looking at *the whole picture* rather than one person over
> another. . . . We can't judge apparitions presently we can only wait to see

the results but to dismiss them in my opinion is a mistake. The year
2000 is fast approaching and we as Catholics must be prepared. Jacci.[39]

To summarize, the apocalyptic landscape that has now prevailed in
Marian apparitions, especially in America, in part due to Protestant influence—and as we have seen the American apparitions are currently the
most important ones, second only to Medjugorje and Garabandal—is progressively losing all transcendence and becoming an immanent script for
events that are about to take place on earth, a script that requires millenarianistic purification and demands not only spiritual preparation but also
material preparation. In that panorama, Saint Augustine's cosmic vision
of the Apocalypse, a milestone in the official Catholic interpretation, is
replaced by a concrete, historic, event-based vision, recognized and confirmed in the daily economic, political, and scientific news from around
the world. It is based on the interpretation of daily world events, taken
from the planetary news circuit, providing the whole picture of prophecies
and messages in hundreds of ideologically unified texts.

In this religious universe, so profoundly restructured, one figure that
has been marginalized is that of the Devil. In a certain sense, the division
between the good and the evil has already taken place, and so there is almost no longer any time for the Devil's chief task, temptation. Taking his
place are new figures of evil, in a sense an expression of the Devil himself,
but now endowed with an independence of operation typical of the end
times. In particular, the Antichrist or the antichrists, in turn Saddam Hus-
sein, Arafat, Bin Laden, Schroeder, Blair, and Clinton, guilty of working
for "world government," the ultimate expression of evil; and then other
institutional figures of wickedness, the United Nations, the World Bank,
the International Monetary Fund, the Euro, all guilty of expressing political trends that the American visionaries and their devotees consider diabolical, confusing their own visions of national economic interests with
the cosmic good.

There remains unresolved a central question of the apocalyptic horizon, which is that the various widespread prophecies unfailingly prove to
be inaccurate. How can an operative landscape for common sense function when the evidence to the contrary is provided so regularly, and clear
evidence in favor is so difficult to find? For instance, let us consider just
how many predictions of the end of the world in the year 2000 were shown
to be false.

In effect, while on the one hand the proliferation of prophecies may expose them to the risk of frequent and outright contradiction by the facts, on the other hand it makes it easier to fish among the myriad events that occur in a world that has become a "global village," knit together by the information furnished by the network of the mass media. Earthquakes, hurricanes, floods, famines, local wars, refugees, monetary crises, financial collapses, and other natural disasters or social crises are present every day in newspapers and television news broadcasts all over the world. The interpretive efforts of the visionaries, their spiritual advisors, and the worshipers are easily able to adapt a relatively generic prophecy to a concrete event selected from the vast ocean of current events, and to assemble the physical components of various catastrophes with the metaphysical elements of divine punishment.

> Dear List Members,
> Does the devastation in Nicaragua (about 8,500 killed) so far from Hurricane Mitch and now unknown thousands killed from the erupting volcano remind you of part of the Fatima message that "entire nations will be annihilated?" . . . Ron Smith.[40]

Once a connection has been made, the successive prophecies by the same or other visionaries focus on the same event, confirming it, commenting upon it, and reinterpreting it. Already at Oliveto Citra I had noticed in my research a similar process. When the disaster occurred in the nuclear plant of Chernobyl in the spring of 1986, someone drew a connection to a Marian message from a few months earlier, which mentioned rivers of milk that flowed but could not be drunk. From this generic connection came new Marian messages in which the connection was direct and no longer metaphorical. And so, in May of the same year, it was the Madonna who spoke, but explicitly this time, about the "bad time of the toxic cloud" now past, while other bad times were arriving, and in a certain sense inspired the comment of the parish priest who emphasized that Chernobyl "was giving us a foretaste these days of what might, unfortunately, happen someday."[41]

Sometimes, however, the visionaries prophesy an event with very specific dates and effects, and then the prophecy proves to be inaccurate. How do the worshipers react in such instances?

In these cases, there is a context of apocalyptic interpretations at work, based on "incorrigible propositions," which has the peculiar property of self-confirming even when events would seem to contradict them.

A corrigible proposition is one that you would withdraw and admit to be false if certain things happened in the world. . . . An incorrigible proposition is one which you would never admit to be false *whatever* happens: it therefore does not tell you *what* happens. . . . I think that in a sense it is true to say that it prescribes what you are to *say*—it tells you *how to describe* certain happenings.[42]

The mailing lists provide us with an interesting opportunity to follow in detail an example of the ferment that spreads among the worshipers at the approach of a significant date foretold by some visionary and then at the subsequent failure of the prophecy to come true.

There was a converging prophecy by numerous American visionaries, according to which on 13 October 1998 "something" was going to happen. That day would be the recurrence of the last apparition of Fatima, which had taken place eighty-one years before (eighty-one is a product of 9×9, the number that corresponds to divine judgment in Revelation). On that day, moreover, the visionary Nancy Fowler was scheduled to receive the last public message from the Madonna, and another visionary, Patricia Mundorf, was scheduled to receive a sign over her house. The visionaries announcing the imminent "something" included Joseph Reyes, who called upon Mirjana of Medjugorje, Patricia Mundorf, Nancy Fowler, and others. Immediately discussions began in the mailing list among worshipers in an attempt to establish what it could be. Some said that it would be the Warning, the famous alert announced previously at Garabandal; others spoke of a simple preliminary alert; some thought it would be a miracle; others spoke of a great miracle; some expected the first secret of Medjugorje, finally manifested by divine power; there was even someone who guessed at the arrival of the great triumph of the Virgin Mary, but he was immediately contradicted. That was expected in the year 2000, according to Father Gobbi and others.

Who said it, where did they say it, what did they really mean to say: these were all questions that the correspondents exchanged with one another in an attempt to find a generally accepted interpretation. As the appointed day gradually approached, activity increased and with it, concern. Michael connected this date to a number of other dates that had been foretold: not only by Father Gobbi for the triumph of the Virgin Mary, but also by Father Malachy Martin for the arrival of the Antichrist on the world stage in 1999, for the beginning of the battle between the armies of the Archangel Michael and Lucifer on 1 January 1999, for the Triple

Corrections of Heaven between March and May of the same year, to the end of the century of Satan on 31 December 1999 and the kingdom of God in 2000: all confirmed by a reading of the text of Saint John. Pat, thanks to her Baptist cousin, reported that in other religious worlds as well something was expected for the thirteenth of October. In other words, it seemed to everyone that humanity itself was about to enter the convulsive final phase. On 7 October, with only a few days left to go, a message circulated in numerous discussion groups: "Alert—all catholics!!! Catholic visionaries all over the world are receiving messages of imminent nuclear war!"

But the following day, Joe stopped everyone dead by reminding them that the thirteenth was a Tuesday, and that the Warning would certainly not take place. Why? Because the Lord had already told the visionary Reyes that the Warning would come while everyone was at the stadium attending a football game, and therefore on a Saturday or a Sunday, because he was offended at the fact that his day had become the day of football. A message came immediately from Kathy, who reminded all the others that there was also going to be a very important football game on the evening of Monday the twelfth, and that because of the difference in time zones, when it was being played in the United States, it would already be Tuesday the thirteenth in Europe: therefore the two different versions of the prophecy could perhaps be reconciled, the punishment for football and the date of Tuesday the thirteenth. Then Peter chimed in, claiming that whatever was about to take place—a natural disaster, perhaps a nuclear attack, perhaps a Russian reaction to the possible NATO bombing in Kosovo, according to the prophecy of Carol Ameche—none of it would constitute the Warning proper to his mind. Pat announced that she was beginning to get scared, but someone reminded her that she needed to pray and trust in God, as well as prepare suitable stocks of food and necessaries. Sure, Pat replied, but when I am afraid, it is not out of a lack of faith, but simply because I suffer from anxiety and from panic attacks even though, admittedly, faith ought to be stronger than the frailties of the body and the chemical imbalances of the organism. In any case, she pointed out, that had been a good day for her, "chemically speaking."

Even outside the mailing lists, in many Marian Web pages "documents" were being offered on the impending date. One of the worshipers who was most passionately involved in the debate was William Zambrano, an American oculist who had established one site dedicated to the Jubilee, and another site devoted specifically to the Warning. The latter of the two, called *Eyedoctor's Site: The Warning*,[43] immediately offered, probably with unintentional self-parody, the warning to "be watchful," and it was full of catastrophistic messages taken from a fair array of visionaries and locutionists, as well as from Garabandal and Medjugorje, and from the inevitable Revelation. But the entire Catholic prophetic and apocalyptic baggage concentrated on this Web site was directed toward and was about to culminate on this date and in this location: 13 October, in Conyers.

And then the thirteenth of October arrived. The TV cameras of dozens of television stations arrived in Conyers to view the last message of the Madonna to Nancy Fowler, following which a miracle had been predicted. CNN was preparing to broadcast images in news reports that would then be carried by television stations around the world. The fields around the sanctuary built at Conyers filled with tens of thousands of worshipers, who prayed constantly, watched and participated in the ceremonies, and waited for the sign. Nancy proclaimed the last message, the priests said the last Mass of the day, but no sign appeared, no "something" occurred.

Two days passed, two long days for the correspondents of mailing lists who were used to writing and reading e-mails to and from one another over the course of frenetic days in which they repeatedly signed on to the Marian list. "Why weren't there any 'eyewitnesses' of what had happened in Conyers?" wondered Jim, at last. "How come nobody can tell us what happened in Phoenix. If there's someone who's been there please post" asked Jaime, in *Marian Discussion*.[44] Many must have wondered what had become of the ever-so-active Doctor Zambrano. And he finally surfaced, on the fifteenth, with a long and painful letter:

> So. October 13th has passed. No earth shattering message from
> Conyers. No great sign (though we are told that this was mitigated by
> prayer). No Warning. No rapture. Perhaps you are feeling a little down.
> The "Blessed Hope" that we await appears perhaps a little farther away
> today. I've been there. Many times over the past several years. Times
> when I was sure "something" was going to happen. Only to have the
> day pass by uneventfully. Even someone as stubborn as me has learned
> from these past disappointments. We are told to watch. And watch we
> should. We are told of the conditions of the world prior to the return of
> Jesus. And these conditions are not just surrounding us but at times
> suffocating us. Yet sometimes we go beyond watching to predicting or
> anticipation. And are disappointed. Let's not forget Isaiah 55:8–9: "For
> my thoughts are not your thoughts, neither are your ways my ways"

declares the LORD. "As the heavens are higher than earth, so are my ways higher than your ways and my thoughts than your thoughts."[45]

The letter ended with another pair of quotations from the Bible, with the pope's encouragement to "have no fear," with an invitation to surrender to the will of God, and not to take the words of visionaries as gospel truth.

New arguments broke out. On one side were those who engaged in irony or accused the seers who had proved to be impostors—noting that other seers, clearly more reliable, had predicted nothing—while on the other side were those who employed a hermeneutic strategy in order to confirm the prophecy, either by identifying the Sign or by finding many little signs among the everyday activities of that all too unmemorable day.

In particular, Patricia Mundorf, who had prophesied a sign from heaven directly over her house in Phoenix, diffused a message from the Madonna, who, somewhat offended by the generalized skepticism that had followed the thirteenth, informed everyone that there had been a sign from heaven, and what a sign it had been! Through her intercession, a nuclear war had been prevented, a nuclear war that had been on the verge of breaking out following the NATO attacks on Serbian positions, which had been about to trigger a Russian nuclear attack in defense of the Serbs.[46]

Patricia Mundorf, imitated by others, therefore tried to reformulate the description of what had actually happened on 13 October, in other words, to prescribe a way of describing the events in order to make it possible to confirm the model. After the first few, others joined the process, reporting celestial signs of lesser dimension and less spectacular impact. There were those who claimed to have been "truly" converted, others said that they witnessed the conversion of a nonbelieving neighbor, various others had seen their rosary miraculously transformed into gold, had taken photographs upon which celestial figures had miraculously appeared, had seen the sun move and dance in the sky, had felt no hunger or sleepiness even after hours and days, and so on. Then there were those who believed that the punishment had been averted because the general fear had encouraged conversions, prayers, and repentance. There followed a flood of e-mails, in order to circumscribe and reinforce the various schools of interpretation that had been set forth, discounting the fiercest critics and at the same time restricting the area of possible descriptions.

At a certain point correspondent John Lucas intervened, redirecting the form of descriptions, focusing everyone's attention on the sky and stating that on the night of the thirteenth there had been a visible dimming and reduction in size of the star Sirius. Adrienne asked him or anyone else to tell her about the star in question, because she knew nothing about it. Lisa added: not only would she like someone to explain the importance of the star, but also why "we should be concerned that it is no longer visible."[47]

Thus disappointment began to give way to a new theme of description of the coming Apocalypse, allowing the resumption of the incessant interplay of interpretations, discussions, and disagreements about the end of the world.

And so, a hermeneutic conversation among worshipers had helped to digest the refutation of the prophecy, through the reformulation of the descriptions, thus reconfirming the more general prophetic panorama.

In conclusion, this apocalyptic view is a cultural model that feeds itself with growing intensity in the contemporary world due to the convergence of numerous factors: the complete collapse of all progressive ideologies and the consequential disappearance of any expectations of a brighter future; the use that marketing makes of the collective sensibility toward apocalyptic themes; the concurrent concentration of the hermeneutic efforts of various religious faiths and creeds on the "mysterious" meaning to be attributed to the passage from one millennium, just closing, to another, just dawning; the media-driven power of globalized information, presenting the dramatic events of the world. To "enter," as it were, into the apocalyptic model, that is, to allow oneself to be seduced by its manifold allure (for personal, ethnic, economic or political, cultural, or religious reasons, or any combination thereof; rather than being root causes, though, these reasons can be said to be a manner of consumption), is tantamount to putting into operation a very efficient mechanism, whereby everything has a meaning: from Marian prophecies (if that is the door through which one enters) to catastrophe movies, from the New Age to astrology.

In a historic period without any strong ideological structures, so vital in the previous decades, which might allow a guided and orderly analysis of events that increasingly span a global dimension, the Apocalypse is an attractive alternative to the chaos of the depictions of the world and the potential disorder of the information provided by the mass media: "Those who heed My warnings and trust in Me instead of TV, newspapers, magazines and radio commentaries will be at peace both in their hearts and in their homes."[48]

In the final analysis, the Apocalypse accomplishes, on an intellectually impoverished level, yet, in psychological terms, in a strong and reassuring manner, what has eluded the grasp of political ideologies and
philosophies of history: it colors the world in sharp blacks and whites,
extracting it from that diffuse shade of gray in which it is generally seen,
because of the difficulties in clearly identifying things in terms of distinct
and well-defined values; it establishes a meaning, however rudimentary,
in the general chaos of the world; it explains history, which is—alas!—no
longer a history of progress, nor even is it history, by making use of the
cosmic figures of good and evil, of Christ and the Antichrist; it restores all
those things that seemed to be proceeding anarchically and in a condition
of disarray into a state of order, into a protective scheme provided by the
Madonna herself,[49] who protects and reassures just as, paradoxically, she
orients us toward an increasingly muddled outlook, that of the end of the
world, or at least the end of this world. To many, the existence of some
meaning, some order, some understanding of the world, however catastrophic and apocalyptic, is preferable to not ever understanding what is
happening and to never knowing what might happen next.

Chapter 3

SCIENCE, TECHNOLOGY, AND APPARITIONS

Photography of the Supernatural

Photography of apparitions and, to a lesser degree, videos, constitute the most substantial case of technological colonization
of the practices and the imaginary world of Catholic visionaries (and not them alone). A plastic box made of lenses and
microchips, with a film or a floppy disk, is considered capable
of capturing and rendering visible to anyone at all an invisible
image from the world beyond, which she can then take home,
put in a drawer, and pull out on any occasion, like any other
object. With the photography of the supernatural, there is a
transition from the personal experience of a human being to
an object, a technological product, and in the final analysis, a
merchandise, that may be purchased and paid for online and
with a credit card.

Photographs and videos of the supernatural render completely obsolete the tension between charism and institution,
since in order to obtain a contact with heaven through an image and an accompanying message, the worshiper no longer
needs either the charismatic or visionary or the ecclesiastical

institution. All that he or she needs is the appropriate technology or money to purchase the appropriate products.

Catholicism has been accustomed, from the very earliest centuries, to a form of religious education based on the devotional image, in which the physicality of the representation or even the display of the divine played a central role. This educational model was the subject of ferocious debate and dispute, right from the earliest centuries. There is no real need to describe the dramatic historical episodes of the conflict that divided the iconoclasts and the iconophiles, and not only in the eighth century. The distinction that progressively took hold in the earliest centuries between idols and images[1] offered at least the theoretical possibility of distinguishing between the correct and orthodox use of images and their idolatrous use, between that which referred to a transcendent God and that which identified an immanent power. In effect, however, the theological distinction could be upheld only through a continuous practical recognition, case by case, of that which was idolatrous and that which was not. And of course that process occurred on the terrain of a struggle for power between popular customs and ecclesiastical attitudes, in the general landscape of political considerations and diplomatic compromises.

But the current state of photography of the supernatural gives an entirely different status to the devotional image, which could scarcely be understood within the context of the age-old discussions on the use and abuse of images.

Let us begin by noting that photography of the silhouette of the Madonna or of the face of Jesus in the apparitions is neither a recent nor an unexpected development, either from the point of view of the Catholic devotional tradition nor in terms of the history of photography. Epiphanous images of the Catholic supernatural, on the one hand, and photographic applications of the yearnings for contact with the beyond, on the other, are historical forerunners of the present-day photography of the supernatural.

One much-discussed and famous epiphanic image is the Holy Shroud, or Sindon, which according to common belief is the winding cloth upon which, at the moment of the resurrection of Christ, almost the same process took place that is produced on a piece of photographic film when it is struck by rays of light. We should actually use the plural, and speak of Shrouds, because before the Shroud of Turin was officially named the Shroud, at the behest of Saint Charles Borromeo, there were at least nine others in circulation throughout Europe, each contending for official authenticity; there were shrouds in Saint John Lateran, Saint Mary Major, and Saint Peter's.

Another miraculous image recognized by the church is that of the Madonna of Guadalupe, in Mexico, who supposedly impressed her image, like some photograph *ante litteram,* on the cape (*tilma*) of Juan Diego, an Indian who was said to have had this vision at the turn of the sixteenth century.[2] As Wojcik notes, "Descriptions of the creation of such images suggest the features of photographs, as emanations and luminous imprints, and like these previous divine images, miraculous photographs appear similarly free from human influence."[3]

The Shroud and the *tilma,* then, are miraculous photographs preceding the era of photography, and the miraculous photographs are so many Shrouds of the New Age. A virtuous circle reinforces the plausibility of both: theological and technological plausibility.

Photography, after all, in itself has certain "apparitional qualities," as Wojcik notes, and the Polaroid in particular accentuates that quality, inasmuch as it produces "images [that] appear instantaneously and seemingly of their own accord, through a chemical-optical process that produces spectral doubles of reality."[4]

It is not entirely surprising that in the nineteenth century, a century that was growing increasingly dependent upon technology, ancient beliefs concerning relations with the world beyond should find new instruments to use in the new devices offered by technology. The documentary quality of photography was immediately accompanied by the recognition of a certain visionary power that it possessed. Indeed, just sixteen short years after the invention of the first photographic process, the daguerreotype (1839), we have the first spirit photographs:

The first examples of what would later be called "spirit photographs" dated back to 1855, when it was first discovered that, during the course of a number of seances, photographic plates could be impressed with strange whitish spots. Insistent use of the medium, on the part of a wide and diverse array of European experimenters, would in time lead to results that were considered to be more important. Fleeting images, fragments of a "fluidic" body, in some exceptional cases, entire figures took form in what were called, at the time, "materializations" (i.e., of the souls of the deceased). These "materializations" could be "visible," that is, they could cause an impression upon the human retina, or "invisible," causing an impression only upon the photographic plate.[5]

These photographs played an important role in the construction of the "scientific demonstration of the existence of souls in the afterlife" which at the end of the nineteenth century so impassioned the fervid minds of the Western scientific and cultural milieu, split between supporters and critics of spiritism.[6] In substance, the photograph, considered as an instrument for the objective understanding of reality, which the subjective limitations of the human being could never hope to equal, was ordained with a function of knowledge that extended right up to the boundaries of the world beyond, boundaries that it even tried to venture across.

Francesco Faeta notes that many have considered photography to be an ideal instrument for a rising middle class, precisely because it seems to provide documentation and certainty:

> The photograph embodies the nexus that links sight and knowledge, reconfirming the primacy of vision but, at the same time, removing the sense of sight from the subject context in which it is perceived, and transforming it into an undeniable document, endowed with social significance. No one can doubt that what I have seen and what I state, as a witness of a natural or human event, is reliable and collectively accessible.[7]

That which had been entirely overlooked in photography, according to Faeta, was precisely the fact that it possessed a subjective dimension, that it was an interpretation of reality.

Precisely its presumed objectivity and its concealed subjectivity made photography an ideal new "site" for the marvelous and the wonderful.

A miracle that appeared fairly early in the history of photography had to do with the photographs themselves, on the surface of which supposedly miraculous phenomena occurred—and still occur today. In the 1930s, at Ezkioga, in the Basque Country of northern Spain, there were photographs of images of the Madonna and Jesus which bled. In fact, in 1933, bleeding actually occurred from a photograph that depicted a collage of two photographs of Jesus and the Madonna which had, previously, also bled. If we consider that the subject of the first photograph was the Christ of Limpias, a crucifix that had bled in 1918, we find ourselves in the presence of a series of transitions of scale: a bleeding statue, a bleeding photograph of the statue, a bleeding photograph of the photograph of the statue.[8]

In cases of this sort, the photograph simply takes the place of the more traditional painted or carved images that either weep or come to life, which populate devotional history right up to the present day: among the most recent examples, in Baton Rouge, Louisiana, in 1993, a heartbeat was detected in a life-sized photograph of the Virgin of Guadalupe.

It should be recalled that at least one other "marvelous" use was made of photography in the nineteenth century, worth remembering because it constitutes the prehistory of contemporary phenomena: "psychography." Claiming that it was possible receive messages from the deceased upon photographs, psychography was a forerunner of those celestial messages that—as we shall see—worshipers from all over the world now "read" upon their miraculous photographs.[9] Recently, this belief has been extended to television: on the screens of television sets tuned to unused channels it is possible to decipher, at least according to those who practice these forms of "channeling," messages from the dead.

Finally, photography also influenced beliefs concerning other miraculous images which we encounter today:

> Nineteenth-century ideas about supernatural photography are also suggested by numerous legends concerning flashes of lightning imprinting extraordinary photographic images on glass window panes. Early accounts often refer to the miraculous or supernatural nature of these lightning prints, some of which included faces of ghosts and the recently deceased, as well as ineradicable images that served as supernatural reminders of the miscarriage of justice or divine retribution for blasphemy. . . . In a study of this subject, Barbara Allen (1982) notes that these lightning print legends began circulating after the new technology of glass-plate negatives was first used in studio photography in 1851. The lack of understanding of the photographic process at the time, and the mental association of glass plates, a flash of light, and the creation of photographic images in studio portraiture may have given rise to the belief that lightning could similarly create photographic images on a pane of glass.[10]

It is hardly surprising that in the age of supernatural Marian photography, even these last-mentioned beliefs should become popular again, though of course changing in orientation. It was no longer ghosts (even though people still believed in ghosts) but the Madonna who now appeared unexpectedly on glass panels. Among the images of this sort—and new cases are reported on a continual basis—one of the best known is certainly the one reported in Clearwater, Florida. In December 1996 a number of plants were cleared away from the side of a glass-walled office building, headquarters of the Seminole Finance Company. Someone then noticed on the plate-glass windows the impression of a silhouette extending over an area 15 meters wide and 10 meters tall; the shape was immediately recognized as an image of the Madonna. A pilgrimage began which, within the course of a few weeks, swelled to over a million people, all praying or asking for miracle cures or simply milling about curiously. Someone theorized that the image had been produced by the cleaning fluids used on the plate glass, but the worshipers pointed out that it was quite odd that the fluids should have created precisely that unmistakable image, and that in any case it was strange that the image did not vanish with the passage of time. The following spring, one night, unknown vandals tried to damage the image with chemical solvents. Despite the evident modifications, the overall image remained substantially intact. The owner of the office building, Mike Krizmanich, promised that he would transform the building into a sanctuary. In the end, he sold it to the Catholic religious organization of the Shepherds of Christ Ministries, mentioned above, which turned it into a sort of devotional museum, as well as the business headquarters of its ministry.

Another case is more recent. On 26 March 2000, in the full turmoil of the international crisis that had erupted over the case of the little boy Elian Gonzales who survived the sinking of a boatload of Cuban refugees trying to reach the coast of the United States, the *Miami Herald* reported the existence of a pane of glass in a bank in Miami, not far from the house where Elian's relatives were trying to keep him from being sent back to Cuba, upon which an image very like a cloud had appeared, in which many claimed to recognize the figure of the Madonna.[11]

In recent years, miraculous images have appeared on other materials besides glass, and I have already offered a lengthy list of the materials. Sometimes an image is discovered by chance, and its origin is not known; in other cases there is a specific event to which its origin is traced.

Rose petals in particular tend to recur in the context of visionary geography. We find them in San Francisco at the house of Carmelo Cortez, at Betania in Venezuela, at the home of Maria Esperanza, in Lipa in the Philippines, in Bayside, New York, and in many other places. And then there are miraculous photographs impressed on ordinary everyday objects. For instance, in 1996, a man found the image of Jesus on a bandage that had just been removed from a cut on his grandson's knee. Reproductions of this image, in large and small format, now circulate on the Web and can be ordered online.[12]

As was the case a century ago, then, we are today witnessing a proliferation of phenomena, generated by fascination with the photographic process, and through the effect of analogous imitation of that process, which is thought to provide an objective knowledge of reality.

But alongside these "classical" features, others now appear, on the specific terrain of visionary Marianism: the obfuscation of the traditional dialectic between charisma and institution, with the delegitimation of each; the candidacy of the camera—and the video camera—as a new central and democratic medium for contacts between heaven and earth; the weakening of the protagonists of the contacts themselves, both human and celestial subjects; and lastly, with the Web, a delocalization of the prodigious events, including the technological events. Let us see, in a series of approximations, just how these new elements are making headway.

Let us begin with the numerous photographs of the "true face of Jesus" or of the Madonna that circulate around the world. Sometimes the photographer who succeeds in taking a picture of this sort has been explicitly chosen by heaven. At Colma di Valduggia, near the city of Vicenza, during a meeting of a prayer group on 13 August 1983, the photographer, painter, and visionary Pino Casagrande felt "an inner impulse to take a picture of the altar where the Monstrance stood among flowers and candles." During the course of the meeting, the liturgical director had been secretly asking God to send him a sign to help him decide whether or not to join the Jesuit order; one worshiper, a woman, had been asking Jesus to appear to her at least once. And so, when the image developed on the Polaroid, there emerged "nothing less than the Holy Face of Jesus, with an expression of sweet sadness."[13] The hoped-for sign had arrived. This photograph was followed by more than two hundred more, taken on various occasions, which were to make Casagrande a recognized "photographer of the world beyond."[14]

Even Sister Anna Ali—a member of the religious order founded by Emanuel Milingo, the famous African bishop—claimed that she had taken real and direct photographs of Jesus on more than one occasion. The most successful of these pictures, previously published in magazines and books, is now found on the Internet, along with this message attributed to Jesus: "I allow myself to be seen after many warnings. . . . I make myself visible in order to bring back souls. . . . I love mankind and I make myself visible in order to give my warnings of mercy. . . . Many do not listen to me because they do not believe in my reality."[15]

These images would not seem to be all that different from other, much older "true" images of the face of Jesus, such as for instance the famous "Veronica," that is "vera icona" or "true icon," venerated in Rome ever since the Middle Ages, which consisted of a cloth that was said to have been placed by a woman upon the face of Jesus in his death throes to wipe away the blood and sweat (there was another one in Laon, France, and others still, though much less famous).[16] In all three cases we find a person upon whom a charism was conferred by a heavenly decision: the woman of the shroud, who was considered holy over the centuries, and was in fact Saint Veronica; the photographer of the world beyond, driven by an inner impulse; and Sister Anna, to whom Jesus communicated explicitly his decision to have his picture taken. But we should not overlook the difference between the ethical nature of the act of the woman who approached Jesus and the technical nature of the act of the two contemporary photographers. The charism of Saint Veronica derived from the pity she felt for that sweaty, blood-stained face, while the charism of Casagrande and Ali derived from their skill at using a camera. Moreover, the authenticity of the Veronica itself is based on the oral tradition of the legends that surround it, and therefore upon a collective consensus, and it is legitimized by the official cult that the Roman ecclesiastical institution accords it. The authenticity of the photograph of Jesus derives primarily from the prestige accorded to the "objective" recording device that captures the images of reality, whether visible or invisible, rather than from the statements of the photographers *qua* visionaries. The power of the functional affirmation of technology prevails over the dimension of charismatic testimonial of the visionaries: Pino Casagrande and Sister Anna were photographers, and that is why they were able to produce a photograph of Jesus, and not the other way around.

It becomes especially clear that authenticity is more an attribute of the technology than of the subject that uses the technology when images of the "True Face" are obtained by chance, without any intention on the part of the photographer. One of numerous possible examples: in 1982 Jackie Haas made a pilgrimage to the Holy Land where, as is normal for any traveler and contemporary pilgrim, she took many photographs. When she got back home to Scranton, Pennsylvania, she discovered a portrait of Jesus among the pictures that she had developed. She was sure that she had not photographed any images, and she was positive that she had never seen anything like the one in question. She asked her husband, and the priest who had led the pilgrimage, and the travel agent, but nobody could come up with a reasonable explanation. Since she knew that miraculous photographs had been reported on more than one occasion, at Medjugorje, Conyers, and Lubbock, she became convinced that she had taken one. Deeply moved by this miracle, she decided to distribute copies of the picture to her friends, relatives, and anyone else she could reach. After a few years, a priest from Garabandal found a copy of this photograph in his hands, and, in a condition of "charismatic knowledge," he declared that it was an image of the true face of Jesus. This declaration was later confirmed variously in Garabandal by José Ramon, who had the "gift of locution"; in Gijón, in Asturias, Spain, by the visionary Maria del Rosario Frechoso; in Sacramento, California, by the visionary Denise Morgan Estrada; and later by Father Robert Burns, a Jesuit visionary, and by others still.[17] All of these visionaries declared that Jesus had intended to give humanity an image of his true face in order to strengthen humanity's faith.

In this case, the tipping point that makes it possible to move from the idea of having obtained an image, produced in a mysterious manner but not necessarily celestial in origin, to the idea of possessing a "true" image of Jesus is the awareness that there exist in the world, and are therefore possible, photographs that have captured miracles. And so if other such photographs exist, then this too may be one. Certainly, in a subsequent phase, charismatics intervene in order to offer confirmation, but in effect they confirm themselves much more than they confirm the photograph: many visionaries, including those of Medjugorje, have at times expressed their views, authenticating this or that miraculous photograph that circulates among worshipers, precisely because the alleged objectivity of that photograph, in feedback, provided an excellent instrument confirming the charisma of the visionary in question.

It is even more evident that there is no need to be either a seer or a charismatic in order to obtain a celestial photograph, and that all that is needed is a camera, in those cases where the result is not the "true face," but silhouettes, blurry figures, signs that will then be decoded and explained in terms of celestial messages. In all these cases, the photography of the supernatural attains the peak of the process of democratization of the extraordinary, of the proliferation of private Holy Shrouds, of the multiplication ad infinitum of the unique and therefore extraordinary epiphany of the sepulchral winding cloth or the *tilma* of Juan Diego.

According to the worshipers of Bayside, New York, one of the most famous cases of an American apparition, repeatedly condemned by the local ecclesiastical authorities, the Madonna confided to Veronica Lueken (the visionary, who died in 1995) that God himself had decided to make use of modern technology in order to communicate with "a fallen generation," "a generation whose hearts are so hardened, and eyes so blinded, that they need some kind of tangible proof" in order to accept the apparitions.[18] This meant, according to the worshipers, that through the intermediary person of Veronica, it had been God himself who had asked them to take photographs on the site of the apparitions. Moreover, they had been advised to use Polaroid cameras, which printed the photographs just seconds after they were taken, and therefore eliminated the objections of the skeptics, who thought that the miraculous photographs were the product of artful manipulations of the negatives in the photo lab: the Polaroid camera offered a photograph that could not be modified, and therefore left no room for doubt as to authenticity.

Every worshiper, every pilgrim, even every onlooker, could take a photograph and have his own personal proof of the existence of the afterlife, as well as evidence of the presence of the Madonna in Bayside and his own personal contact with her.[19]

At Bayside, if someone had a personal problem and directed a specific question to the Madonna, she could expect to receive an answer, roughly as specific as the question, from the picture that she had taken, through the images, writings, and signs that appeared miraculously on the photograph, and which could be easily recognized or decoded with the assistance of some expert or the guidelines provided in the sanctuary's publications. Once, Daniel Wojcik, during his field research at Bayside, was surrounded by numerous friendly worshipers after taking a Polaroid photograph of one of them; they each offered an interpretation of the signs, scratches, and shapes that appeared on the picture. When faced with a sign that no one knew how to decode, they told Wojcik to speak to Veronica Lueken herself to find out its meaning.[20]

Many of the images that miraculously appeared in the photographs referred to the content of messages from the Madonna, and therefore had to do with the impending end of the world, the punishments, the tribulations, the second coming of Christ, and so on.

In general, the symbols that appeared were organized into four categories:

Numbers, letters of the alphabet, concrete symbols, and colors. For instance, the number 2 symbolizes a man or woman; the number 3 means warning; the letter M means Mary; W is for worldwide warning; and the omega means the end is at hand. Concrete symbols often include snakes, which represent the forces of hell, and colors; blue is for the Virgin Mary; pink, Jesus Christ; green, St. Michael; and purple means suffering or sorrow.[21]

But the images also served to provide personal answers to existential doubts, private dilemmas. After the first photograph, mentioned above, Wojcik took another:

Later, after I took another photograph that had streaks of light in it, I asked the man who suggested that I take a photo, and from whom I borrowed a Polaroid camera, what it meant. He replied, "Well, do you see anything in it that relates to your own life? What did you ask for?" When I responded that I had no idea what it meant, he told me to take another photo, this time concentrating on a specific subject or "asking heaven" a specific question.[22]

During the visionary appointments, as soon as Veronica Lueken informed the worshipers that the Madonna had arrived, at times accompanied by Jesus, another frequent visitor to the visionary, "The sound of clicking and fluttering camera shutters and then the whirl-buzz of film being ejected from hundreds of Polaroid cameras could be heard all over the apparition site."[23]

The same effect occurred in the Mojave Desert, at the beginning of the apparition to Maria Paula Acuna, near California City, when, on the thirteenth of each month, the visionary would murmur "Our Mother is with us," and then, "suddenly the air is filled with the whir of [P]olaroid cameras snapping directly at the sun."[24]

Numerous miraculous photographs were taken at Conyers, as well, during the appointment of 13 October 1998, mentioned previously in connection with the failure of the apocalyptic prophecy to come true, an event at which thousands of people took miraculous photographs. Here is an eyewitness account:

I arrived at Conyers around 4:30am, after that there were so many cars! There were so many people there that early! Around 11:00 someone there was speaking in the apparition room about Bolivia. We prayed the Rosary (15 mysteries) but I don't think anyone saw the Miracle of the Sun! (I didn't see it) I did get many MIRACULOUS PHOTOS. When Our Lady was arriving and we were singing the FATIMA SONG I took a picture of the SUN and I saw a Diamond like figure on the bottom While Nancy was speaking and announced the message I took pictures of the sun and Our Lady's Figure appeared and a thin door to heaven appeared. I took pictures after Nancy announced the messages and Our Lady's Figure didn't show up anymore, only the door to heaven. . . . John Paul.[25]

In Hillside, Chicago, too, pilgrims visit the site of the visions of Joseph Reinholtz and try to take photographs of heaven "who often capture special photographs at this site: glimpses of Our Lady, angels, phenomena of light that are difficult to explain."[26]

But there are dozens of places in the world at which miraculous photographs can be taken, beginning with Medjugorje, which is in absolute terms the place where the greatest number of images is in circulation.

The fact that the possibility of seeing heaven lies not in some inscrutable decision from on high, but rather in the availability of technological resources, is a clear effect of an increasing democratization of consumption, which goes so far as to intertwine the verticality of heaven itself in the horizontality of the freedom of the consumer. But this technological democracy produces an unexpected effect in religious terms. In fact, after it comes into play it is followed by depersonalization and decentralization of the subjects involved, in favor of a technological prosthesis. Anyone can enter into contact with the world beyond, but not because they are someone in particular—a child of God, a worshiper, one of the faithful, a Christian, or whatever else—but rather because they have something in particular, i.e., a technological instrument. It is no longer necessary to be good, humble, worshipful, children, charismatics, saints, or whatever conditions traditionally typified the visionaries in the history of apparitions; all that is needed is to own a camera or, nowadays, to have access to the Internet.

There are numerous traditional devotional histories that attribute the painting of the True Face to Saint Luke; others describe an artist who, just as he was about to complete a holy image, stopped short of painting the face of Jesus or the Virgin Mary. The implied meaning is that human art ventures no further when faced with what is not given to humans to know, the face of the divine. All of the traditional images of the True Face, from the Shroud of Turin to the *tilma* of Juan Diego, to the Veronica, are the fruit of single, specific events, and as we have seen, base their authenticity upon traditional accounts that have been sanctioned by the community and then legitimized by a cult more or less officially reserved to them: behind the Veronica, the *tilma,* and the Shroud, there is the power of myth and the authority of the church. Today, on the other hand, the terms of the problem are quite different. For example, here are the technical specifications of a miraculous photograph taken by a worshiper at Conyers, in place of the more traditional eyewitness testimonial: "The image was shot with Kodak Gold 200, conditions were partly cloudy at the time with no direct sunlight. Unfortunately, I did not note the f stop of the camera at the time."[27]

Technical data have replaced spiritual and human "data." Lighting, exposure, film speed, and lens size have replaced the life of devotion, humility, ecclesiastical authority, and much more.

In a certain sense, the technological image is the apparition itself in the era of technology: democratic, generalized, horizontal, manifold, subject to exchange and consumption. No longer a Madonna appearing in institutional locations—the sky, a grotto, a church—no longer a Madonna who decides the times, manners, and persons to whom she wishes to appear, confirming the abyss of difference and otherness. Unquestionably the action of the camera owner seems to be responsible, active, far from the passivity of the traditional visionary surprised by an apparition. Technology offers a chance to take control of the dialogue, the relationship, the gaze. The Madonna, invisible, is here, someplace; she shows herself to someone but not to me; I take my camera and shoot a picture: something will emerge. And indeed from the Polaroid there emerges a personal, self-produced divine epiphany, in defiance of the choices of the Madonna herself. The experience of power associated with the act of photographing the supernatural, though covered by the thousand ritual scruples of humility and modesty, cannot be overlooked: the lightning bolt, the god, the light, the epiphany, the classical apparition, here they all are, captured by any passing pilgrim, without any particular qualities or charisms. Captured, literally, in his hands, by that familiar little machine that is used to take pictures of family celebrations, personal remembrances, weekend outings, and which can also be used to record celestial figures, to block them in a personal snapshot, to be kept among the family pictures, to be shown to one's friends, to give to those one loves. One pilgrim wrote, "During a return flight after my attendance at one of the anniversary celebrations of Mrs. Lueken's visions, the Baysiders I travelled with spent much of their time sharing photos, discussing them, and analysing their prophetic meaning. Many had dozens of photos and had already put them into albums that were circulated among passengers on the airplane."[28]

This is the same experience of power generally associated with the means of modern technology, widely used, praised, or directly suggested by advertising.

Attention, however, should be paid to a detail that we have already noted: in effect, this power, this positive ability to interact, is not a product of any quality of the individual—bravery, strength, skill, or even a greater ability than the celestial figure that she is capturing—but rather of what she possess. She is not the active source of this epiphanous capture; the active source is the object that she possesses: the camera or video camera.

And indeed, in the end, the camera can even exclude entirely the presence of humans. A camera is not an extension of the eye, inasmuch as it is sufficient for it to exist in a certain place and then function—one might even say that a camera need only be a camera, while humans must be satisfied with having a camera. The fact that the human eye behind the viewfinder does not see what the lens "sees" and captures opens the way to the possibility of automatic optical mechanisms in which the human eye—that is, human beings—intervene only after the technological process, and no longer before, because in the phase "before" they have been entirely replaced by the machine, the camera.

The vision machine[29] renders humans obsolete; it produces that which can be seen and transmits it to humans, who are at this point nothing more than a passive final terminus, not even really necessary and certainly not essential. The procedures for verifying reality have bypassed humans: the objective eye of the camera, the faithful documentation that it permits, the test that it puts into action—all trigger technical mechanisms in comparison with which the human subject is increasingly obsolete.

At the *Second International Video Festival* in Montbéliard in 1984, the Grand Prix went to a German film by Michael Klier called *Der Riese* (The Giant). This was a simple montage of images recorded by automatic surveillance cameras in major German cities (airports, roads, supermarkets . . .). Klier asserts that the surveillance video represents "the end and the recapitulation of his art. Whereas in the news report

the photographer (cameraman) remained the sole witness implicated
in the business of documentation, here no one at all is implicated. . . .
This solemn farewell to the man behind the camera, the complete
evaporation of visual subjectivity into an ambient technical effect . . . [30]

In the context of technological and visionary religiosity, this "solemn
farewell" has already taken place. One of the most popular and widely discussed photographs on the Internet among Marian worshipers is one of
the many that the Hubble Space Telescope was able to take, thanks to its
remarkable power, in 1995, successfully capturing in an astonishing series of images a cloud of luminescent gas that was produced at a distance
of seven thousand light years, in the context of the process of formation
of a group of stars from the interstellar mass Aquila, in the constellation
of Draco. Once these photographs had been broadcast by CNN, though
with an appropriate scientific explanation of their source and origin, the
switchboard was jammed with hundreds of telephone calls. In one of
the photographs, somebody claimed to see cows; in another somebody
else saw dogs. But in one photograph in particular, most of the callers
claimed to have seen the face of Jesus. Despite the denials of the astro-
physicists in charge of the telescope, who patiently explained the origin
and the structure of the image, this photograph became for many worshipers emblematic of the presence of Jesus in the cosmos. Then, after
Jesus, the Madonna: another photograph taken by the same telescope was
interpreted as a miraculous depiction of the Virgin Mary. And there were
precedents for this. In connection with a well-known astronomical photograph, taken by a satellite orbiting Mars more than twenty years earlier,
and known as the "faces on Mars," there were some who claimed that,
when the picture was enlarged to a sufficient degree, you could see the
silhouettes of the Virgin Mary and the Christ Child,[31] while others, instead, suggested a curious optical game involving a stereogram similar to
the one used in the "magic eye": if you looked at the picture according to
the technique that was carefully explained, you would be able to glimpse
in it three faces: the face of the "traditional western Jesus," another face
of a Jesus who appears upset, and a third face, close to the hand of the
previous image, which is referred to as the "face on Mars."[32]

With the photographs taken by the Hubble Space Telescope, we have
reached an extreme in terms of the disempowerment of the human subject. A technological mechanism is able to obtain, according to the worshipers, photographs of Jesus and the Madonna taken by an automatic

and impersonal eye at a distance of thousands of light years: the relationship is limited to a contact between the distant cosmic deities and the complex technological resources that are capable of capturing them visually in the interstellar remoteness of their vast otherness. That a human eye might in the end actually see the final product is entirely irrelevant and immaterial to the context of the dialogue that is taking place between the powers of the lens and magnifications of the telescope and the power of the celestial figures. With respect to this "dialogue," humans are entirely on the sidelines, and undergo a twofold alienation: an alienation from the celestial figures, who hover at distances of thousands of light years like so many mute images for humans, suitable only to be fed into the digital circuits of technological equipment and then the virtual universe of the Web; and a second alienation from technology, which in a case of this sort validates the ideas of those who point out its metamorphosis from "instrument" to "environment," of which humans are merely a product.[33]

In light of this drastic enfeebling of the human subject, in this period of technological achievements in the relationship between heaven and earth, what is happening on the other side, in heaven?

Technology reduces the margin of subjectivity of those who are involved in its devotional use, in one way or another. In the extreme case of the photographs of the Hubble Space Telescope, celestial subjectivity has become a pure digital image, an algorithm subject to manipulation, infinitely transformable and transmittable. In general, however, heaven, in the collective technological practice, has lost nearly all the prerogatives of absolute freedom that are still acknowledged in the conventional beliefs that concern it.

Even though it is never explicitly declared, what is done by the photographers of the "world beyond" is based less on someone who allows themselves to be seen, in virtue of a special relationship with those who see them, and more upon someone who is seen in virtue of the technical equipment that captures the objective fact of that someone's presence in a given place.

Let us compare two types of attitude. The first is found among many of the visionaries who see apparitions. Once they believe that they have seen the Madonna, and that they can actually speak to her, they ask: "Why do you allow yourself to be seen by me in particular?" Surprise, amazement, and the recognition that they have been chosen. The second attitude, on the other hand, is exemplified in the following forms of behavior, recorded on sites of apparitions: in Oliveto Citra, a young man saw the Madonna and exclaimed; his mother, standing next to him, could not see her. And so she put on her eyeglasses and squinted at the sky.[34] At Medjugorje, Father Janko Bubalo, looking toward the cross on the hill next to the rectory, could not see the Madonna. And so, fully aware that his eyesight was not good, he asked for a pair of binoculars, and with them, he succeeded in glimpsing the figure of a woman with her arms spread wide.[35] The binoculars were handed among the other three monks present, who all saw the same figure.[36] At Turzovka, in Moravia, in 1966, Hans Steiner, who was very nearsighted, asked other pilgrims to point him in the exact direction in which they were seeing a white cloud containing the Madonna. He then took a photograph that, once it was developed, showed a veiled female figure.[37]

In the first type, the idea is clearly implicit that the Madonna is selecting the person to whom she appears. In the second type, the protagonists are not as focused on the idea of being chosen by the Madonna, as much as they are on the power of the instrument with which they are able to see what the naked eye misses. Certainly, eyeglasses and binoculars are still extensions of the human eye, while the camera has an autonomy of optical operation that is now clearly independent of humans; in both cases, however, the freedom of the celestial figures has vanished.

In pretechnological apparitions, the Madonna was thought to be present in a given place and visible to a given person, the visionary; the others, to whom the Madonna was invisible, took it for granted that there was a subjective decision on the part of the Madonna to allow herself to be seen by one but not by others. But when a piece of equipment intervenes, in technological apparitions, then the age-old subjectivity of the decision made by the Madonna gives way to the objectivity of her presence captured by a camera, like any other object in the world. The subjective choice of invisibility has to do with the relationship between the Madonna and humans, not the relationship between the Madonna and the camera: to the camera, the Virgin Mary is an "object" like any other, and she is not allowed to make the choice of invisibility, because in some way the camera is more powerful than she is: unless we are to think that heaven has somehow decided to offer a testimonial for the photographic industry in hopes of encouraging it, inviting the faithful to buy cameras and film in order to gain access to holy images.

Finally, when a photograph of the supernatural is uploaded onto the Web, the process of the strengthening of the machine and the definitive weakening of the subjects, both human and divine, is joined by a further delocalization of the sacred routes. Indeed, it will no longer be necessary to reach the sacred place chosen by the Madonna to appear to humans in order to make a photograph. Before the Internet, although she might have been captured by a technology that deprived her of the choice of showing herself to Bernadette and no one else, or to Lucia and no one else, the Madonna could at least select the place in which she would be captured, and she could impose a sacred aura upon that place. With the Web she lost even that possibility: on the Web site of the apparitions of Cojutepeque, El Salvador, you can see through a miracle photo that which the visionary Nelly Hurtado has been "seeing" directly since 1991. In fact, in that picture you can see a clump of trees, and "if you look closely at the photograph— right in the center—you can see the image of Our Lady."[38] For Medjugorje, too, the Web offers this possibility: millions of pilgrims have traveled to the Bosnian sanctuary without seeing anything exceptional. But on the Web it is possible to eliminate entirely the physical voyage and, at the same time, see a supernatural image provided from the repertoire of the virtual. If you go to the Web site of "Servant Son," the pseudonym of an American visionary, you will be able to see a photograph taken on the hill of Medjugorje during a miracle of the sun, accompanied by the following invitation: "Stare at the photo and you begin to see the image of Crucified Jesus."[39]

Two questions remain.

The first question. We might suppose that, if we consider the photographs taken in accordance with the request made by heaven in expectation of a response, as at Bayside or in California City, in certain cases there can still be an active relationship between heaven and earth in the production of a photograph. The photograph would be a mere vehicle, a channel, like a telephone, and it serves only to link requests and responses, leaving the initiative entirely up to the human and celestial subjects: each person with his or her own personal requests, and for each person, personalized responses. In a world that is opaque to comprehension, complex, in which the meaning of human events and experiences is obscure, fragmented, and elusive, indeed, often seems not to exist, we see that photography of the supernatural would offer unexpectedly a new resource, simple, clear, and immediate, without any inequality of access to the sources of knowledge. The relationship with heaven by which it is possible to attain a sense of things is now a direct one; it is no longer mediated by any others—priest, confessor, visionary—and it is available to anyone. Indeed, no other type of relationship, mediated by any of an infinite array of vehicles—the Book, the church, the other, the conscience, the Eucharist, the rite, and so on—can boast the clarity, the immediacy, and the absence of ambiguity that governs the media-based relationship governed by the camera.

But the medium is the message. The question does not particularly have to do with the fact that meaning is no longer sought in the difficult tests of experience or in the darkness of the mysteries of dogma, in the eloquent silence of faith or in the heart of a devout community, but instead in the camera obscura of photography. The real issue is that everything that happens in the camera depends entirely upon the camera. And indeed the test of the interaction between demand and response, question and answer, will no longer occur on spiritual terrain, but rather on technological grounds: did the camera function properly, or was there a malfunction? Was the film good or was it too old? Would a different type of camera or film have yielded clearer results? Was the lens adequate? And so on: the whole set of questions that determine the quality of the dialogue lies within the perimeter of technology. Therefore, the human "subject" winds up seeking contact with heaven through a total delegation of control to the technological instrument, to which he or she entrusts the organization of demand and response, and from which derives the unequivocal and unexceptionable meaning.

The second unresolved question about photography of the supernatural is this: the "true face" of past tradition,[40] from the Shroud to the *tilma* to the Veronica, was endowed with sacred status, as we have seen above, by the legendary traditions that surrounded it and by the legitimation of ecclesiastical authority. Can we maintain that the technological process confers sacred status on photographic images? Can we imagine that the sacred is produced in the very citadel of disenchantment? In the final analysis, instruments that render visible the invisible, for instance, those that produce x-rays or sonograms, are used widely in modern-day life and yet they do not seem to produce images endowed with any particular sacred value.

Perhaps, however, we should distinguish between a disenchanted technological procedure and the private use of its results. An x-ray or a CAT scan, cradled jealously in the hands of a worried patient waiting his turn to see a physician, well aware that the images that he holds in his hands contain the "secret" of his life, obviously do not hold the emotionally neutral value for him that they might for the technician who produced them. Likewise for an ordinary photograph of a wedding, for the bride and groom and for the photographer, or a little plaster statuette of the Madonna of Medjugorje for the artisan who makes dozens of them at a time and a specific statuette, perhaps produced by the same workshop, which wept bloody tears in the hands of Bishop Girolamo Grillo in Civitavecchia. The difference, obviously, lies in the investment of differential value that different people place in the same object. And the same person might even make different uses and different investments of value in the same object at different times of her life. The sonogram of a fetus loses much of its value when it is replaced by a picture of a newborn on its first day of life. And so on: new degrees of significance replace old ones.

That is why Clara Gallini revised the "premature enthusiasm of Walter Benjamin, who believed that the path of the desacralization of social and esthetic values led directly through the process of the progressive diffusion of the techniques of the mass production of objects and images."[41]

And so, technology does not exclude a potential labor to sacralize its objects; rather, it privatizes that labor, it fragments it, rendering it increasingly provisional, variable, never definitive. On one hand, the multiplication, the serialization, the copying of technological objects is a harsh test of any possibility of sacred value, while on the other hand, the penetration of technology into the most intimate recesses of individual and collective life triggers new and unpredictable processes whereby sacred status is conferred.

It is no accident that I should mention x-rays and sonograms. They, just like photographs of the supernatural—but in contrast with ordinary photography—are the products of technological processes in which the nonvisible is rendered visible. I do not believe that there is any opposition between photographs of the supernatural and these other processes, any radical distinction in terms of the sacred and the profane. But there may be, in the personal uses that can be made of them, a difference of degree: both of them are or can be subject to a process of sacralization, which is not limited to the religious field in the narrowest sense, but, to use the words of Giovanni Filoramo, "is triggered wherever individuals or groups of people, in order to give meaning to their individual or collective lives, confer an absolute value to objects or symbols (consecrating them, and thereby separating them)."[42]

Among the miraculous photographs that I have collected in the course of my research, one in particular, anonymous, with a caption in English, possibly from an American source, seems to confirm the thesis that I have set forth here:

Look to the right of the picture. The white "image" surrounding the
darker image (the Fetus) resembles the Virgin Mary. My son was born
a Preemie and his esophogus [*sic*] was not connected to his stomach
but rather to his lungs. Doctors said it was a miracle he didn't swallow
any fluid as this would have gone straight to his lungs and killed him
instantly. IS IT THE VIRGIN MARY?? We like to think so . . . what do
you think??[43]

The image in question is a sonogram, and the caption quoted above
is a personal interpretation by the parent who put it on the Web. The
malformation of a son, a tragic experience for a parent, is associated, in
the description of the sonographic image, with a miracle. The senseless
drama of pain, grief, and misfortune is recognized as a celestial sign, no
longer just a misfortune but almost a privilege, as in the case of Audrey
Santo (the comatose "victim soul" described above in section 1.2). Thus,
the image of the sonogram of the fetus merges with the miraculous image
of the Madonna, it is the same image interpreted in a twofold manner.

In this exceptional case, we see clearly that which normally remains
concealed, that is, the fact that the process of sacralization can effect, to
a greater or lesser degree, not only the photography of the supernatural,
but also x-rays, sonograms, and even more.

There is a difference however: an alleged Marian photographic image
has a culture, a visionary culture, underlying its process of sacralization; a
sonogram of a fetus has, instead, only a personal and private investment of
meaning, all the weaker the more it is dependent upon a reenchantment,
which to the very degree that is made possible by technology lies within
its general regime of disenchantment.

Apparitions on Television

The terrain of the photography of the supernatural sketched out above is
confirmed, especially inasmuch as the delegation to and reliance upon the
technological medium is concerned, in the use that is typically made of
video, from broadcast television to the private use of videotape.

The belief that it is possible to see entities from the world beyond and
the resulting practices have found a new legitimacy and a new foundation
precisely in the shared experience of a universal visibility and a familiarity
with the objects seen, effects produced by television. The dematerialization of the world that is so characteristic of television, that is, the passage

from concrete bodies to their televised images, has encouraged the ancient, but newly updated, phenomenon of visions of ethereal, decorpo-
realized images of the world beyond. Television offers an excellent field
for religious visionary possibilities, by placing under the eyes of everyone
that which is not present. We may feel like smiling at the vain expectations of thousands of Texans, on 25 March 1998, as they waited for the
apparition of God on Channel 18, a religious TV station in Dallas, at the
behest of Hon Ming Chen, a televangelist and the founder of the True
Way Church.[44] But for those who believe in the possibility that the world
beyond will reveal itself to human eyes in this world, the only difference
lies in a not-impossible shift from a physical world beyond, that of televised images, to a metaphysical world beyond, that of the images of God.
And within this logic, it is not even impossible for the images of the celestial world beyond to overlap with the images of the world beyond of
the screen: according to the "Marian" theologian René Laurentin, that is
what happened in Russia in 1987. A local television station in Grushevo,
a city in Ukraine, was broadcasting a program in which an apparition of
the Madonna announced by a number of visionaries was being debunked,
when the Madonna herself appeared on the screen, blocking out the images being broadcast.[45]

Television, in fact, has supplied a strong and everyday instrument for
the construction of a shared visionary sensibility. This is reflected in the
fact that the visionaries often describe their experiences making use of
references to television. At Medjugorje, Vicka Ivankovic described having seen Ivanka's dead mother, "once, just a passing glimpse, like on
television"[46]; another time she saw, "like in a movie," the parish priest,
who had been put in prison for "subversive activities."[47] The same young
woman explained the way in which the symbols—the cross, the heart,
the sun—would disappear after the Madonna would show them, sometimes, during her appearances: "like images on television."[48] And hagiographic commentators use similar images: "Sometimes, when she shows
the young people scenes or images outside her person, they run past their
eyes like fragments of a film of mysterious origin."[49] And the same thing
happened when the Madonna appeared for "eight minutes" and showed
to Mirjana, who burst into tears, an impending punishment that would
strike a part of the world,[50] and then again a few days later, both times, "as
if it were a movie."[51] Stanley Villavicencio, a Filipino visionary who was
said to have "returned to life after death," claimed that when they showed
him his past life in the world beyond, it was as if he were looking at a

"video screen," and that "the moments in his life when he had committed sins were shown back to him on the screen, enlarged and in slow motion, as if they were sequences on a film projector."[52]

Another decisive influence of television can be seen in prolonged serial contemporary apparitions, a new development in the history of Marian apparitions. Television has not only accustomed people to the perception of distant persons and realities, but also to the daily repetition of the same images, the same faces, the same settings. At Lourdes, Bernadette had eighteen visions; at La Salette, Maximin and Mélanie spoke of only one apparition; at Fatima, Lucia and Jacinto received six visions. Even if in the past mystics and saints have described receiving frequent celestial visions, the most significant apparitions have been quite limited in number and duration. But in the television era, daily apparitions take place for years. At Medjugorje there have been visions of the Madonna since 1981: the visionaries, who in the meantime have grown up, married, and had children, for years have had daily visions of the Gospa; three of them continue to have those visions, though not as frequently. Throughout the world, visionaries and locutionists carry on daily interactions with the Madonna and with Jesus: "daily visions, daily conversations" is the recurrent slogan on their Web sites. The American visionary John Leary has already published seventeen volumes of celestial messages (and in one year the first two volumes sold 25,000 copies), while his fellow American Gianna Talone Sullivan has published four books. The Bolivian visionary Catalina Rivas has published eight books of messages from Jesus and the Virgin Mary. Laura Zink has received almost two thousand messages. Throughout the world, in brief, a flood of daily visions and messages attributed to these two sacred figures washes over the visionaries and worshipers like a special network of television stations constantly broadcasting.

Even the believers in the apparitions explain their serial nature by referring to the characteristics of the "messages" of television. In the words of Laurentin and Rupčíc, "We live in a repetitive world. Television broadcasts everyday. That which is not repeated is overwhelmed, submerged. This means that a message must be repeated, over and over."[53] And this repetition seems to occur at will, as if by means of an on/off switch. Let us recall the words of Bishop Peric, "the 'Madonna' appears at the 'fiat' of the 'visionaries.' "[54]

Moreover, the recent so-called "new television," characterized by an emphasis on "everyday life," conviviality, "being together,"[55] finds an echo and is mirrored in a convivial relationship that the new seers have with the Madonna and Jesus, displaying great intimacy and familiarity, interacting frequently, and even joking around. Far different from the serious approach of Bernadette or the terror of Mélanie and Maximin at La Salette.

Finally, overlap and interaction between the television and the world beyond have become common and even obvious phenomena for those who subscribe to the visionary ideology. Here is an example, taken at random from a vast array of case histories. Christopher, from California, whom we have already encountered, told his friends on a mailing list that he was planning to go to Boston to visit his niece. The circumstances of his decision are especially significant for us: he had been chatting with his niece on the Internet—he was in California, she was in Boston—when she asked him to come see her. But he decided to wait for a sign from heaven before traveling, that is, a sign that would communicate to him that the right time had come to go. The next day, while he was at the computer, he was interrupted by his nine-year-old daughter, who told him that she wanted to go to Boston. Why this sudden, unexpected request, Christopher wondered. He had spoken with no one of his niece's invitation. So could this be the sign from heaven? Christopher asked his guardian angel, with whom he has regular contact, for an opinion. The guardian angel's response was positive. Then, his curiosity led him to ask his daughter why she had made the suggestion: she explained to him that she had been watching the television series *Touched by an Angel,* when for some reason that she could not explain, she had felt an urge to go to Boston. In the episode that she was watching, had there been any reference to faraway relatives, Christopher prodded, his amazement growing as he asked his daughter, his wife, and his sister, who were all present. Nothing. The next day Christopher reserved two tickets for Boston, for himself and for his daughter.[56] Here is a case of complete overlapping between an angel from heaven and an angel on television: through the angel of a television show, heaven had sent a sign, confirmed by a real angel, with whom the worshiper spoke regularly.

One consequence of the growing importance of television in the contemporary world is the power that accrues to reality as presented through the television screen. Not only do the devotional promoters seem to be aware of this fact, and therefore produce increasing numbers of videos documenting miraculous events, but even the Jesus and the Madonna of visionary culture seem to understand it. In April 1999, while preparing a documentary about the case of the Bolivian visionary Catalina Rivas, a television crew from the Australian Fox Network was given something like an appointment from Jesus himself to film the formation of the stigmata that were produced on the hands and feet of Catalina on special religious holidays. In fact, in response to Rivas's requests, made at the behest of the television film crew, who had already traveled to Bolivia twice, only to return empty-handed, "Jesus said [to Catalina] she will experience the stigmata on the 4th of June."

The crew flew once again from Australia to Bolivia for the appointment, set this time by Jesus himself, and they "were not disappointed": "The team was to capture on film a very painful sign of Christ's Love for broadcast to the world. A sign that is a vivid, visual expression of suffering in Love that could not help but touch and move the hearts of viewers. It is a sign today of Christ's Passion, a sign of His continuing, infinite Love for mankind."[57]

In the context of visionary culture, Jesus himself makes use of the network to attain greater visibility of his "Passion" and his "Love," in order to leave a "contemporary sign" of them.

The video camera is thus given a more prestigious role than the mere eye of the human witness. It is capable of producing the miraculous event directly, with or without the awareness of the worshipers.

For the first case: in Boston, in 1991, in the Italian-American community, the procession of the Madonna del Soccorso was held, organized by the Sciacca Society. Someone was filming with a video camera. When the person reviewed the images, he discovered that the statue of the Madonna was winking. Doubt, skepticism. But the worshipers on the Web knew exactly how to answer those doubts:

> Many people consider the "blinking Madonna" a miracle, while others, including two video technicians who examined the videotape, believe the camera's shifting autofocus mechanism was responsible for the phenomenon. Two video experts from Harvard, however, said the autofocus theory could not be proven conclusively even after a careful analysis of the videotape.[58]

The celestial sign, the winking of the Madonna, was not intended for the immediate perception by the faithful who were taking part in the procession; it actually took place in the darkness of the magnetic codes of the videotape, and waited before it could be revealed—which has nothing to do with its actual realization—to the eyes of spectators through the medium of the television set.

Now let us examine the second case, the famous miracle of the sun, documented on video.

Frankie S., from Houston, Texas, a devotee of the apparitions of Conyers, provided an account of the miracle of the sun in the forum of the Conyers Web page for an episode that took place on 13 October 1998, during one of the apparitions of the Madonna to Nancy Fowler. The real protagonist of the episode was his daughter, who was filming the event with a video camera:

> Then the unexpected happened to my daughter while she was filming. She pointed the camera to the sun, and in the beginning, the sun appeared "still" in the video. Then all of a sudden, an "aura" like a rainbow appeared around the sun, with my daughter saying, "Oh my God, it is huge!" We [Frankie and his wife] did not know the meaning of it. What had happened, was that the sun had started pulsating at a tremendous rate of speed (this lasted for two or three minutes). At this time, I had not seen this "video" of hers, but she kept asking me to see it. I didn't see this video until a week later, after we had returned home to Houston, Texas. Much to my surprise, when I first saw the video, I thought that something had gone wrong with her camera, or maybe it had malfunctioned. What I saw in this video, was amazing! It was something that you only hear someone else talk about! We have now shown this video, not only to our prayer group here at St. Frances Cabrini Church, but to every prayer group or person/persons that want to see it, including our own parish Priest.[59]

In this account, we have a pretty clear description of how the so-called miracle of the sun takes place today (this is not the context for an analysis of a corresponding type of miracle in the pretechnological era), a type of miracle that is common on the sites of apparitions and among the religious groups that are attracted by those sites. Frankie was present when his daughter was filming, but he did not see the miracle that she saw in the video camera. He did not see it himself until he finally agreed to watch it on the television screen. What is referred to as a video reproduction of a miracle is in reality a video production of a miracle. Here I will quote the words of Corrado Malanga and Roberto Pinotti, two Italian UFO experts, who have noted that the phenomenon occurs at shutter speeds of less than 1/150 of second, and only after one second after the beginning of shooting. And so we see that does not always happen, but only in the special conditions to which a video camera is subjected during an event believed to be miraculous in nature. . . . In other words, when too much light strikes the video camera's electronic circuits, they automatically tend to shut the electronic diaphragm which, on an automatic setting, remains closed, but on a manual setting opens up, to return to the conditions determined by the camera operator, thus producing the phenomenon cyclically.[60]

Here we should emphasize, among other things, the considerable contrast among the various versions of the miracle of the sun generally provided by eyewitnesses; the versions are often at odds with one another, while there is a single, very clear video recording of the same event. The direct human visual experience appears to be confused and problematic, while the video recording provides certainty and clarity. I have personally witnessed various alleged miracles of the sun, and they were triggered by someone operating a video camera who, by inviting everyone to pay close attention to something that he, and only he, could see very clearly in the viewfinder of his camera, focused the collective attention and established a hermeneutic current of the worshipers who began to see thousands of tricks of the sun, which danced in the sky, changed color, and pulsated.

We may well wonder how celestial phenomena came to acquire such a central role in the visionary culture of this century. We should therefore indulge in a slight digression.

Heaven and Earth

The Christian religion has always been heaven-focused, but now we are seeing a shift from the metaphorical heaven or heavens to the real heavens or sky as the site of the divine, and from the metaphor of light to the identification of light with Christ (or the Madonna). Certainly, Fatima was influential, not the first but certainly the most famous site of apparitions in which the miracle of the sun was reported. But there has also—and perhaps primarily—been, a growing physical dimension of the world beyond, closely linked to the central role of technology and therefore to the custom of verifiability, testability, and the automatic and impersonal production of real objects.

The heaven of Marian worshipers is crisscrossed by flocks of angels, Madonnas, and Jesuses who appear in all shapes and colors. The proof of the existence of these presences is, to worshipers, provided primarily, though not exclusively, by hundreds of different photographs, in which we can see a face here, a silhouette there, or a man with a beard or a woman with a veil.

Celestial phenomena are directly called upon to form part of the list of miracles and portentous phenomena caused by heaven, to summon the earth to return to the authentic faith. Even when the presence of Jesus's face is not taken for granted, astronomical photographs, such as pictures of the comet Hale-Bopp and other astrophysical phenomena, are inserted as links in Web pages devoted to apparitions, such as in *Stepping Stones to Catholic Apparitions and Miracles,* which includes a link to "Natural Wonders," alongside links to "The Message," "Miracles," and "Catholic Apparitions." In other words, the sky, the light of the sun, and the light of the stars are all so many "stepping stones," milestones of the apparitions, examples of the cosmic nature of the divine. Sometimes, even photographs of perfectly ordinary atmospheric phenomena become miraculous. For instance, the photograph of a cloud that had been made phosphorescent due to an electric storm, published as a curiosity by a Massachusetts newspaper, the *Worcester Telegram & Gazette,* was posted to devotional Web sites, and transmitted as a "miraculous light."[61]

One of the most widespread images is that of a "gate of heaven" or a "gate of paradise," a luminous arch superimposed upon the sky, the effect of the refraction of sunlight upon a convex lens, which is interpreted as a miraculous signal of the opening of paradise, in accordance with Revelation 4:1.

In religious settings, visionary Catholicism is not alone in believing that the divine materializes in the astronomical sky. For instance, the star Sirius was considered by adherents of the Solar Temple (fifty-three of whom killed themselves in October 1994, and sixteen more in December 1995), the home of the "ascended masters," a spiritual center that could be attained through suicide.[62] And the approach of the comet Hale-Bopp, in March 1997, triggered another mass suicide in California, leaving thirty-nine members of the sect Heaven's Gate dead; before they died, they had put out a final appeal on their Internet site, Higher Source: "Red Alert—Hale-Bopp brings closure to: Heaven's Gate. As was promised—the keys to Heaven's Gate are here again in Ti and Do (the UFO Two) as they were in Jesus and His Father 2000 yrs. ago . . ."[63]

On the other hand, the religious cults that have the sky—or heaven—as a strictly physical reference, as well as a metaphorical idea, present numerous shared features in common with visionary Catholicism. In a list of seven characteristic features of UFO cults developed by Jean-Bruno Renard and quoted by Massimo Introvigne, we find—alongside the transcendental nature and perfection of the extraterrestrials, the idea of a new Revelation, which will uncover the true meaning of the Bible; an apocalyptic catastrophism analogous to that of visionary Catholicism; an impending manifestation of the extraterrestrials on earth, corresponding to the Second Coming of Christ.[64] Certainly, we may say that it was the UFO cults that took on features of millenarianistic Catholicism, which is much older. But the point is that nowadays these cults influence one another in turn in the context of a syncretistic ideological framework, from which each one uses certain elements to construct new intertwinings.

Returning to visionary Catholicism, the transformation of heaven from a metaphor to the physical reality of the divine site, encouraged by the central role of technology, has produced countless forms of materialization—and now, digitalization—of the divine. For instance, in the case mentioned above of Cojutepeque, El Salvador, the seer Nelly Hurtado spoke of rays that were sent by the Madonna to heal the sick. A camera captured those rays, and now on the site *El Salvador—Our Lady of Fatima,* there are four photographs of the "rays of healing light":[65] a spiritual heaven, and then a physical heaven, has finally become a virtual heaven.

A direct form of physicalization of the divine is given by the idea that the Marian apparitions on earth have an implicit, although incomprehensible, message in strictly geographic terms. For instance, Flavio Vettorel, an airport topographer, claims that the Marian apparitions of Lourdes, Fatima, Medjugorje, and Akita all lie in a strip around the 40th parallel north, and that the distance between the grotto of Lourdes and the church of Saint-Jean in Tarbes (the see of the bishopric with jurisdiction) and the distance between the Podbrdo hill (site of the first apparitions of Medjugorje) and the Serbian Orthodox church of Mostar (the see of the bishopric with jurisdiction) are practically identical, respectively 18.568 and 18.569 kilometers.[66] Vincenzo Aversano, a professor of geography at the University of Salerno, claims that there is a special relationship between the direction in which the statue of Lourdes, in the grotto of the apparitions, is looking, and the pole star, symmetrical with the center of the vault of the heavens; moreover, he has determined that Lourdes, Assisi, Medjugorje,

Fatima, Pompeii, San Giovanni Rotondo, and Santiago de Compostela all lie between 43 and 38 degrees north latitude, which leads him to ask:

> Should we then think of a geographic spiritual belt . . . no further
> across than 4 or 5 degrees (400 to 500 km. on the ground)? . . . I cannot
> say whether the coincidences and similarities are the product of pure
> statistical chance; whether there is a physical and natural determinism
> at work on certain events and certain forms of human behavior in the
> area of faith; whether these are signs from Heaven. . . . Caution and
> a critical spirit prevent me from looking to relationships or cause and
> effect of any sort.[67]

But this faith in the physical presence of Jesus and the Virgin Mary in heaven, in light, on parallels and meridians, does not come without a price. Their physicality—documentable, capturable, storable, and then translatable into the digital signals potentially capable of attaining still other forms: sounds, colors, traces, volumes, and everything else that digital technology, "interfacing," and the virtual dimension of the Web can invent—destroys their subjectivity, transforming them into objects among other objects, multiplying them into figures and counterfigures, mirrors seen in mirrors, fragmenting them, virtualizing and actualizing them, rendering them a homogenized material of technological treatment, reducing substantially their otherworldly sense and their value of otherness—or reformulating it in the form of a cyber-otherness.

God is swallowed up by the power of technological systems that attest his signs; he has become a test result; he exists because he himself, or perhaps we should say, his envoys and his miracles, have been photographed, filmed, recorded, documented, and stored. The sacred, with all of its attributes and requirements, with the correlative processes of de- and resacralization, has been transferred into the structure of technology.

The Experiment of the Supernatural

If photography of the supernatural constitutes the technological democratization of the apparition, then the scientific experiment on the supernatural is in contrast a more aristocratic and elitist path to the technologizing of the apparition. All worshipers own cameras or some other technological instrument, but only a very few enjoy access to laboratories and experimental equipment, or instruments for scientific testing. Those few often mean to evaluate through their equipment the claims of visions and miraculous phenomena on the part of seers and visionaries, in order to test their authenticity, but implicitly—and perhaps involuntarily—they are seeking to provide a scientific confirmation of heaven, its realms, and its power.

Precisely the better educated worshipers—technicians, scholars, scientists in various fields—gave the definitive push to the technologizing of Marian apparitions, capturing them in the laboratory and bending them to scientific logic.

On 13 June 1993, Nancy Fowler, a visionary from Conyers, had an appointment with the Madonna. It was a special day because she had authorized a team of scholars to carry out medical and scientific tests. The medical tests were designed to rule out the possibility that her visions derived from a cerebral pathology of some sort or a psychiatric problem; the scientific tests were intended "for the purpose of detection and analysis of certain changes in atmospheric radiation that were found to take place during Nancy's apparition."[68]

The group was led by Ricardo Castañon, a professor of neuropsychophysiology at the Catholic University of Bolivia, a former professor in Italy and Germany who had written extensively on the brain, stress, and the nervous system. The other members of the team were neurologists Ramon Sanchez and Norma Augosto Maury, respectively from Atlanta and Puerto Rico; electroencephalogram technicians Scott Prandy and Ted Blume; New York psychiatrist George Hogben; radiation specialist Umberto Velasquez, from Florida; biophysicist Philip Callahan, also from Florida; Australian cameraman William Stellar; and Ron Tesoriero, a lawyer who was observing the documentation and recording of the tests for a video and a book he was working on.

The equipment was already in place and running when Nancy announced that she was beginning to see the Madonna. At that precise moment, Castañon wrote in his report, the instruments detected a surge in energy, and the instruments for monitoring radiation indicated the arrival of gamma rays from the angle of the apparition. A researcher was watching the waves produced by Nancy's voice, translated into visual signals on a monitor: they were very small waves. But when the visionary fell silent and the onlookers guessed that she was listening to the voice of the Madonna, very big waves appeared on the monitor: nothing could be heard, but the instruments registered clearly the presence of a voice. At the same time, Castañon was monitoring Nancy's cerebral activity, through

measurements of the electrical conductivity of her skin. To his great surprise, he noted that there was no electrical activity whatsoever on the
woman's skin: "I can say her brain is dead; her brain is in coma state.
I don't have any result; she has a very deep, deep state of relaxation."
Sanchez was using other instruments to monitor Nancy's brain waves: he
recorded delta waves, 4 hertz a second. Normally, these waves are recorded
in a state of deep sleep, according to researchers, but Nancy was wide
awake. A third researcher, Callahan, was monitoring yet another type of
waves present in the air around Nancy Fowler's body, with the use of a
Schumman detector. Prior to the apparition, the wave frequency was 14
hertz, with an amplitude of 1 millivolt. But as soon as Nancy said, "I see
the Virgin Mary," the waves dropped to 8 hertz, and when she said, "The
Virgin Mary is speaking to me," they dropped sharply to 4; meanwhile,
the amplitude dropped to 2, then dropped again to 4 millivolts. Nancy
should have been sleeping, according to these indicators, according to the
researchers. Even if it were not evident that Nancy was neither in a coma
nor sleeping, Tesoriero adds, the footage is there to document that the visionary was dictating to a note taker sitting near her just what she was seeing and hearing. At a certain point, then, Nancy moved to another room
where there was a wooden crucifix. There she announced that Jesus was
speaking to her and that a light had formed on the crucifix, though no one
saw or heard anything. Then Callahan moved a probe over to the crucifix
to record any potential signs of electrical activity. As if it were alive, the
crucifix began to transmit electric signals, especially close to the hands,
where Nancy saw the light. Then when Callahan moved the probe to the
height of the statue's "heart," the energy began to pulsate, like a heartbeat. When Nancy said that Jesus said to her, "That is all," the electrical
activity ceased.

Thus the report of Castañon. Ron Tesoriero provides information
about other experiments. Doctor Sanchez, in his clinic in Atlanta, had
already done some tests of the cerebral activity of Nancy and another seer,
with whom there had been some cases of shared visions. And here the
recording of the brain waves had yielded some surprising results. When
the two women declared that they were seeing Jesus, the activity of their
delta waves was measured as 3 hertz, with a recurring pattern of 333.
But when they saw the Madonna, the activity rose to 4. And finally, when
they claimed that they were seeing Satan, the level rose to 6 hertz, with a
recurrent and nonrandom pattern equal to 666.[69] As we know, the number

666 is the number of the diabolical beast of Revelation. The technological pattern coincided with the religious symbol, as if to express the wonder of the reenchanted world.

The lengthy and elaborate report on the tests done upon Nancy Fowler, which until recently could be found the Web site *Conyers Apparition Web*,[70] confirms in another area what has already been noted in connection with photographs of the supernatural. Technology, in the current phase of Marian apparitions, reaches where the human senses fail to reach; the relationship with heaven runs through the field of technological mediation with greater strength and clarity than it does through the spiritual field. Jesus and the Madonna do not so much allow themselves to be recognized—in their obscure and mysterious being in the world beyond—by the path of faith and devotion as much as they clearly present themselves here, revealing themselves through probes, monitors, and computers, as in the previous section by film, lenses, video cameras, and the chips of machinery.

If this experimentation on Fowler had not been a rigorous laboratory study performed by scientists and researchers who appear to be members of the institutional scientific world—clinics, universities, laboratories—it might seem like an intentional caricature of a scientific experiment. These waves that come and go with the Madonna and Jesus, these hertz levels—with a 333 pattern for Jesus, which we cannot help but interpret as related to the 33 years of his life, while the hertz levels for the Devil are at the apocalyptic number of 666—and these small waves of Nancy's voice, with the large waves of the Madonna's voice (imperceptible to the human ear, but registered by the sensors, wires, and chips of the equipment) represent, as no other evidence could do, the technologization of religion in visionary Catholicism. The scientists report that while Nancy was receiving the consecrated host of the Eucharist, the monitors showed an increase of energy and a shift in her brain to delta waves. The mystery of transubstantiation, revealed by machinery: yes, it is true, Christians can proclaim to the world, bread really does become the body of Jesus, and if you don't believe us, just take a look at the computer screens in the laboratories that determined that it was true. This implication which, I repeat, borders on caricature, is not contrived, but is experienced in devotional practice as being as clear as day, even though it may unconsciously result in the obsolescence of faith.

That the case of Conyers is not isolated, but simply one of the best articulated, is shown by the fact that several of the occurrences noted there can be found in other noted vision sites; for instance, at Medjugorje. A few references will suffice.

In the tests carried out in Conyers, Professor Velasquez, the radiation expert, tested for the presence of ionizing radiation in the room where the apparitions occurred. In Medjugorje, a similar test was done, with even more precise details. An American doctor of Polish descent, Doctor Boguslav Lipinski, made use of a device called the "Spiritual Energy Machine," and ascertained that on the sites of the apparitions there was a level of radioactivity ten times the normal level, 100,000 millirads, which allowed him to indicate the presence in those sites of a powerful spiritual energy.[71] But these experiments were disputed by the Genoan researcher Emanuele Mor, "director of the Institute for Marine Corrosion of Metals of the C.N.R. (the only such center in Italy and one of the most important in Europe),"[72] according to whom, as quoted by Sala and Mantero: "Lipinski's research, though exceedingly interesting, was quite superficial, inasmuch as it failed to establish in advance all of the relationships between positive ions and negative ions."[73]

Indeed, Mor, after Lipinski, carried out a number of experiments that led him to state that there is no spiritual radioactivity, in contrast with the claims of the American physician.[74] According to Laurentin, who weighed in on the matter, Mor's experiments suggested that the hypothesis of detectable spiritual energy, claimed by Lipinski, was "illusory and non-scientific."[75] Later, however, in subsequent experiments, Mor himself detected a level of ionized air ten times the average. On those grounds, the physicist no longer rejected entirely the idea of spiritual experimentation, but instead suggested further testing with more sophisticated equipment, which would open up "new space for scientific investigation in reference to the mysteries of the supernatural."[76]

I have already suggested in another context the distinction between a technological test and a scientific analysis.[77] I maintained in that publication, based on the examples taken from Medjugorje, that

> the test, entirely blind and "idiotic," because it fails to comply with any rules of scientific hypothesis and verification (how can we hypothesize the presence of the Madonna and how can we hope to verify that presence in compliance with the scientific principles of knowledge of the world?) reports, on one occasion, "x," the next time, under the same conditions, "y." Obviously, the testing of a miracle is not a

laboratory instrument of scientific knowledge, but rather the staging of an experimental verification of a supernatural miracle. It seems to attest to the givenness of the miraculous event, but in reality it creates it, endowing it with local standing and phenomenology. "Local," as it is used here, means that the ascertainment done in this context cannot be related to scientifically demonstrable general conditions that it either confirms or disproves because, as we saw above, the verification provided at one point contradicts another comparable test performed at another time. The purpose of these tests, then, is to demonstrate that the miracle is not offensive to scientific reason, and not because that reason explains it, but rather because the experimental technology that is used by scientific reason, registers the miracles in the receptive sensors used to ascertain a "state of the world."[78]

Even though not all worshipers of apparitions look favorably upon scientific experimentation, this naïve reliance upon laboratory confirmations of the truth of the apparitions on the one hand documents, ambiguously, a dependence upon the scientistic ideology that is central to the contemporary world, holding science to be the supreme case of the quest for "truth," and on the other shows a certain ambition to make use of science to confirm the truth of faith and religion. In a vicious circle, the laboratory is asked to prove the validity of an affirmation of faith, which is then given absolute priority over any other sort of affirmation, including scientific affirmations.

Another scientistic phantom that wanders through the sites of Marian apparitions is that of ecstasy as evidence of authenticity.

In Medjugorje the visionaries were subjected on numerous occasions to experiments and tests to measure the degree of dissociation of the surrounding atmosphere and the modification of the neurological, psychological, and physiological indices of the normal conditions found in everyday life.

The first studies were done in 1984 by a French team led by the oncologist Henri Joyeux, and including Laurentin as well,[79] and in 1985 by an Italian research group, supervised by a gynecologist from the University of Milan, Luigi Frigerio, on behalf of the Associazione Regina della Pace (Queen of Peace Association).[80] These studies were followed by many less systematic studies, which did however add new data to the information gathered by the two groups mentioned above. *Press Bulletin* reported that a new and systematic study had been undertaken on 22 and 23 April 1998 in

the Casa di Incontro Cristiano in Capiago-Como upon three visionaries—
Ivan Dragicevic, Marija Pavlovic-Lunetti, and Vicka Ivankovic—by a scientific team led by Andreas Resch and Giorgio Gagliardi, and that the results
would be made public soon.[81] A brief report, which stated only that the
study had confirmed the data observed in 1985, was then published in the
Press Bulletin at the end of 1998 and in May 2000.[82]

These types of investigations are designed to document, through clin-
ical diagnoses and instrument-based experiments, the neurological and
psychic conditions of the visionaries both before and after the visions.
After a preliminary examination rules out personality disturbances, psy-
choses, or other psychic pathologies, the examiners then test the operative
state of the brain, before and after the phenomena. The brain waves that
are documented in an electroencephalogram are recorded; perceptive and
cognitive sensory contacts with the outside world are ascertained through
visual, auditory, and pain-generating stimuli; and the electrical activity on
the surface of the skin is even recorded, in order to gain information about
the functionality of the neurovegetative system and the state of awareness
of the visionary. The researchers also record heartbeats and the tone of
the "precapillary sphincters of the fingertip (plethysmography)," and finally they try to ascertain whether the visionary's lips move during the
apparition, suggesting a soundless speech, corresponding to movements
of speech-producing muscles in the larynx.

This array of studies, not always homogeneous in all the research
projects undertaken, but not entirely devoid of correlations either, has
led scholars to conclude that the visionaries of Medjugorje enter into a
psychic and physical state that can be termed "ecstasy," and that this state
is typical of—though not exclusive to—Christian, perhaps even Catholic,
mystical experiences, as distinguished from the mystical experiences of
other religions, such as Hinduism or Buddhism.[83] Scholars involved in
this type of research insist on the fact that the ecstasy in question is not a
pathological state. This statement is by no means universally accepted
in scientific circles, where quite to the contrary there is a widespread
tendency to place what is described as ecstasy in the array of symptoms
associated with hysteria or similar categories.[84] As early as the nineteenth
century, the phenomena associated with apparitions, mysticism, stigma-
tizations, and the sort were the focus of ferocious debates, not merely
scientific in nature but also, and especially, ideological, though generally
masked by scientific motivations, among the supporters of religious and
antireligious points of view. And this is a fact that we should not fail to take

into consideration: studying ecstasy with a scientific approach is not the same thing as studying sleep, hypnosis, or epilepsy, psychic and physical states that are often referred to in these studies. In contrast with studies of phenomena that are universally recognized as entirely physical and of this world, studies of ecstasy tend to mix physical states that are ascertainable (or suspect) with, in contrast, hopes of otherworldly presences; often the scholars work with the body, placing the sensors and probes of scientific research, in order to "prove" the existence of the soul, which is normally the field of observation of the theologian.

The research model proposed by Gagliardi and Margnelli—who seem, nonetheless, to be carrying out serious and reliable investigations and tests—is broken down into six phases. The fifth phase is a "theological analysis" while the sixth phase is a "scientific and theological final judgment."[85] These two latter phases certainly have nothing to do with the context of the scientific method, which does not include religious options among its procedures. In fact, in the Western tradition, and especially in scientific culture, there is a sharp separation between that which can be considered the field of scientific investigation, ascertainable, quantifiable, and if necessary, possible to reconstruct in accordance with hypotheses and theories apart from any factual or empirical basis—though with the provision that one will continue to seek those elements, leaving the door open for them, waiting for their eventual arrival—and that which belongs to a very different field, the field of theological speculation, whose source of inspiration is faith, not empirical reality, with a methodological approach proper to philosophical thought, not mathematics. Margnelli and Gagliardi, along with others, are working on a model of Catholic ecstasy as a differential and specific state, not classifiable with other states such as hysteria, neurosis, hallucination, and so on. In this connection, they insert into their model a substantial series of neurological and psychological indications that are said to be specifically characteristic of the general picture of Catholic ecstasy, and refer the reader to their other works. But what makes this model particularly muddled in terms of scientific method is the hypothesis of a direct intervention on the part of God. In fact, how could this hypothesis be tested with scientific instruments? A scientific model serves to explain the things that it is able to describe, and proving the existence of God is not one of those things. Alongside a scientific judgment, a believer can adduce a theological judgment: but the two judgments do not refer in a linear manner one to another; at the very most they can add up in the conscience of the believer, that is, when they do not cancel each other out entirely. In fact, in order to identify a presumed specific psychic and physical state, that of Catholic ecstasy, it is necessary to make use of empirical data taken from a given worldly and cultural context, that of the world of charismatic Catholics; therefore, one cannot dispense with neurology and anthropology, but one must dispense with God. On the other hand, a theologian could do without the first two disciplines, but could not do without God, for obvious reasons having to do with the foundation of his field of study. And so a synthesis between theology and science is possible only within an ideological context that intends to overlap the two fields, imagining that one is consequential to the other. That is not necessary, however, for an evaluation, scientific or theological, of a given ecstatic phenomenon.

And then, even if an instrumental test revealed in a subject all of the indications called for by the theoretical model of ecstasy, would that be proof that there was a genuine apparition? That the Madonna was there, before the eyes of the subject? We have already seen that at Garabandal one of the visionaries confessed that she had never seen anything at all, causing a crisis in the cult that had developed out of the visions.[86] Well, one aspect that caused quite an impression among the spectators, inducing them to believe in the reality of the apparitions, was the fact that the four girls all fell into a trance simultaneously, a phenomenon that could only be explained, according to the worshipers, by the real presence of the Madonna.

Margnelli and Gagliardi themselves identified two phases for Medjugorje: the first, with the earliest apparitions, in which "the state of consciousness during the visions is not very different from ordinary consciousness"; the second, of the well-consolidated apparitions, in which "the state of consciousness during the visions is that of ecstasy, and synchronisms have begun to appear,"[87] given the fact that during the initial prayer "Suddenly and all together, perhaps cutting off a word in the middle (and it was not the same word each time), they would stop speaking and drop to their knees in ecstasy."[88]

The conclusion of the two researchers, as they themselves point out with a conditional—"this would be of no small importance"—is that "ecstasy can be learned."[89] Far from being evidence of the presence of the Madonna, ecstasy could be evidence, instead, of a process of initiation, not culturally formalized yet quite effective, which has brought the visionaries from a preliminary stage of confused and uncoordinated visionary experience to a stage in which they have learned to control that experience, to orient it, and to make it simultaneous. And this does not mean that there has been fraud or anything of that sort. It means that the visionaries have attained a state of control of their states of altered consciousness that is typologically similar to the countless examples, found all over the world, of the learning of and initiation into the control of trance states.[90] If it were not already scientifically untenable to claim an automatic correlation between the presence of neuropsychological indices of ecstasy and a celestial presence, these examples of training and initiation to the trance state would be a clear demonstration of the fideistic and nonscientific dimension of the automatic correlation. And we can therefore view as an act of faith and not a scientific stance, the claim of that correlation sustained in all the areas of spreading visionary Catholicism, beginning with what the researchers state in such an ambiguous manner. For example, Frigerio declared that at Medjugorje "the children are experiencing an authentic mystical ecstasy."[91]

As if this statement had any real meaning, and were not simply ignoring the fact, previously mentioned, that, "in the field of neuroscience . . . one is even obliged . . . to prove the existence of ecstasy."[92]

Even if the theoretical model of ecstasy were to be universally recognized, it would remain obviously impossible to demonstrate that there is anything divine underlying a real ecstasy. Frigerio's scientific demonstration is therefore a mask covering his personal faith. And he goes on to state, further on in the same text, concerning the experiments done on the states of perception during the visions: "This is a genuine ecstasy, which is not scientifically explicable in terms of purely natural phenomena."[93]

We are thus asked to believe that a scientific investigation could provide a definitive conclusion that something cannot be explained in "natural" terms. The scientific explanation of a phenomenon must necessarily fall within the realm of natural explicability without any secondary prefix, whether we are talking about supernatural, infranatural, or paranatural. Moreover, that explanation is made possible by virtue of a theoretical model that provides coherence and congruence to the observed data and, at the same time, takes its legitimation from those same data. Even the research on ecstasy done by Margnelli and Gagliardi—members of Frigerio's research team and supervisors of the experiments discussed by Frigerio—is based on a theoretical model, set forth by Roland Fischer,[94] and they attempt to show its applicability. A model is adopted or rejected in terms of its ability to explain and reconcile a given array of empirical data. When the data cannot be explained, then we must change our theoretical model or reformulate the questions that the research was undertaken to answer, or reconsider our methods of observation and perhaps revise them; but in no case is it acceptable, in scientific terms, to conclude with a reference to the supernatural, as Frigerio does, since that is incompatible with a scientific approach and is an unacceptable outcome for a scientific experiment.

Unless we suppose that these ordinary procedures of scientific study and professional ethics in the reporting of the findings of research were not known to Frigerio and others, we must consider other explanations.

Over the course of the second half of the nineteenth century, a rivalry of enormous importance was played out between the Catholic Church, medical and institutional equipment, and unorthodox therapies as magnetism and somnambulism, on a territory that seemed to belong, in the eyes of one constituency, to the realm of the "marvels" of nature, and to the eyes of the others either to the realm of the supernaturally miraculous, or to the depths of a pathological hystericism. A rivalry, substantially speaking, for the control of the bodies.[95] The competition touched numerous fields of human life, and strongest of all was the demand for health and welfare. But this conflict between antagonist and competitors was, curiously enough, played out in the context of a shared point of reference, that of the recognized supremacy of science, that is, on the basis of a radical scientistic ideology, strongly encouraged by the general climate of positivism. As Clara Gallini observes, "It is precisely scientism that is the great myth, pitting all the competitors in a race on a single track, so that all the forms of miracle-working—whether orthodox or heterodox—advance the same demand to operate in accordance with scientifically valid and demonstrable methods involving the objective verification of data."[96]

It was in that cultural environment that those views developed, which still exercise a powerful hold upon many of the religious scholars who devote themselves to the experiment of visionary Catholicism, and who continue to ask laboratories to provide the final proof of the truth of their faith.

Among other things, in this case more than the standing of the miraculous is under discussion: that is, whether it is legitimate to invoke a divine origin, after having demonstrated "human inexplicability" of a given phenomenon, or whether it is not more reasonable to consider further improvements of the tools of scientific research. If that were the only issue at hand, the religious sphere would still enjoy a certain degree of ideological independence.

What is under discussion in the experiments done by Castañon, Lipinski, and Frigerio, and in the use made of those experiments by Margnelli and Gagliardi, is whether it is possible to prove by means of technological tests the presence of the Madonna, Jesus, and various saints in a room, on the body of a person, on the surface of a statue, to capture and definitively demonstrate the physical traces of God in social life. The presence of the Christian God in things, obscure and uncertain as it has always been, becomes something tested, proven, and complete: that which has been the object of faith for millennia is now plotted in graphs, recorded on screens, and depicted in images. Neither science nor religion, then, emerges as the winner of a centuries-old contest in which they were always rivals and, in the final analysis, mutually respectful; rather, technology has beaten them both, imposing the law of laboratory instrumentation, which on the one hand coopts the practical function of science, and on the other an ultimate concentration of the truth of faith.

Let us set aside the doubt as to whether there is any awareness of this fact on the part of scholars and scientists performing experiments on the supernatural, or if there is some hidden and Machiavellian strategy to gain consensus in an era of profound reliance upon science and technology. But I hardly think that there can be any question about which of the two sides is winning the match between religion and technology.

The laboratory test, abstracted from its scientific background, and with that background deprived of its experimental meaning—that it, its reliance upon scientific and not theological hypotheses, the fact of being part of a model, and therefore comparable or "disprovable" in the light of other models and other hypotheses, capable of "speaking" only within the panorama of scientific discourse—becomes an absolute that resolves within itself all of the questions of this world and the world beyond, something that is capable of speaking on its own and silencing everything else: the results of the test, distributed, cited, restated, and reformulated, become the keystone, the axis of the world, that which renders obsolete everything else, including the darkness, doubt, and silence, that envelops the God of Christian faith. Photographs, videos, laboratory tests: evidence of the supernatural proliferates, intertwines, offering cross-referenced documentation. Everything converges to capture the event, to certify it, placing it in the light of truth, isolating it from all the rest: from the dynamic of theoretical models, experimental methodologies, and observational data, from the complexity of sources of authentication, from the contexts in which it was produced, from the subjects who were actors or protagonists, from the forces at work, from history. And so the test gains access to the eternity of divine truth, in reality itself producing that truth and becoming its yardstick.

When Castañon visited Catalina Rivas, the seer of Cochabamba, for the first time in 1994, he was fairly skeptical about her claims to have received messages from Jesus and the Madonna. Catalina had been married three times, the scholar later stated, and in his opinion that made her claims harder to believe. Moreover, the test of electrical activity on her skin did not yield the same results obtained with Nancy Fowler. Castañon admitted to Catalina:

> I don't think you are lying to me, but to say that you have authentic experiences, I must have some register in my instruments, and I have nothing. Then if it's from God, what you have, and if he wants that everybody knows that you spread His messages, he must give you a proof that we can test, that we can measure, that we can see, and it must be repeatable. Then if it doesn't happen, it's only for you, this experience.[97]

Two years later, in 1996, Castañon received a telephone call from a friend of Catalina: "Ricardo, I think that the proof that you were waiting for has arrived; come to the hospital." Catalina had been taken to the hospital with the first manifestations of stigmata. "When I was there"—Castañon recalls—she said, 'Now I have the proof, something is happening with me.'"[98]

If what you have comes from God, it must be tested, measured, observed repeatedly and upon command. And then, behold God, who complies with the instrument of Castañon and allows himself to be tested, measured, observed repeatedly and upon command.

In conclusion, the quest for proof to eliminate all doubts about the existence of the world beyond and the reliability of faith require a materialization of the divine to subject to testing. The tools of this evidence are of course technological. This produces a doubly paradoxical result: the reduction of the spiritual standing of faith and dependency on the technological order to attain it. The technological laboratory, however, is a field from which one cannot escape, once one has entered it. Whatever technology can prove, it can also debunk or cast doubt upon, and a prior reliance upon it prevents a subsequent distancing.

Something similar has happened among groups that have a relationship with their own dead, in the world beyond. Traditionally, in Western cultures, this relationship operated primarily through dreams. From the point when human relations were extended past the moment of death, dreams, conceived as an intermediate space between the life of the living and the death of the dead, were accorded full legitimacy to be considered a valid channel. Some subjects, recognized as being particularly endowed with charism, became points of reference. Then, however, dreams were transformed into the psychoanalytic site of the subconscious; consequently, it became difficult to consider them as a channel to anything extending beyond the subject actually doing the dreaming; the locus of the relationship with the world beyond, necessarily, shifted. And attention turned, among the other so-called paranormal media, to technology, and especially to audio recording devices, televisions, and radios. Following the abandonment of dreams, which are difficult to confirm, subjective, and archaic, came the fortuitous tuning in of radio stations, recorded on tape machines; or the direct recording of voices from the world beyond, captured by a tape recorder left to record freely a magnetic track close to the charismatic. Sounds and noises of various sorts were thus transformed into phrases, words, the chants of the dead, promptly identified by the charismatic and then recognized by the relatives of the loved one. And this method worked superbly for the numerous adepts. But if dreams could not be verified, neither could they be disproved. Instead, an audio track can be completely isolated and identified with the use of other sophisticated technological equipment, and then decoded and explained as having nothing to do with the voices of the dead, but quite simply as a given audio source definitely present in the world of the living. Technology allows itself to be used and it may fascinate its users. It does not, however, allow its users to go beyond the technology itself. Everything that technology produces, it explains, and it does so in worldly, empirical, nonsupernatural terms.

And we can only view as pathetic this abandonment of age-old beliefs, still capable of cultural autonomy, in favor of beliefs that are technologically supported, and yet which no longer have any margins of independence, and which allow themselves to be dismantled by a rigorous critique. And the world is truly, in this way, culturally unified within the dominion of technology.

Chapter 4

INTERNET

The Surfer and the Web: A Preamble

What happens to the devotee of Marian apparitions, when the habitual use of the PC and the Web modifies his relations with the world of his practices and beliefs? The same thing that happens to anyone when such a powerful new tool of knowledge, social communication, and symbolic mediation intervenes, restructuring all his relations with reality, other people, and the very form of the social contract.

It is useful, then, before we enter the archipelago of worshipful surfing, to provide a preamble upon the surfer and his or her virtual sea.

> The new system will be the telecomputer, a personal computer adapted for video processing and connected by fiber-optic threads to other telecomputers all around the world. . . . The telecomputer may even reverse the effects of the television age. Rather than exalting mass culture, the telecomputer will enhance individualism. Rather than cultivating passivity, the telecomputer will promote creativity.[1]

The author of the passage quoted, George Gilder, is an American corporate consultant, and he states, further on in the same text, that:

> With artful programming of telecomputers, you could spend a day
> interacting on the screen with Henry Kissinger, Kim Basinger, or
> Billy Graham. . . . You could take a fully interactive course in physics
> or computer science with the world's most exciting professors, who
> respond to your questions and let you move at your own learning speed.
> You could have a fully interactive workday without commuting to the
> office or run a global corporation without ever getting on a plane.
> You could watch your child play baseball at a high school across the
> county, view the Super Bowl from any point in the stadium that you
> choose, or soar above the basket with Michael Jordan. You could fly
> an airplane over the Alps or climb Mount Everest—all on a powerful
> high-resolution display.[2]

The tone of enthusiasm is fairly emblematic of a diffuse optimism concerning the resources of freedom and creativity available to the telematic individual.

Even the most balanced and philosophically reliable scholars insist upon the aspects of creativity offered by the computerized interaction of human and machine. Pierre Lévy, a French philosopher engaged in a vast undertaking to reconsider the general epistemological aspects, as well as the ethical and political aspects, imposed by the progressive computerization of existence, has no doubts about the resources of creativity that spring from this interaction, which should not be confused with the purely logical determinism of the unfolding of a computer program that "moves by itself," with all its automatic mechanisms.[3]

Others appear to be more concerned about the resources and spaces of humanity in its relationship with machines. Ellen Ullman, a software specialist, writes: "We will be 'talking' to programs that have already been 'talked to' (programmed). . . . [In the end] the system contains them. It reproduces and reenacts life as engineers know it: alone, out-of-time, disdainful of anyone far from the machine."[4]

Aside from the personal emotional inclinations with regard to the near future, what disconcerts some and excites others is the fact that "in the symbiosis between operator and computer, a part of the nervous system belongs to the person, while part is in the computer."[5]

Derrick De Kerckhove, a student of Marshall McLuhan, identifies in this interaction a new and decisive corpus callosum, external to the one that links the right hemisphere with the left hemisphere of the brain:

> The new electronic media are working to become intermediary environments, which offer access to the interior reality of our individual psyche and create a bridge to the outside world. They carry out a form of social mediation in a single, continuous extension of our individual powers of imagination, concentration, and action, and which function, by and large, as a "second mind." A mind that will soon be endowed with a greater degree of autonomy than we might wish.[6]

Clearly, these new instruments and models of humanity's relationship with reality profoundly modify that same relationship, and as a result, impose a restructuring of the categories of thought and analysis. De Kerckhove proposes a psychotechnology with which to study both the technological devices for the treatment and processing of information and the restructuring and modification of the correlative psychological characteristics.[7] This shift, in the traditional way of thinking about humans, of the center of gravity from the human subject to the corpus callosum between humans and machines, is one of the most delicate questions in the contemporary debate, the evaluations of which, whether alarmist or enthusiastic, change radically, as Formenti emphasizes, "according to whether what prevails is the point of view favoring the expansion of the body through new channels of interaction with the outside world, or, in contrast, that of the invasion of the body by "nonintegratable" sensations and experiences."[8]

It would be a mistake to think that the "teleputer" is transforming a world that had been static prior to its arrival. The crisis afflicting community networks, the shared culture of a world in common, and centralized ideological systems is not a consequence of telematic technology; if anything, it has developed in the context of this larger crisis, which is a historic phenomenon of earlier roots and much grander scale. It is no accident that currently the greatest number of Internet access points, both in absolute terms and in percentage, should be in the United States, and that 84 percent of Web pages are created there.[9] Certainly, one factor may be the country's wealth, and we cannot ignore the scale of the technological revolution that has taken place in the United States, but we should also look to the weakness of the ideology of the traditional community and the ideological—and practical—centrality of individualism and the rhetoric of individual independence. Evidence to the contrary can be seen in the case of Japan: in a research project undertaken by John Quartermann of Texas Internet Consulting concerning the correlation between gross domestic product and the number of Internet sites, Japan proved to have fewer Web sites than other European nations with relatively comparable GDPs, such as Norway and Finland.[10] Japan's cultural tradition has always been and continues to be incomparably less individualistic than American culture; it is much more group-based, much more founded upon community networks. De Kerckhove quotes the Italian scholar Fosco Maraini, describing the tenacity of the resistance among the Japanese in the past to the temptation to purchase private automobiles: "An automobile implies individualism, independence, immediate decisions, all things that contrast with a Japanese mentality. In a country that is marked by such a close-knit social fabric, individual initiative is basically suspect."[11]

The setting of contemporary life speaks eloquently of a collapse of the forms of community cohesion, a fragmentation of the social bonds into myriad loyalties, affiliations, and identifications, all weak, fungible, and each incapable of providing orientations that are definitive, stable, and applicable to one and all. It also clearly bespeaks a failure of what Marc Augé calls the "intermediate cosmologies," which include

> both cosmologies traditionally studied by ethnology—they began to suffer with the advent of colonial penetration—and those representations particular to what Durkheim called intermediate bodies, namely political parties and trade unions, representations which for many played the role of a "vision of the world" capable of organizing and orienting their everyday lives, just as religion does for those who believe (or at least for those who practice). We should note that individual initiative is being asserted today in the religious domain itself. There are many Catholics, for example, who intend to practice "my way"—as if religion's capacity to organize and orient each person's daily life, its ability to function as an intermediate cosmology, were diminishing in its turn.[12]

In the absence of general and centralized orientations and local or intermediate points of reference, the individual is summoned to respond directly and personally to the stimuli deriving from the "acceleration of history,"[13] the shrinking spaces, the pluralization of ideological and symbolic worlds. Each person, individually summoned to create her own individual cosmology for herself, to seek out a foundation in the unstoppable and unconfigurable flow of things, tends to sense the dizzying loneliness of her condition: "Each person is or thinks he is somehow 'in relation with' the whole world. There are no longer any intermediary rhetorics to protect the individual from direct confrontation with the informal whole of the planet or—what comes to the same thing—the vertiginous image of his solitude."[14]

And while this is a process that is in some sense already present in modernity, which to Jean Starobinski was characterized by a twofold aspect "Loss of the subject among the crowd—or, inversely, absolute power, claimed by the individual consciousness,"[15] there can be no doubt that precisely the media-driven present contributes more than anything else to accelerate this process, since it is "the media in general, advertising images, the news . . . ," that imply

> what is, from the anthropological point of view, the paradox of contemporaneity: while their truth is not local—mediatized images and messages instantly put any person into relation with the entire world—their immediate meaning, the type of relation they allow us to establish, involves the individual more than the group.[16]

This decisive role of individuality, however, is not an affirmation of the individual taken as an autonomous and sovereign subject. The reduction of intermediate cosmologies does not translate into an affirmation of individual liberty. On the contrary, a fragmentation of the social sphere corresponds to an equal fragmentation of the individual, which has itself become a paradoxical site of symbolic conflicts among diverse considerations, all obviously originating in the relationships with otherness, that is, in the social sphere.

A long debate on the pluralization of identities, on the fragmentation of individuality, on the weakening of the ego, the fading of the self, accompanied all Western thinking over the course of the twentieth century, but in truth it had already begun long before. An allusion to its existential drama is expressed nicely in this passage from the description of Sula, the protagonist of the novel of the same name by Toni Morrison: "The first experience taught her there was no other that you could count on; the second that there was no self to count on either. She had no center, no speck around which to grow."[17]

Then came the Web, which certainly did not create on its own the isolation of the individual, the fragmentation of cosmologies, and the collapse of collective points of reference. Those things already existed. But the Web changed them, transforming them from tragic elements to aspects that were in a certain sense festive, exciting, consciously touted, promised, and achieved. In the words of George Gilder, the Internet "liberates . . . individuals from the chains of bureaucracy and geography and makes it possible . . . to work and exchange ideas with the right people anywhere in the world."[18]

Furio Colombo, a member of the sizable group of the "alarmists," to use a term that appears on the back cover of his book, cautions, "On the one hand, we do not know the boundary of our mind. And on the other hand, we do not know the boundary of a voyage through the Web. These two undefined entities, touching and intermingling, cannot but help but induce a sense of euphoria, an almost hallucinogenic feeling of pure power, expansion, exaltation of the mind, exactly the same thing that so many seek from drugs."[19] Colombo refers to the theme of the isolation that is produced by the "new drug" (for that matter already sketched out by Augé):

> But it also leads to isolation, loneliness. It is a solitude that no longer
> knows its limitations and believes that it is in contact with the world.
> And in a certain sense, perhaps it is, and we should not undervalue the
> practical aspects of "surfing." But it is not in the sense that one remains
> a captive of an internal and mental space, a mysterious space that,
> before computers, was the province of artists and mystics, and which
> could not be explored without some degree of risk. Now a machine that
> costs a thousand dollars can provide this experience to anyone, a risky
> exaltation. We can't live without the machine, but we cannot conceal
> from ourselves that the voyage is a lonely, solitary one.[20]

This solitude, which as we have seen is not generated by the Internet, is well concealed in the Internet. Indeed, the sensation is that one is in touch with everyone, that one is in the company of the hundreds of thousands of correspondents that one can reach. One of the characteristics of the Web is the proliferation of "virtual communities," experiments in new forms of community building, obviously quite distant from the traditional models of communities found throughout the history of human groups.

One radically distinctive aspect, Colombo notes, is found in the fact that personal identities on the Web are not comparable to their external counterparts: "The absence of faces and identities is no longer a theatrical expedient but rather a technical datum which forms part of the nerve circuits of the new world."[21]

It is likely, however, that this is just a phase in the development of the Web. Soon the dizzying growth of technological resources will make it possible, much more easily than is the case today with "teleconferencing," to have contacts that will be visual, and more, with other surfers. The problem, therefore, will not be the face, as much as the lack of any complex and localized community links, institutional and civic obligations, allowing a constant oscillation of identities, an interplay of roles that will introduce—and to an even greater degree introduces today—a certain lightness in the communities that form and dissolve on the basis of rapid identifications and disidentifications. There are now tens of thousands of discussion groups, newsgroups, and mailing lists, and they are continuously increasing. Whoever posts a topic on the Web and finds someone else to read it has formed a small group that might grow, or shrink, depending on the interest that is attracted or lost. As Colombo tells us, "Usenet is a giant network of ten thousand discussion groups scattered within the Internet, and dedicated to every possible discussion of news. Usenet seems to be the perfect antidote to the traditional mass media. Instead of submitting to the lowest common denominator in order to reach the largest possible audience, Usenet is regulated by its own users."[22]

Even more fragile are the chat lines, the real-time discussion groups that are held on specialized Web sites for whoever happens to be passing by the site at that moment. The gratuitous nature of the presence and the conversation in these systems is almost total, and the personal identities are entirely unknowable and impossible to reconstruct. In fact, you cannot enter a chat without equipping yourself with a nickname, which becomes your own emblem of identity. Chats tend to make it difficult to make real contacts outside their context, both because of the technical difficulties involved, and because in certain cases to do so is expressly forbidden. This is true, for example, of the chat line created for children in Italy by the Disney corporation. The first and the fifth rules of the site are eloquent: "1. Never transmit personal information, whether your own, or that of your family or friends, which would let others identify you: this applies to your first name, your last name, your phone number or your fax number. . . . 5. Never make appointments to meet anyone outside the Web."[23]

The objective is to protect children who want to join in the conversation from child molesters and other ill-intentioned individuals. The result is the creation of a relationship among children that is entirely devoid of concrete points of reference, a relationship with others in which the dimension of personal imagination, fantasy, and dream world is absolute and unmitigated, at a very impressionable age, by the fact of the physical presence of the interlocutor. It might seem safe to describe it as an unreal relationship. But that is not the case. It is a mistake to think of these new dimensions as being something separate from reality. Far from it: what we need to learn is that alongside the realities that we perceive with our shared senses as the only ones, there are other realities, virtual realities.

The case of chat lines is fairly persuasive. In effect, entering into a discussion in a chat line, by means of a nickname that serves to mask one's true identity, entails a series of operations that are anything but neutral. First of all, the operation involved in concealing one's own true identity, which corresponds to the operations whereby one's correspondents conceal their own identities, obliges you to speak with others as if, in a sort of dreamlike dimension, one were speaking as well with and among one's own inner phantoms, with, however, the unexpected and added factor of originality—that the pretext is entirely external, and derives from one's correspondents—conferring a greater attraction. In fact, constructing a discourse without necessarily having to consider social roles, identities, or personal or logical consistency allows one to assemble, condense, and overlap as one pleases. Let us be clear on this: it is possible of course to take into account—and people often do—roles, identities, and all of that; but it is no longer necessary in order to cause the mechanism of communication to function, and it is not required in order to take part in a chat. This is true for the "outgoing," so to speak, that is, with respect to one's correspondents, but it is also true for the "incoming," that is, on the part of the correspondents in their turn. It means that anyone, like a novelist faced with a blank page, can construct characters which, certainly, though they may derive from real corollaries—yourself on the outgoing, your correspondents on the incoming—are in any case projections of inner phantoms and ghosts, with respect to whom the correspondents in any dialogue will eventually be forced to adapt and accept. If they fail to do so, in fact, it is as easy as can be to switch correspondents. And so—precisely like a novelist who, having once created a character, suddenly sees that character acting as if it had a life of its own, and is obliged to strike a sort of creative compromise in the continuation of the story—the user of a chat line establishes a stabilizing compromise with his various correspondents, conferring to them the characteristics of the personalities that have been constructed and that he watches moving, as if they too were endowed with lives of their own.

At this point, we are ready to go back to focus on the worshipful surfer, setting sail with him or her in the visionary Catholic archipelago.

Virtual Voyages

For centuries, the sacred status of certain places has been central to the European Catholic religion. Sanctuaries, miracles, visions, devotions—everything worked together to reinforce local communities; everything was contained within their symbolic context, in relation to exchanges with other communities, with unspoiled nature, and with nature that had been tamed and cultivated. In the wake of the Industrial Revolution, the growth in spatial mobility, and the development of the mass media—as well as the responses of the church to these processes of transformation—as has been demonstrated for Spain by William Christian, local sacred statuses have progressively declined in importance.[24] The Turners have claimed that as far as Marian devotion is concerned, over the course of the nineteenth and twentieth centuries, centuries that witnessed the creation of several of the most important Marian sanctuaries of the modern Catholic world—Lourdes and Fatima foremost among them—there has been, instead, a transformation rather than a simple weakening. The transition has been from the medieval "shepherd's cycle," in which "the Virgin instructed the individual visionary to found a shrine to her," to a new cycle, based upon messages that contained "a general call to all humankind to repent and be saved."[25] Although Lourdes, Fatima, and other modern apparition sites might also entail the construction of a sanctuary in a physical location, the cultural significance has extended beyond the confines of a local dimension, organizing itself into the form of a universal message. It is no accident that the two locations, one French and the other Portuguese, should have become, from the local sanctuaries that they originally were, national and finally universal sanctuaries. Inevitably, then, there was a progression from strictly local dimensions to "Catholic" dimensions, that is, to a general delocalization of the sacred.

In the case of Lourdes, however, a peculiar form of delocalization was imposed as early as the 1870s with the spread of imitation grottoes, modeled on the original grotto of Lourdes. "A singular cloning of a sacred landscape that eliminated geographic distances," emphasizes Clara Gallini, "and translates into the terms of a miniaturized familiarity the arcane distances of a mystical space, the very presence of the Grotto, as was written at the time, 'transports Lourdes to the various cities. . . .' "[26]

In general, copies, reproductions, and imitations have played a crucial role in the delocalization of sacred statuses. Fatima has propagated a great number of "original copies" of its Marian statue, to which special powers, even visionary powers, were often attributed. And nowadays Medjugorje is no less active, exporting throughout the world miraculous statuettes, including one that in 1995 wept tears of blood in Civitavecchia. In turn, the images of the Virgin of Guadalupe in Latin America, and especially in Mexico, have an ancient record of widespread miracles, a tradition that is now being powerfully revived. In the world of contemporary apparitions, new visions are often announced as copies of famous earlier visions, as was the case with the anonymous American visionary "S," who saw an apparition of the Madonna of Fatima on the headrest of her own bed.[27] Sometimes the process of the delocalization of the sacred through the medium of copies has to do with several famous images and apparitions at once: the weeping statue of Christ in Cochabamba, Bolivia, in 1995 was a copy of the Christ of Limpias, a statue that wept in 1918;[28] but it is also an exact copy of another statue of the Christ of Limpias, the one kept in the home of Nancy Fowler, the American visionary from Conyers, Georgia. Moreover, it was purchased by Catalina Rivas, who herself became a visionary a few months later. The case of the statue of the Christ of Limpias and the visions of Catalina Rivas originated with its links to Conyers. According to worshipers, Jesus told Nancy when she was in Bolivia in March 1995, "I will leave a sign of My presence in this country." Two days later, just as Nancy was flying back to the United States, the statue began its lacrimation.[29] This intertwining seems to me to be an eloquent commentary on how the universalizing culture of modern apparitions and the tendency of the new visionaries to extend their own influence have played an important role in the processes of the delocalization of the sacred.

All the same, in general the cases of the visionary movement begin with a clearly local dimension. The visionaries must first and foremost gain acceptance from the local communities in which they live, and so it is fairly obvious that the "messages" are intended for the parishioners, the parish priest, the leaders, and the faithful of their own territory. In these phases the cultural dimension of the phenomena must reflect or in any case take into account the local models of worship, faith, ritual, symbolism, and so on. In some cases, there is an ethnic emphasis, in the context of which the apparition appeals to the specific community. For example, in San Bruno, California, Carlos Lopez and Jorge Zavala, immigrants from El Salvador, received their messages in their own language, Spanish.[30] In Washington state, the worshipers who flocked to Yakima, in 1997 because the policeman Chico Rodriguez had seen the Madonna, were mostly members of the Hispanic community.[31] A good many of the faithful who visit the house of the visionary Nasreen, in Los Angeles, are Arabs, as is Nasreen herself, originally from Kuwait.[32]

The very acceptance of new miracles is restricted by criteria of local religious and cultural recognizability. For instance, the reason that the miracle of the lacrimation of a statue of the Madonna dei Fiori (Our Lady of the Flowers) claimed at Sannicola, near Lecce in southern Italy, was not accepted was that, according to the investigation undertaken by a committee appointed by the bishop of Nardò-Gallipoli, the liquid that issued was found to be an "oily vegetal substance";[33] and that was, on the contrary, precisely the reason why the exudations of the image owned by Myrna of Damascus, and the copy of that image owned by Nasreen in Los Angeles, were recognized as authentic by the Arab Christian communities.

When the apparition gains local credence and consensus, however, and visitors begin to arrive from elsewhere, or when articles begin to appear in the press or coverage appears on television, then the local dimension is gradually revised to its proper proportions, if not eliminated entirely. If, then, the apparition acquires international renown, the local and ethnic dimensions are quickly relegated to the background, or they disappear entirely. They may reemerge later in special circumstances, as was the case in Medjugorje, where, as a result of the war in Bosnia, a marked nationalistic element came to light that had previously been relegated to the background. In other words, in general terms, when a place where apparitions are reported grows in importance, it results in changes in the organization of both ritual and communications; the influence of the local community wanes, replaced by a reliance upon other entities imposed by the growing importance: ecclesiastical institutions, the various cultures of pilgrims from elsewhere, and the mass media. While the first phases of an apparition are heavily shaped by local symbolic and ritual structures, in later phases the new factors at work modify the whole, no longer as a function of the circumscribed local universe, but now in consideration of a much broader horizon—these days, a planetary panorama—which becomes accessible to the new cult.[34]

With the Internet, finally, the long process of transformation of the relationship between celestial visions, the site of the visions, and the visionaries themselves comes to an end, while the delocalization of the sacred epiphany reaches its culmination. The Web no longer connects physical places—as television still does—but rather it composes a network of virtual places, the Web sites. "When you can transfer the Library of Congress from one place to another in under a minute," writes Howard Rheingold, "the very notion of what it means to have a place called the Library of Congress changes."[35]

There are still apparitions that preserve distinct elements of localization, through references to the archaic model of apparitions, with requests for the construction of a church or a sanctuary to renew local faith.[36] In Litmanova, Poland, the Madonna asked that an alcoholic woman be brought to the site of the apparitions in order to cure her: "It is necessary to take her to the place where the apparitions occur," inasmuch as, according to the commentary of the visionaries, "the Madonna gave us the message that her power is especially strong in the field" of the apparitions.[37] Kurescek, Slovenia, is praised in a message from the Madonna of February 1990 on the Web page that describes the visions that take place there: "This will be a place of grace, a place of healing of diseases and wounds of the soul. Whoever, in this place, takes refuge in My Heart and in the Heart of My Son, will be healed and will receive that peace that can only be given by Heaven."[38]

But ultimately, on the Web, for Litmanova and Kurescek as well, what counts is not the richness of their local importance, but rather the fact that they are links in the larger visionary network, "words" in the virtual vocabulary of the apparitions of the Madonna. And that, like all the other sites of apparitions around the world, they are possible sites for physical—but most important, virtual—visits with the Madonna.

Outside the Web, the traditional pilgrimage has not vanished; indeed it has been reinvigorated in a jubilee-related period marked by an enormous development of religious tourism. But a new type of pilgrimage has become possible on the Web, and it is quite attractive, allowing one to reach the venerated sacred image instantly; it could even make the physical trip unnecessary. The exploration of Web sites makes it possible to obtain maps of the physical sites, suggestions of potential geographic itineraries, and even advertising for travel agencies. At the same time, however, it offers virtual stopovers and way stations, where physical movement is replaced by a shuttling from one link to another, with accompanying prayers and other ritual practices: on the one hand, there are information and pictures of holy places and historical sites related to the apparition, and on the other hand, you are invited to recite prayers or listen to sacred music, with an image, the face of the Madonna or Jesus, or perhaps simply a legend reading: "recite the Hail Mary."

But is a virtual tour merely a voyage that does not happen to involve physical movement, leaving unaltered all the rest of the devotional experience? Apparently, at least, nothing changes in the context of apparitions. The visionaries and the community of Medjugorje, for instance, continue to constitute quite specific identities, with an unequivocal and unmistakable location, in the heart of a region that has notoriously been riven by many years of warfare; the messages proclaimed in Medjugorje, as in the apparitions that emulate those of Medjugorje, feature appeals for an immediate conversion, because our times (or time in general) are coming to an end. But when this set of events, significances, and symbolic productions passes into the Internet, it is altered, inevitably, and perhaps definitively. On the Web, space, time, and external identities undergo destructuring metamorphoses; new forms and new events are created, as pervasive as they are subtle, as powerful as they are unpredictable.

In order to understand the forces of change at work it is time to examine the issue of the virtual dimension, mentioned above.

A clear and fascinating theorization is offered by Pierre Lévy. In agreement with Gilles Deleuze, he suggests two pairs of terms: "real" and "possible," on the one hand; "actual" and "virtual" on the other. Through the first two pass the processes of "realization" and "derealization"; between the other two, "actualization" and "virtualization." In contrast with what is often thought, the virtual is not an antireal, it is not the opposite of the real; rather it is the opposite of the actual, whereas that which is the opposite of the real is the possible:

> The possible is already fully constituted, but exists in a state of
> limbo. . . . The possible is exactly like the real, the only thing missing
> being existence. The realization of a possible is not an act of creation
> in the fullest sense of the word, for creation implies the innovative
> production of an idea or form. . . . Unlike the possible, which is static
> and already constituted, the virtual is a kind of problematic complex,
> the knot of tendencies or forces that accompanies a situation, event,
> object, or entity, and which invokes a process of resolution: actualiza-
> tion. . . . Actualization thus appears as the solution to a problem, a

solution not previously contained in its formulation. It is the creation, the invention of a form on the basis of a dynamic configuration of forces and finalities. . . . We now have a better idea of the difference between realization (the occurrence of a predetermined possible) and actualization (the invention of a solution required by a problematic complex). But what is virtualization? . . . Virtualization can be defined as the movement of actualization in reverse. It consists in the transition from the actual to the virtual, an *exponentiation* of the entity under consideration. Virtualization is not a derealization (the transformation of a reality into a collection of possibles) but a change of identity. . . . The virtualization of a given entity consists in determining the general question to which it responds, in mutating the entity in the direction of this question and redefining the initial actuality as the response to a specific question.[39]

To put it in Lévy's terms, then, the physical Medjugorje is a place where a set of possibilities of ritual practices exists, and the individual pilgrimage, whether performed by a group or a single person, is a realization of that possibility. It is from that set of possibilities, then, organized or controlled by the local Franciscans, and in turn set within a framework of Catholic "possibilities," that a given ritual practice emerges: any deviation that is not contemplated in what "is possible" would be immediately attacked; for that matter, the institutional and the spatial and temporal arrangement would in any case prevent it in advance.

Online, on the other hand, there is no complete, defined, given Medjugorje, to which we can gain access. In fact, the physical Medjugorje does not automatically upload to the official Web site, or to any other Web site. Now it belongs to a "problematic complex," a "node of trends and forces" which certainly refers to the cases of the most famous Marian apparitions in the world, but which also expands to include flows of the religious imagination in the broader sense, and then also to even vaster levels of symbolism, and which stands ready to be actualized, that is, taken to a specific and unforeseen solution. Only a given actualization of the surfer brings into play Medjugorje on the Web. But every given actualization is a peculiar and given "solution to a problem," which was not so much a necessary prerequisite—as a possibility—of the action of browsing or navigating, but which instead emerged from the creative activity of the corpus callosum on the Web. It is evident that this fact alone already places the virtual pilgrim outside the given local symbolic context of Medjugorje.

The physical pilgrim immerses herself into a binding symbolic context, which orients her intellectually and emotionally, selecting for her the
correct interpretations of what she is doing and of what is occurring in the
place where she finds herself, directing her actions, setting the event of
the pilgrimage into the hierarchic order of the collective symbolic frame-
works, which she uses and, at the same time, which she processes as a
necessarily disciplined user.

The virtual pilgrim, on the contrary, has no strong contexts that restrict
his movements or that offer him an anchorage and a compass. His is a
voyage in which every stop—every actualization that is determined—is
the center of the world, temporary but unquestionable, and removed from
any hierarchic structure. The suggestions of direction and orthodox interpretation that he may receive are on the order of virtualizations, which
await his actualization, or, as we have seen, transformation.

Every actualization is thus also a virtualization. Let us continue with
Lévy: "[The] actualization itself produces new messages and new information, micro-virtualizations . . . , everything that is an event is part of a
dynamic of actualization (territorialization, instantiation in the here and
now, particular solution) and virtualization (deterritorialization, detachment, sharing, elevation to a problematic). Events and information about
events exchange their identities and functions at each stage of the dialectic
of signifying processes."[40]

In other words, if we consider that on the Web, Medjugorje—let us
continue to use the Bosnian apparition as an example—lies at the convergence of a countless array of problematics, each process of actualization or
virtualization shifts and reconfigures incessantly the larger picture, drifting away relentlessly from the given symbolic configuration that exists
offline (the physical Medjugorje), whose production is carefully controlled
by the hierarchic order, but which online is replaced by the current configuration created by the browser, eluding the monitoring of any institutional
auctoritas, remaining entirely subjective. That any individual surfer might
attempt, eventually, to copy or imitate its symbolic configuration offline,
is another matter, eventual, in fact.

The action of the surfer, then, modifies the physical relationships of
space and time through the twofold mechanisms of delocalization (Medjugorje, there) and relocalization (the navigation that actualizes a Medjugorje, here), unlinking (the collective symbolic context, there) and determination (the actual use, here), general problematization (prophetic and
apocalyptic visionarism, open to the signs of the paranormal and the New

Age) and circumscribed specification (the specific manner in which the "problem" is reformulated and solved, here).

No visionary phenomenon can pass through these processes intact without a radical transformation of its original characteristics. What come into play first and foremost are the identities of the sacred places, which undergo processes of weakening, obscurement, and syncretic overlapping; the localizations, which disappear into myriad places created in a nonplace that cannot establish itself as a collective center, and the space-time rhythms and pacings, which are eliminated in synchronicities and ubiquities that eliminate the before and the after, the here and the there. Medjugorje on the Web—like Hillside and Lipa—belongs to a fluid virtual scenario, not definitive, a problematic visionary background, prophetic and apocalyptic, which is accessed for "localized" uses that may be quite differentiated one from another, fragmenting the Bosnian reality, so sharply determined offline, into an array of extremely articulated problematic refractions, repositioned in countless actualizations and then re-launched into new placeless virtual horizons.

The Risks of Surfing and Erotic Shipwrecks

Christine, . . . for every hour on the internet there are 3 days added to your time in purgatory.[41]

I didn't know that Jesus King of all Nations was on the internet, but it is.[42]

Which of the two devotional interpretations of the Internet is true? Both are true, since each corresponds to an actualization that a surfer has accomplished of the devout virtualities that can be actualized on the Net. When you move through the Internet, you are not moving toward a secure deposit of definite meaning, a certain destination where you will find the hierarchy of meanings that you left behind you upon your departure: in Lévy's words, "Interpretation, the production of meaning, no longer refers exclusively to the interiority of an intention, to hierarchies of esoteric signification, but to the individual appropriations of a navigator or surfer. Meaning is based on local effects, it is formed at the intersection of a deterritorialized semiotic plane, and its goals are efficiency and pleasure."[43]

The Internet, as we have already seen, is not an asteroid that fell out of the sky, upsetting well established and functional equilibriums and configurations. The present-day world, as so many say and find, is a world where movement, transformation, and mixing are common and often incomprehensible. "Movement plus uncertainty," goes the formula that Georges Balandier coined to summarize the dimension of modernity.[44] "Much, if not everything, is subject to cancellation, substitution, or transformation—but we also see the recovery of certain forms handed down from the past. The upheaval of social and cultural landscapes, references, tools, and 'know how,' just like the multiple connections that govern the relationship of the individual with his or her environment and social context, all of this contributes to the emergence, and then to the reinforcement of an awareness of the disorder."[45]

The wide-ranging and apparently endless debate over postmodernism abounds with analysis and references to a world that appears increasingly under the aspect of incomprehensibility, at the same time due to an excess and an absence of rules, and the general loss of boundaries: boundaries, first and foremost, between order and disorder, then boundaries between everything that we think of when we consider a model of traditional society—and perhaps to an even greater degree in our imaginations than in the actual experience of the past—as being well regulated, circumscribed, and contained, in contrast with the chaotic, confused, hybrid experience of the present day.

From this point of view, the Internet has added nothing new to the existing world. Except, perhaps, for one decisive thing: the fact that the "disorder," without boundaries and without rules, now arrives on the screen of the surfer as an automatic factor, as an obvious feature, as "the way things are." While this aspect, outside the precincts of visionary culture, does nothing to disturb in any particular way those who experience this type of reality—almost entirely devoid of stable points of reference offline— in a favorable manner, either wittingly or unconsciously, that is certainly not the case with those who search the Internet for a confirmation of the grueling daily task that they have set for themselves: discovering a powerful principle of order in the religious panorama, in devotional practice, in transcendental metaphysics. Because in these cases, there is an exceedingly high risk that the Web might entirely undermine their efforts. There may be no one better suited than a scholar who is accustomed to spending time in devotional contexts—pilgrimages, sanctuaries—and accustomed to identifying in those contexts strenuous, even noble, efforts to find a new foundation for solid and centralized order in the world, as well as to recognizing the features of symbolic universes that are meant to be orderly and cosmic—no one could be better equipped to discern the radical difference between these contexts and the sites of virtual pilgrimages, where there is almost nothing to ensure the solidity of the desired centralized order, the vertical thrust toward the transcendental, the clear definition of the boundaries between good and evil, order and disorder, salvation and damnation.

The Internet is amorphous, polyvalent, transformational, holistic, and fragmented, all at the same time. The Internet is volatile: Web pages open and close; that which is there one day may disappear the next, as I have more than once realized, alas!, when I suffered the loss of data that I failed to record during the course of my research.[46] Everything that is introduced into the Internet tends to take on the nature of the medium itself, becoming reticulated, punctiform, erratic, and mingled: the medium is the message. For this reason alone, it is not hard to guess how dramatically this dynamic affects a religious world based upon powerful and radical choices, as is the world of visionary Catholicism, an especially conservative "province" of the Catholic "confederation."

As is known, the English term most often used to describe browsing the Internet is "surfing," and the person browsing or navigating the Web is described as the "surfer." In Italian, the corresponding terms are *navigazione* (navigation) and *navigatore* (navigator). Both languages use the metaphor of the ocean and those who ply its waves. In the English there is an implicit reference to the frequent possibility of falls and loss of control that is typical of surfing; in Italian there is a greater implication of safety, with a reference to boats and ships, which are far more stable than surfboards. But there is also an implied reference to another type of risk, that of becoming lost in the open sea, which is less of an imminent danger to a surfer. In both cases, the unpredictable factor of losing one's way, wandering off course, and finally shipwreck is intrinsically linked to the term itself. But while wandering off course and shipwreck could perhaps prove exciting eventualities for someone who navigates or surfs for fun or as a game, and could even prove to be a creative resource with potential economic returns in the utopian versions of the new economy,[47] or perhaps be nothing more than a slight delay for a surfer who is browsing for work, those risks become catastrophic for the worshipful surfer, for her faith, her devotion, her very existential orientation.

For that matter, the opportunities for worshipful surfing on the Internet are immense. Catholic sites, especially in English, are in the thousands and are continually growing in number. Each of them, moreover, is connected to other sites through links, that is, the points of connection that make it possible to pass from site to site with a simple click of the mouse. There are sites whose chief purpose is to assemble lists and links to the greatest possible number of other Catholic sites. The Web site *Catholic Goldmine*,[48] for example, in 1997 had links to a thousand Catholic Web sites, and a year later, to eighteen hundred. In Italy, the Web site *Lista dei siti cattolici in Italia* (List of Catholic Sites in Italy), administered by Francesco Diani,[49] had 987 entries at the end of October 1998, while in June 2000 it had grown to 3,280 entries, and as of this writing it has more than 5,000 links. In Italy, moreover, there is now a Catholic search engine, called Profeta, which in August 2001 boasted links to 6,320 Catholic Web sites. Numerous books have already been published listing Catholic Web sites and e-mail addresses. For example, there is *Catholics on the Internet*, by Brother John Raymond, cofounder and member of the order of the Monks of Adoration;[50] *Catholicism on the Web*, by Tom Fox,[51] publisher of the *National Catholic Reporter*; in Italy, *Il Web sia con voi*, by Igino Domanin and Stefano Porro.[52]

It is impossible to have a complete list of the Catholic Web sites, inasmuch as the way in which sites are constructed on the Internet is entirely free, and needs no authorization or controlling authority that must take note of the creation of a site in a worldwide categorized registry. This is especially true of the enormous number of sites created by individual Web users, the so-called personal home pages. With minimal expense, or even entirely without cost, worshipers can create their own personal Web sites, consisting of a variable number of pages—ranging from a very few to thousands—and post them on the Web, at the disposal of whoever manages to track them down or happens upon them by pure chance.

Among these Catholic sites, then, those devoted to the Madonna and her apparitions are among the most widespread, determined, and combative.

The simplest and most immediate way to reach these sites is to type in the URL,[53] that is, the set of characters that allow the teleputer to contact the desired site directly. But one does not always have the exact address, and then one needs to make use of one of the "search engines," that is, a fast keyword search system that hunts through the hundreds of millions of Web pages scattered throughout the Web.

And it is precisely with this method of browsing that the first dangers of shipwreck begin to loom for a worshipful surfer in search of Marian Web sites. Keywords, in fact, are not capable of distinguishing contents and including or excluding. I have already observed that, for instance, if I type in the word "Madonna" in order to obtain information concerning the Web sites on the subject, I will find on my screen a list of several hundred or thousand possible references, according to the search engine that I have used, but that there is no distinction between the sites relating to the Madonna and to apparitions and the sites devoted to Madonna, the rock singer. The problem is that the references concerning the singer are quite often linked to pornographic or erotic Web sites, or Web sites that are closely linked to them. This first risk can be avoided by typing "Our Lady" or "Virgin Mary" or "Immaculate." That does not entirely eliminate all risks—because references to the singer include such wordplay as "Immaculate Madonna," while others derive from the name of her daughter, Lourdes Maria—but they are thus drastically reduced.

In fact, even before we typed in a URL or did an initial search with a search engine, we ran another risk: in order to enter the Web at all, in fact, you need to make use of a special software, a browser, which provides access to a portal, which is to say, a virtual location in which categories of sites are assembled by subject, ranging from current events to politics, from sports to vacations, culture, and so on. These portals tend to present an attractive screen, with invitations to visit specific sites of all sorts, including the most popular, the top sites of the day, the week, or the month. And among them, of course, are sites that, while they may not be pornographic, are often close to it. That is, however, a risk not unlike the risk that you run by going to purchase a copy of *Catholic Digest* at a newsstand, where your eye could easily be attracted by any of a number of visually striking porn magazines. If you want to avoid the risk, you simply configure your Internet access so that as soon as you log on to the Web through your modem, the first site that you are taken to will automatically be a Marian Web site.

Unless we introduce blocking filters, such as those that prevent access to pornographic sites and ward off child molesters, when even involuntarily we happen on these sorts of Web pages, the risks of going off course or experiencing shipwreck will always accompany the worshipful surfer in every moment of his or her navigation, and not merely through the chosen Web browser or certain search engines. The most important risks are those entailed by a fundamental element of navigation on the Internet: links.

Let's start over from the beginning: a Web site is a location on the Internet, where any sort of information is published. In comparison with the Internet's early days, when sites were composed exclusively of texts, the Web now has sites with hypertexts, or we should say, hypermedia, that is, not only written words, but also images, pictures, and sounds. The hypertext is a "text about texts," which need not be read in a linear, obligatory form, as is the case with a book (that is, a book without footnotes or endnotes, since notes are really a "text about a text," and allow nonlinear shifts and circuits). Instead it becomes possible to leap forward, go back, follow tangents, and so on. Links are a fundamental element of hypertext since they make it possible with a click of the mouse to make nonlinear jumps and transitions to related text within the same Web site or to altogether different Web sites. Alberto Berretti and Vittorio Zambardino explain that "technically speaking, in a hypertext the linear structure of the discourse is 'broken' by links that connect remote sections of that discourse, endowing it with an arbitrary structure in terms of the connections, and no longer strictly serial in nature."[54]

Think of a text, a book, or an article, and consider how the sections succeed each other one after the other, forcing the reader to follow their sequential development. But on the Web, it is impossible to be sequential. A Web hypertext page, especially a home page, presents itself as a set of links, each represented by a small icon, which you can access by clicking upon it.

Compared to a few years ago, the Web masters now tend to limit the number of links. Franco Carlini explains: "In an Internet that is less altruistic than it used to be, the authors of webpages now try to keep the visitor hooked into the site, and to offer the visitor the smallest number of ways out. And so, some sites offer no links to external sites, but only links to their own pages. . . . The purpose is not to spread and increase communication, but to glorify one's own website."[55]

In any case, the system of links remains one of the principal features of the Web.

There are various types of links: those which a Web master inserts intentionally to construct his or her own hypertext with paths, relational structures, and information hierarchies, making it possible to go to other pages in the site or to other sites that form part of the same category. Then there are the banners, graphics, and text references inviting the surfer to leap into other types of sites, and which can be inserted by the host, that is, the company that supplies the computer and technical substrate to open a site, or by the Web master as a swap with other Web masters: you post a banner on my site, and I'll put one on yours. There are organizations that allow individuals to join together in order to place their own banners on many sites. Then there are the icons of the awards, citations, special mentions, or prizes that are bestowed upon the most popular, attractive, amusing, and crazy sites by various organizations on a daily, weekly, or monthly basis. The sites that have received an award, obviously, insert its icon to announce it to the various surfers. Finally, there are links consisting of the icons of Web rings: this is a system of obligatory links, whereby a click of the mouse in a special little panel will move you from one site to another, always and rigorously remaining in the same order and type of sites. The Web rings serve the function of limiting surfing to within a ring of sites all adhering to the standards set by the organizers of the Web ring, in our case, a relatively strong control over the characteristics of devotion and orthodoxy.

The hypertext structure is the basis for the processes of virtualization and actualization, inasmuch as it allows us to construct routes that do not already exist as potentialities waiting to be implemented, which are creations of the Web master, as well as of the surfer. As a Web master, that is, as a developer of Web pages for a personal site or an organization, I can create a hypertext structure that links information that was previously unrelated, or that did not even exist, actualizing a virtuality that existed in the background of the collective cultural phantoms and that did not exist before I created it, as an event, a cluster of information, an act of communication. But as a surfer as well, I will be able to develop networks of information that I will view or save on my computer's hard drive according to an entirely personal map; and I will then be able to interact with Web pages with a series of possibilities that will be provided to me or that I will obtain from the options of the computer system that I use.

Now, the hypertext or hypermedia structure is practically infinite, that is, able to extend until it encompasses not so much the whole of all possible information as much as, theoretically, the whole of all virtualities present in electronic communications. Even though a surfer will, in practice, end her voyage, due to limits of relevance, interest, time, and money, at the point where she has exhausted her impulse or resources, in theory there is nothing preventing an infinite browse. This means in reality that a hypertext on the Web can never be entirely enclosed, limited, concluded. A specific hypertext created as a site by a Web master has a certain degree of circumscribability, of course. But that same hypertext, once it is on the Web, becomes part of the hypertextuality and hypermediality that the surfer who encounters it at any point on the Web will freely produce in accordance with her own creativity. This hypermedia hypertext has, in effect, no place—if it did, it would be easy to censor, limit, and control it—and it is produced by the very act of surfing and it disappears when that act comes to an end, leaving its only traces in the memory of the surfer or the surfer's computer. And that is a memory that belongs, simultaneously, to the surfing person and the surfing machine, a collective product of the new corpus callosum discussed by de Kerckhove.

The actualization of the hypertext, precisely because of its characteristic of individualized creativity—admittedly, within the technological possibilities where it operates—cannot be premeditated, prefigured, and calculated. Technological resources make it possible for each of us to roam freely throughout the Web, with no constraints whatsoever. The methods of and the obstacles to moving from one site to another are always technical in nature, never a question of content: this may be an audio link, so you will need a certain piece of hardware or software; another link may be video, you will need yet other resources; for this text link all you need is the computer's basic software and hardware, and so on. But in no case will it be possible to separate in absolute terms one site from another by such criteria, as say, ideological diversity or opposition. Everything is horizontally arrayed in the face of the possibility of being viewed on an individual screen. If you rule out a few cases of extrinsic limitations, such as filters, passwords, and credit cards, the limits to navigation can be established only by the will of the surfer.

Among these decisive limitations facing the surfer, Web rings play an important role. As we have seen, these are mechanisms limiting individual hypertext constructions. They provide a system of controlled browsing, in which instead of venturing out into the open sea, you remain in an archipelago made up of sites all of the same type. There remains a certain sense of open navigation, with the accompanying surprises and discoveries, provided by the fact that often the transitions from one site to another within the Web ring of linked sites can be done through a random system, that is, a random search function. Generally speaking, Catholic Web rings, for the most part American, are organized by Catholic associations of various sorts, but sometimes also by individual Web masters (also known as ringmasters), who want to supply a set of tools to limit the risk of navigating in the open Web. The authors of personal Web sites who want to enter one of these Web rings must submit their own sites to inspection by the organizer of the ring, and if the Web site is accepted, then it is placed among the other sites, all marked by the distinctive logo of the Web ring in question. Obviously, the level of acceptance and control is established by the authors of the Web ring, and the criteria can vary widely. They may range from the admission of sites that present "a Catholic nature and spirituality"[56] to those that demonstrate "a strong veneration to Mary,"[57] from those that "do not necessarily have anything to do with Our Lady and might contain other sorts of material"[58] to those that are "Christian Based from a Catholic Perspective."[59]

The Web ring operates only if the surfer browses exclusively by using the icon that indicates that Web ring. But if the surfer moves from the Web site in which he is browsing by clicking on any other link contained in it, then the Web ring no longer protects against risk, because from any given link it is possible to browse through any other link and reach any other Web site, that is, to browse the open Web. In order to avoid risk entirely, the surfer should also refrain from hopping from one Web ring to another Web ring found on the same Web page, that is, passing from one archipelago to another. In fact, quite often the sites linked into Web rings are included in more than one circuit, and so at the foot of the Web page you will see the icons of the various Web rings to which the Web page itself belongs. Now, passing from one Web ring to another can entail a whole new set of risks, because not all the Web rings shown on a Web page that belongs to the Catholic persuasion are necessarily Catholic in observance. And so if you hop from one to another, you could soon find yourself out of bounds, for example, in Protestant territory, or in circuits that are not religious in subject.

With the exclusion of Web rings, nothing can limit the surfing in the open sea. However controlled the sites devoted to Marian worship may be, they cannot eliminate entirely links that may prove to be quite dangerous. And so even the best-intentioned surfer may find himself wandering far off the course that he had originally set for his voyage; he may be tempted off course by alluring sirens, and he may even run ruinously onto shoals and reefs quite distant from his original objectives.

Crossing the boundary between devotional sites and other sorts of sites is in any case a continually present possibility. An overwhelming proportion of the sites found on Web rings of Catholic inspiration consist of personal home pages, which as we shall see almost never focus only on faith-related subjects and have more than just religious links. This has a number of important consequences in terms of the itineraries that can be virtually activated.

Let us now enter the Web as surfers in search of information and images of the Marian apparitions around the world, in search of prayers, sounds, and films that can carry us to the territories of Marian devotion.

Carmine is a site present in the List of Catholic Sites in Italy (*Lista dei siti cattolici in Italia*); it entertains the worshipful surfer with sacred music, images of Medjugorje, the "principal prophecies of the last few centuries," "pages of spirituality," and so on.[60] The site is presented as a floor plan of a house in which the children, Carmine, Pino, and Raffaella, and their parents, Gennaro and Teresa, each occupy their own rooms. The "room" of Gennaro and Teresa, however, houses the site of the Parish of the Immaculate Heart of the Virgin Mary of Brindisi.

The charming Web site of the Romano family has won four awards, which are cited on the home page, along with a counter showing the number of visits, which reported that I personally was—during a "browse" I did in 1998—visitor number 3,022. The worshipful surfer might have a legitimate interest in seeing which awards these were, and that is where the first risk of shipwreck arises. The first award takes me to a site called *Agenda Internet,* and once that site is opened I find myself on the personal Web site of Felice Marra, the organizer of this award. The next link— second click, just a few seconds away from the home page of the extremely religious Romano family—takes me to *Freeonline,* which offers a "guide to free resources." Here, among the possibilities available, I can click (and this would be the third click) on "recommended links." Of course, a surfer who chooses to click the third and even the fourth time has clearly decided to move beyond the narrow boundaries of the Catholic *Carmine* site, but an undertaking of the sort, which only requires a few seconds, and which does not require moving away from chair or computer screen, and which had its beginnings in a reputable Catholic Web site, hardly seems dangerous. For that matter, it is hardly surprising that someone who admires the Romano family Web site should want to know more about whoever awarded it a prize. With a third click, then, the worshipful surfer will find a list of banners, including the reassuring legend: "We don't want to conquer the WORLD . . . we only want to make a NEW ONE," from the Gruppo Missionario Parrocchia S. Croce—Salerno. The worshipful surfer, then, can continue, feeling that he or she is at home on this list. But things are different from what they appear. If he goes on looking, another banner would open directly into a pornographic Web site: *eroschange.* And if, slightly surprised, the surfer should choose to investigate whether this is really a pornographic Web site or if there has simply been a misunderstanding, he will open it with a click and, even before the

Web page in question has time to appear, a small panel will spring open at the top of the screen: "eroschange Italia recommends . . . ," and from there another even smaller window will open up, with a presentation of— unexpected and unmistakable—on the left Bill Clinton, and on the right Monica Lewinski, and by means of a photomontage, there is a cigar and a phallus next to her. Above the pair is the phrase, "Watch Bill Cum on Monica," which needs no commentary. It is an obscene videogame, and it is not hard to guess how it works. Four clicks—suggested involuntarily by the devotional site itself—from Medjugorje and from the Renewal of the Spirit of the parish of the Immaculate Heart of the Virgin Mary of the Romano family, and there on the screen appears an irreverent porno-graphic Web site, inspired by the questionable erotic escapades of the White House. Let us proceed no further.

Another banner, close to that of the Missionary Group of the Parish of the Holy Cross, opens *Thriller,* which offers a list of other links within the site: chats, photographs, guestbooks, software, and, among other things, an enigmatic "XXX V.M. 18" (Italian for "X-rated") which, once opened, has a small photograph of a tiny naked woman, her legs spread wide open, and beneath her, an invitation: "click on the pussy." The sirens sing their alluring songs terribly close to the gunwales of the vessel of the worship-ful navigator. The very same Missionary Group of the Parish of the Holy Cross is publicized by *Freeonline* which, in return, is publicized on the home page of the Salerno parish church in question. This is a curious and circular invitation to the devil and to the holy water, a miracle of the Internet.

There is already something quite similar outside the Web, in the pro-liferation of television channels. But in this case the worshipful viewer has better options. First of all, she can exclude pornographic channels or channels likely to feature questionable material when she programs her television set. In the second place, once she is tuned to a "safe" channel, she is unlikely to find any invitations to switch to another channel where she could encounter unpleasant surprises. Lastly, the television lacks the individualized and interactive structure of use that we find in the teleputer.

The awards for the Romano family, the banner of the Missionary Group placed on a site that also features the banners of *Thriller* and *eroschange,* are only a few examples of the traps that links can pose for devotional surfers. From any given devotional site, it would never take many leaps between links to reach a pornographic site.

In order to avoid the potential pitfall of banners, an Italian Catholic

Web site dedicated to the Virgin Mary, *Miriam*,[61] has decided to establish a Catholic Network Banner Exchange, as a first initiative toward the creation of a "virtual Catholic network" designed to "promote online evangelization." Those who decide to join this service will have, in exchange for every two banners displayed on their own Web sites, their own banners publicized on the Web sites of other members of the service. But the problem is that the very same home page *Miriam*, inasmuch as it is in turn a member of other banner exchange networks,[62] contains five banners that change every so often, periodically offering potential leaps not only into other archipelagoes, but into other "worlds." I myself saw what can come out of these banners, when I was surfing the Web: I had added to my list of favorites, as was my habit during my research, the Web site *Non-Believer's Guide to Jesus and Mary*, which, with the slogan "Just because you're an atheist . . . (it doesn't mean there *isn't* an afterlife)," had placed on the Web a number of "miraculous" photographs from Medjugorje. When I was done with my browsing, I went back to explore the sites that I had found, in order to study their texts and graphics at my leisure. Imagine my surprise when suddenly, from the Web site mentioned above, I saw a pornographic banner pop up (literally, since it was a "pop-up"), with the invitation to enter "deeply" into the site, to see images of Pamela Anderson nude. Now I have repeated the same Web path many other times, online, without encountering any pornographic results, finding only ordinary advertising. What happened was that when I saved it as a favorite, I did so in the very few seconds when the pop-up banner of the pornographic Web site, which however did not seem to be a pornographic Web site, happened to have appeared on the Web page *Non-Believer's Guide to Jesus and Mary*, and it was recorded on my computer as such (with the entirely benign heading of "index").

It is not easy to get shed of a pornographic Web site; once you have loaded one of these onto your computer, even if you hurry to close it immediately, for a few minutes there is a bombardment of new sites and banners flying open on your screen, and a hapless surfer who stumbles onto them in perfectly good faith can do little to prevent them—leaving aside the fact that they have also entered the memory of the computer in the folder Temporary Internet Files.

You might think that, as extreme as they are, these closely neighboring dangers are avoidable pitfalls along the route, and all that is needed is a little extra care. In reality, however, there is no way to control the horizontal nature of the Web—the borderless and ruleless disorder—and its basic, characteristic element, the fact that that every point can theoretically be reached by every other point. With some bitterness, the Web master of *David Spiritual Links* points this out about the Web: "Call it undesirable literature and pictures, filth, dirt, pornography or what you will, it ranges from the subtle to the overt. It is so ubiquitous in its presence that, not infrequently, an honest web search with innocent keywords can rake in one of these things."[63]

We should also point out that the same subjective impulse that drives a surfer to construct his own cognitive route, a genuine actualized hypertext, shifting from one to another of the countless virtual realities, cannot be fully administered. Indeed, certainly, the links can continually cause the surfer to drift, overlap, and disconnect from the central territory to which he feels he belongs, but he can also detour, wandering in search, out of curiosity, by mistake, instinct, or temptation.

There is a sort of "compelling vacuum," as Lévy puts it,[64] underlying all movement on the Web. Against a relatively well-defined background of ideological orientations, the surfer goes in search of a path all her own to conquer, without foreseeing what she will find, and in a certain sense, not even what she will be looking for. The question that drives her will not accept a single response, potentially already implied in some part of the world or of the Web. The response, entirely provisional and incapable of filling in the compelling vacuum is on the order of actualization. But this is an actualization that does not correspond to the process of awareness that the surfer might find outside the Web, where, being able to distinguish between one place and another—entertainment, books, newspapers, conversations, all of which are contexts that are already broken down into and organized by sectors and orientations—she would know in advance the direction she was going. Here the simultaneity of the matrices, the total correspondence, the unpredictability of the door that opens, rendering nonobjectifiable and therefore impossible to circumscribe the process of assembling the hypertext, which is not the result of a process entirely contained within the mind of the surfer, but rather a product of that fruitful and as yet unexplored relationship between the human mind and the machine, the corpus callosum described by de Kerckhove.

In the case of the worshipful surfer, at the end of the voyage the "compelling vacuum" can encounter a plenitude of disturbing pornographic images. To judge by some of the recent developments among the new sites, the companies that own pornographic Web sites have become well aware of this, and seem to be laying siege to the archipelagoes of Marian sites, almost as if they considered them target sites for an expansion campaign.

A few years ago, the press carried stories about the Web site of the Internet Entertainment Group, which provided detailed reports on the route and dates of the pope's trip to Saint Louis in January 1999. Tucked away at the bottom of each Web page could be seen icons advertising a pornographic Web site, *Clublove*, owned by the company that managed the Web page. In this case a lawsuit brought by the bishop of Saint Louis resulted in a temporary restraining order shutting down the site.[65] It seemed at the time like an isolated case, the first and last of its kind. Probably, however, it was just a glimmer of a larger operation seeking new customers.

One of the targets is the field of apparitions newsgroups. If you browse the Internet using the term "alt.religion.apparitions," you will see an increasing presence of messages about pornographic Web sites or advice about effective erotic or sexual gadgets; to offer just one example, on 2 April 2001 readers were advised in a message with the subject line "instant sex appeal" to make use of a pheromone-based product, which "attracts more women easily!!!" In Italy, too, the path of discussion groups has been used in an effort to penetrate the Marian archipelago. A very curious case is that of a newsgroup present in www.yahoo.it, called "The Madonna of Medjugorje." When I clicked to enter this newsgroup in May 2001, I noticed that until then there had been only one correspondent, who was also the founder of the newsgroup, a certain Fabrizio Salomone. I thought that he must just be getting started and so, diligently, I opened the personal Web site that the founder of the newsgroup had prepared, and to my naïve surprise I found, among the links for the not very numerous hobbies of the Web master, a "naturalist and nudist" link, which immediately plunged me into the pornographic archipelago. Quite clearly, then, this was a lure-site for the "compelling vacuum" of Marian devotees. And to judge from the proliferation of lure-sites, the effectiveness of these temptations must be substantial. In fact, there is more.

The Web master of the respected American Catholic Web site *Catholic Goldmine*, on 4 July 2001, put a curious warning on his portal: "I have been notified recently some Catholic sites have turned into porn sites. Please let me know if you come across any and I will immediately remove it from the site."

I did a little bit of surfing myself to get a better sense of the range of the phenomenon. An extremely crude but effective way of doing it was to use keywords in the search engines. Here are some figures: in August 2001, the string "Virgin Mary porno" gave a result of no fewer than six thousand pages in Google. I opened only the first ten: many of them had to do with the dispute over the position taken by New York mayor Rudy Giuliani against the Brooklyn Museum for its exhibition "Sensation," which included a work by the English artist Chris Ofili featuring an image of the Madonna surrounded by photographs of female body parts cut out of pornographic magazines.

Aside from these sites, a series of results had to do with genuinely pornographic Web sites that have references to the Virgin Mary. For instance, *Mary Beginner, Virgin Mary,* or *Blessed Virgin Mary* were all sites that had nothing religious about them except for their name. Indeed they verged on the blasphemous, because, once you open them, you find phrases like "Virgin Mary showing their nude beauties [*sic*]," as well as invitations to enter deeply into them.

Admittedly, it is unlikely that a devout surfer would do a keyword research like the one I described, adding the word "porno." But the presence on porn Web sites of the expression "Virgin Mary" brings these bait-sites into the great Marian archipelago; in fact, even without using that keyword, search engines might very well snag pornographic Web sites that contain the expression "Virgin Mary." It is useless at this point to offer numbers or information about the other critical phrase, "Madonna porno."

Other sites are midway between pornography, open blasphemy, and irony; but the irony is heavy-handed and quite far from the lighthearted standards that I will discuss in section 4.5. One emblematic example is the Web site entitled the *Official Homepage of Jesus the Porno!!!,* which opens with the phrase "From God to Judas (the apostle you love to hate!) to the 'Virgin' Mary herself. The Jesus Porno tells the story of Jesus' life from conception all the way to . . ." On the main page of the Web site, full of pornographic links, we find an icon of Jesus on the cross, with the legend "Jesusporno.com." If you click on this icon, you will link to nothing less than the Vatican Web site. Here irony, blasphemy, and pornography reach a culmination that would be hard to match offline.

Heaven without Borders in the New Age

Vassula Ryden is a well-known visionary in the international circuit, who represents an emblematic case of the continual threat of religious boundary-crossing present in many Catholic visionary experiences. Her fame has grown progressively, as she has become one of the most famous visionaries on earth. She travels constantly, and only the visionaries of Medjugorje can compare in terms of her capacity to attract the faithful. Her case presents the Vatican authorities with numerous problems related to the control of orthodoxy. Indeed, aside from the fact, mentioned above, that Vassula has been divorced and remarried, in the messages that she attributes to Jesus there are numerous affirmations that are questionable in terms of Catholic orthodoxy. The Congregation for the Doctrine of the Faith issued a note on 6 October 1995 strongly criticizing her ambiguous way of defining the Holy Trinity, as well as her prophecy—quite common among the visionaries—of an impending period of the domination of an Antichrist within the church and of a founding "in the near future [of] a Church which would be a type of pan-Christian community, in contrast with the Catholic doctrine."[66]

Vassula states that Jesus asked her to unify the dates of Easter for all the different religions that celebrate the holiday and to work to bring about a world council of churches. On the other hand, Vassula, although she is still Greek Orthodox, regularly takes part in Catholic ceremonies and rituals, as is critically noted in the Vatican document, and she claims that the two religions are in fact indistinguishable. The consensus among Protestants that she boasts of is yet another sign of this overlapping. And yet Vassula is defended fiercely by illustrious figures in the Catholic world, such as the former primate of Yugoslavia, the archbishop emeritus of Split-Makarska, Frane Franic, who announced in the *Medjugorje* newsletter of Genoa, immediately following the publication of the Vatican note, that in his opinion Vassula is faithful "to all revealed truths as they are taught and explained by the Catholic Church";[67] or Father Guido Sommavilla, who recalled that in the twentieth century the Vatican had already made other errors, with Padre Pio or Blessed Sister Faustina Kowalska; or even Monsignor René Laurentin, who claimed that Cardinal Ratzinger had told the bishops of Mexico that the report on Vassula had not been the result of a thorough investigation.[68]

But if the Vatican, offline, amid difficulties and contradictions, can try to stem the rising tide of religious boundary-crossing, online overlapping is almost the rule, not the exception. In fact, the church can take action against events that have a space-time location, but it has no valid tools to influence the delocalized events of the Web. This is not limited to the relationship between Catholicism and other institutional religions, but is especially applicable to a sort of evaporation of Catholicism into the folds of an omnivorous media-driven religiosity, creating a mélange of faiths, spiritualistic and scientistic ideologies, both New Age and Next Age.

Here too the Web is not a meteor fallen from the sky onto a well-ordered and balanced earth. Do-it-yourself religion has already been noted by scholars as a new and unexpected phenomenon of the last few decades, rendering superficial an analysis of modernity in rigid terms of a secularization that is a movement generally opposed to religion. Moreover, religion and the sacred are not strictly speaking the same thing,[69] and the latter is being reproduced and presented with unprecedented twists and intertwinings in entirely unexpected social and cultural areas, where it might have been thought that secularization would be a more entrenched phenomenon: aesthetics, politics, science, and so on. Now, if we consider the fact that the Web allows its users a continual movement of hypertext construction, whereby two elements that would be in clear opposition in the offline world are easily seen in parallel online, and in some cases even overlap, then we clearly see that the do-it-yourself aspect of the Web can make use of and enormously reinforce the contemporary development of do-it-yourself religion: on the one hand as an expression of an overlay of the styles, ideologies, and cultural forms typical of the "Neo-Baroque" of the postmodern,[70] and on the other hand as an almost automatic result of the interplay of references and word-based links.

In the devotional mailing lists, there are frequent exhortations to beware of the New Age and its representatives. But the frequency of the attacks corresponds to the diffusion of links and overlappings present on the Web between the Catholic world and tendencies, currents, philosophies, and techniques of New Age spiritualism.

Concerning the risk that certain expressions of the Catholic faith might slip into the hazy archipelago of the New Age—and nowadays of the Next Age—the church is exceedingly watchful, considering the fairly worrisome signals that are coming from the faithful around the world, especially from the more economically and technologically advanced parts of the world. The admonitions, the condemnations, and the qualifications flow in countless numbers at all levels of the hierarchy: from urgent invitations by the pope, who is expected to issue soon an encyclical on these themes, to documents from the Vatican Curia, from messages handed down by National Episcopal Conferences to pastoral directives formulated by individual dioceses. Among the latest controversial positions taken by the Vatican I should mention the August 1998 condemnation of a number of publications by the Jesuit Anthony de Mello.

Within the Catholic Church, however, there is a significant constituency that does not reject all interaction with the New Age. And now, on the Web, it finds a very intriguing possibility of penetration. One English site offers a representative example. It is called the *New Age Catholic* Web site[71] and it is an undertaking of *Housetop*,[72] an English Catholic association that specializes in religious education for adults, offering distance-learning courses by means of technological media, especially video, television, and now Internet as well.

This site opens with the following statement:

> We are committed Christians, but we feel very much part of New Age hopes and aspirations: we acknowledge the primacy of spirit over matter; we are concerned for our environment; we respect what is valuable in all truly spiritual traditions; we accept all human beings as our brothers and sisters; we support the efforts to make ours a better world by all men and women of good will; we believe that salvation affects the whole person in body and soul. We also realise that not everything presented as New Age is sound, healthy or true.

After this introduction, the site allows the surfer to move to a link about New Age thought and spiritualism, through the FAQs, or frequently asked questions, and then to move on to other New Age sites. There is another link to an overview of all the theological and pastoral positions that have been taken by Catholic Church with respect to the New Age. And it is interesting that it is a New Age Web site, or at any rate a Web site that is strongly oriented toward an acceptance of the New Age philosophy, that presents the ecclesiastical positions, which, however varied and nuanced, are almost never favorably disposed toward New Age spirituality. Once again on the Web what is being prompted is the "discernment" of the individual surfer. Here too however the surfer is not motivated by preformed and well-established decisions, nor by any presumed spiritual self-education: what is probably at work here, most of all, is the pure chance of browsing, the product of a moment's curiosity and the latest technological developments, as well as the logic of the hypertextual mechanism of Web navigation, which can overlap and merge with that which would be in conflict or in opposition in the offline world.

The FAQs of this site offer clarifications on reincarnation, miracles, near-death experiences, channeling (more on this below), spirituality, and healing. Typical of the hoped-for new spirituality are the answers to questions about reincarnation. For instance, there is apparently a need to "develop a new language that our contemporaries can understand: regarding death, regarding our absorption into God (heaven) and self-realisation in God (the resurrection of the body)."[73]

Concerning the possible confusion between reincarnation and resurrection, it is clearly stated that they are not at all the same thing, but then it is conceded that they both "are key religious 'myths' in which the word 'myth' should not be understood as something that is not true, but in its academic sense as a cluster of symbols that underlie a religious belief."[74]

Last, in a pastoral context, it is emphasized that the theme of reincarnation, increasingly popular in Europe, could help in presenting the doctrine of Purgatory in a pastoral manner, that is, as an opportunity for a Christian who cannot yet appear in the presence of God after death to mature and attain a state of readiness.

In the FAQs about "miracles," then, we find an immediate reference to the Web page *In search of the Miraculous,*[75] which introduces us to another aspect of the Catholic New Age: healings and holistic medicine. The site, whose title is a reference to a book by Peter Ouspensky, dedicated to his meetings with George Gurdjieff in Moscow before the Russian Revolution,[76] discusses the spread of the New Age in the Catholic world, with references to Teilhard de Chardin, Emmanuel Milingo, Hans Urs von Balthasar, and others, suggesting a reconciliation between the hermetic movement and the church, and glorifying the dimension of the "world in between" discussed by Milingo.[77] In the presentation of the site, we find a discussion of *A Course in Miracles,* a three-volume book published in 1975 by the Foundation for Inner Peace, in California. The book, it points out, "was channelled rather than written by a human author," and goes on to say, "ask me which miracles you should perform. This spares you needless effort because you will be acting under direct communication."

This publication, which has a site dedicated to it,[78] gave rise to the foundation of a church with the same name, under the direction of Rev. Tony Ponticello, who teaches courses, even long-distance courses, over the phone, on resolving relationship problems, health problems, financial difficulties, and more, and who relies upon an "intimate connection" with the Holy Ghost. Each intervention costs between thirty and fifty dollars, even though the Community Miracle Center, which runs these operations, is a nonprofit organization.

In the Web site that we are exploring, then, Catholicism and *A Course in Miracles* appear as realities that are entirely overlapping; indeed, the

Course would seem to be a Catholic text, though an original one, and Ponticello would appear to be a Catholic priest, however atypical. In reality, however, the history of *A Course in Miracles* has nothing to do with Catholicism, since this is a book that Helen Schucman, a psychologist at the Department of Psychiatry at Columbia University's Columbia Presbyterian Hospital in New York, "received" through channeling, and which she transcribed, along with her supervisor, William Thetford, a professor of medical psychology at the same university. Both of these scholars were atheists, though they both had esoteric interests, and the book is quite definitely not Catholic: to give just one example, it rejects divine creation.[79]

But what is channeling? The answer can be found once again in the FAQs of the *New Age Catholic* Web site:

> When someone allows a spirit which is not their own to enter into them and speak through their vocal cords or to propose some kind of psychic knowledge which is essentially alien to them, we talk about channeling. This can mean visions, inner voice dictation or automatic writing. It can also mean something which in the Bible is called 'possession.' "

Evidently, it is within the context of a single site or archipelago of linked sites that the compasses providing orientation disappear and the New Age spirituality accommodates and excludes at the same time, in a mélange that is free of the confines that restrict orthodoxy offline.

These boundaries become quite vague indeed when sites that overlap Catholicism and New Age subjects offer information and images concerning Marian apparitions. *Morgana's Observatory*[80] is a site organized by links that are both mythological and astronomical, with a mingling of Hopi, Cherokee, Lakota, and Navajo prophecies, along with references to Nostradamus, La Salette, the secrets of Fatima, Garabandal, Medjugorje, and Akita. The "Prometheus" link, for instance, adds to the Christian prophecies, from the Revelation to Saint John, the prophecies concerning Maitreya, to which we shall return below, prophecies about Muhammad, a few Hindu prophecies, and finally, "The Signs of the Last Days," where we see Marian apparitions again. If you were to reach this site through a keyword search for Marian apparitions, such as "Virgin Mary" or "apparition"—the most common and direct path for a worshiper of the Virgin Mary—you would not quickly understand what is made clear only if you enter through the home page, where you would read that "This site does not promote any particular religion or theology. I'm simply offering free food for free thought."

Another overlap can be experienced if you go in search of information about the tears of the Madonna around the world, because you will see sites like *Crying Virgins*,[81] a link found in an online magazine *Men in Black*, which mixes together Marian tears, UFOs, Bigfoot, "spontaneous combustion," the movie *Men in Black,* and other "mysterious" phenomena. You can access sites on "unexplained mysteries" and the paranormal in many different ways while seeking information and images concerning Catholic miracles. For instance, if you look for sites on the Shroud, you will eventually run into *Mysteries*,[82] which adds to the "unsolved mystery" of the Shroud such other subjects as Stonehenge, prehistoric monuments in Great Britain, the hidden chambers of the pyramids, the giant footprints of the wild men of the woods, UFOs, and other such mysteries. From this site, then, you can reach Fatima, Medjugorje, Garabandal, and other Marian apparitions.

The presence of New Age sites on the Web is massive, and these are only a few examples of how they tend to appropriate specific historical religions, especially, in this case, visionary Catholicism, to create a standardized, uniform fabric of all-inclusive spirituality.

While seeking Marian apparitions sites, we frequently find links that lead to a fabulous and mysterious personage: Maitreya.

> Who is Maitreya? The teacher of the world. Long has His coming been
> predicted by the major religions. Christians know Him as Christ and
> await His imminent return. The Jews await Him as the Messiah; the
> Hindus await the return of Krishna; the Buddhists await Him as the
> Maitreya Buddha; the Muslims await the Imam Mahdi. The names
> may vary but they all refer to the same Being: The Teacher of the World
> named Maitreya. He is returning now at the dawning of the Age of
> Aquarius, as a teacher and a guide for the people of every religion
> as well as for those who have no religion. . . . Information about the
> emergence of Christ was transmitted principally by Benjamin Creme,
> an English artist and esotericist who has been writing and speaking
> about this event since 1975. According to Creme, Maitreya, the Christ,
> descended from His retreat in the Himalayas in July 1977 and took up
> residence in the Asian community of London. There He lives and works
> as an ordinary man. His true being is known only to a few. He has

revealed himself gradually to the public so as to keep from disturbing mankind's free will.[83]

This passage is taken from a long article that a member of soc.culture .italian, an Italian newsgroup on new religions, sent to his correspondents on 26 May 1998; it harks back the theme "return of the Teacher of the World," already present at the origins of the New Age, in the writings of Alice Bailey.[84]

The practice of the Web sites that refer to Maitreya has been to assimilate the Marian apparitions as just one of the phenomena that announce the imminent manifestation of Maitreya and the resulting beginning of a new era. They assemble detailed and exhaustive information about the phenomena of visionary Catholicism precisely with a view to the advent of Jesus-Maitreya: the face of Jesus photographed by Sister Anna Ali; the tears of the statue of the Madonna in Santiago, Chile; the miraculous water of Tlacote, Mexico;[85] the numerous Marian apparitions of recent years;[86] and the lacrimations of statues and paintings,[87] as well as angels, crosses made of light, phantom hitchhikers, and still more, all fantastic events that are recounted and inserted into the context of Maitreya. The overlapping of these with Jesus is confirmed by apparitions of Jesus, immediately photographed, in white robes, the same white robes in which Maitreya appears miraculously, and likewise photographed. For instance, in 1988, in Kenya, six thousand people saw Jesus suddenly appear and then vanish; he was tall and dressed in white, and he was speaking in Swahili. But this description perfectly matches the appearance of Maitreya when he was "miraculously" photographed, in Kenya as well as many other places around the world; some recognize the mysterious character dressed in white as Jesus, others as Maitreya.[88]

It is clear why certain correspondents in the mailing lists warn others against this character, identified as the Antichrist,[89] and called "python," like Eve's serpent, or precisely why it is accused, among other things, of muddying with its presence the phenomenology of Marian apparitions. But such warnings can reach only those who frequent the mailing lists in which it is discussed, and however popular those mailing lists may be, they do not reach all the devotees of the apparitions who surf the Web. For the others, it will be much more difficult to elude the sticky tentacles of sites that refer to the New Age and to Maitreya.

The overlapping of Jesus and Maitreya is in a certain sense a product of the decontextualizing automatic mechanisms of the Web, where blending, substitution, and shifting of identities are normal. This is true especially of images, which move along communications flows outside the context from which they were originally taken and which are therefore tumbled and confused in decontextualized collages. For example, *SpiritWeb* is an archipelago of sites whose purpose is "promoting spiritual consciousness on the internet."[90] It includes numerous sites featuring religious hodgepodges typical of the New Age, including some that contain images of Masters, ETs, angels, astral guides, UFOs, lights, and sacred symbols. In particular, we should mention *Image Gallery: Masters, ETs, Angels* which is an array of postage-stamp-sized images, among which the surfer can choose by clicking, and thus obtain a larger format picture, to print or save on the hard drive of her own computer.[91] And so amid Athena, Confucius, Gautama-Buddha, Helios, Venusian, Serapis-Bei, and many other masters and extraterrestrials, we find Jesus-Sananda, the Archangel Raphael, Gabriel, Jesus, and Mary Mother of Jesus. You would have to turn elsewhere to find any information about these figures, since there is none in the page of the small icons. And when you do, you learn that Jesus-Sananda is an incarnation of the third dimension, that Jesus of Nazareth is in turn an incarnation of Sananda, now represented by Maitreya, and that Mary of Nazareth is a master connected with the Temple of Resurrection, an "ethereal" kingdom of Israel/Palestine. The overlay, the interchangeability—for which the theme of the "incarnation" is an unintentional metaphor—is total. Already, offline, Sananda and Jesus are confused in the religious ideology that, by merging UFOs and transcendentalism, leads to a proliferation of astral spirits that establish, and in the future will establish to an even greater degree, close relations with the earth.[92] But online, the confusion is no longer limited to the restricted and scanty ranks of the worshipers of these cults. It appears everywhere, through short hypertext links.

In the final analysis, images with no (or very little) context to refer to produce a certain depersonalization of the very subjects of the images, a division between the representation of a "real" subject and the subject itself, one being a replaceable copy of another: inasmuch as images resembling one another, Sananda, Kuthumi, Melchizedek, and Jesus wind up being nothing more than different depictions of Jesus, and in fact Jesus will seem to be nothing more than a variant depiction of these.

And here the attack of visionary Catholicism on the citadel is quite radical. Every image captured is an actualization of an infinite chain of virtual depictions of the divine; but a divine that is immanent to the Web, produced by it and imbedded in it. The divine offline, with its well-defined properties and boundaries, evaporates from the images on the Web, vanishes as an otherworldly point of reference, and is replaced by the self-referential universe of the virtual divine.

When a priest posted on the Internet a "remarkable photograph" of Jesus taken by the seer Pino Casagrande, he justified with the following words its unsettling difference from the "true" images of Jesus and the Madonna in circulation: "God is clearly free to show himself, whenever he chooses to do so, with different appearances and semblances, according to circumstance."[93]

In reality this freedom belongs to the Web more than it does to God, inasmuch as the Web produces images: and once those images enter the Web they lose their offline point of reference, or—and this amounts to the same thing—they find a virtually infinite point of reference.

Outside the Web, institutional or syncretic religions can be easily distinguished and separated. The history and the tradition of each religion constitutes its distinctive charter, from which mythologies and rituals derive; the geocultural context is the specific characterization that engenders devotional behaviors and forms of expression. But inside the Web, history and context, time and space are no longer possible in the forms they take on outside the Web. Inside the Web, the external attempts of small groups to transform world religions into a single great universal religion, where all distinctions would be annulled or at least attenuated, encounter—more than an unlooked-for success—an automatic dimension of representation that serves as an adhesive holding together all the depictions of individual religious realities. Inside the Web, in other words, the universalistic and syncretic ideology of the New Age finally achieves success.

Processes of the sort are unthinkable outside the Web, where religious differences are often manifested with religious and extrareligious conflicts. Inside the Web, however, independent of the intentions of individuals, who often deplore those tendencies and try to defend themselves from them, delocalization and depersonalization tend to eliminate religious differences.

Marian apparitions, more than any other Christian religious phenomenon, lend themselves to a role of great importance in the development of a universalistic and boundaryless religiosity within the Web, since, as "extraordinary" phenomena of sensory perception, they stand alongside all the other phenomena that constitute a general background of exceptional signs and signals alluding to an impending time of great change:

UFOs, cosmic lights, channeling, and miracle cures. Apparitions, like all other "extraordinary" phenomena, are decontextualized and projected into a new field of significance within which anyone (sect, group, or individual) can assign them a new and unique meaning, contributing to the construction of an enormous symbolic network, in which everything supports everything else, independent of any individual conflicts of definition and interpretation. And so a new UFO sighting and a new apparition of the Virgin Mary are no longer clashing signals. Admittedly from differing points of view, but still remaining concomitant and specular within the symbolic network, these phenomena are considered to be manifestations of "entities" that pass from a normally invisible dimension to our own, visible dimension, in order to warn us of an imminent change, a new era, or the end times. The significance of such manifestations transcends the boundaries of an individual religious credo: in the interpretative fragmentation produced by the individual surfers, an apparition of the Virgin Mary can be reintroduced into the Web in a Catholic context, or it can instead be considered one of the many extraordinary signals of the present. What counts is that a great many of the significances that can be assigned, whether they are orthodox and official or heterodox, are mirror images of one another, and they reinforce each other reciprocally without clashing, as they might very well offline.

Visionary Catholicism may threaten to overwhelm and invade even other monotheistic religions. Marian apparitions that occur in places where the population is not prevalently Catholic or Christian are treated, in the visionary circuit, as signs from heaven that are aimed at or significant to the faithful of other religions as well. This was the case in Zeitoun, Egypt, in 1968, touted as an apparition that involved Muslims as well. But there were no subsequent announcements of any conversions, any transformations in a strictly Catholic sense. And the fact that on the Web there are accounts of how Pat Robertson and Francis Frangipane, important American Protestant leaders, have declared that the Marian apparitions are manifestations of God,[94] but without converting to Catholicism as a consequence, clearly points in the direction of the establishment of a religious universe in which the differences and the distances are canceled by the shared subscription to the concept of signs and wonders.

It comes as no surprise, then, that some—especially those of Protestant origin, though there are Catholics who level the same accusation—should denounce this syncretism as one of Satan's traps. *The Grandest of All Deceptions, the Apparitions of the Virgin Mary* is the name of a Web site

that considers the enormous diffusion of the Marian apparitions as an exceedingly subtle strategy of the Devil to lead believers away from the true
Word of God, contained in the Bible.[95] Along with New Age beliefs and
UFOs, the Marian movement, according to this Web site, is the product of
a direct channeling from Satan to humans, whose "body, mind, and soul"
he thus captures. The Web master, Bobby Ripp, recounts having traveled
to Medjugorje to determine whether, as so many in the Protestant world
claimed, something closely linked to God was in fact being manifested
there, and he came away with quite the opposite impression: in his view, it
is a place where Satan manifests his most terrible deceptions. The author
was especially impressed, as he sat watching a television documentary
about the annual Youth Day organized by the Catholic Church, by an interview with a young woman who had made a pilgrimage to Medjugorje:

> As I sat there watching this innocent young woman give her testimony,
> a feeling of hopelessness and mourning consumed me beyond human
> comprehension. With boldness I have never witnessed before, this
> young lady, with tears flowing from her beautiful eyes and with the
> greatest show of sincerity, was pleading to humanity to accept the
> "Medjugorje phenomenon." . . . As the young woman concluded her
> plea to humankind, I sat motionless, in a state of shock not wanting to
> contemplate the ramifications of what I had just seen. I just wanted to
> die and go home to my LORD in Heaven. I felt this way because I knew
> that God has placed me in a ministry whereby I was to expose Satan's
> deceptive schemes. . . . The realm of deception which that beautiful and
> innocent young woman was operating from is of the highest degree.[96]

Three thousand eighty-seven hits on this site were recorded on the
day that I myself visited it. This is a significant, and at the same time,
an insignificant statistic. It is significant, because it proves that this is
not a deserted site, but it is insignificant because we will never know the
attitudes and reactions of the visitors.

Unfortunately for the Web master, his warning about the wiles of Satan, which he believes was inspired directly by the Holy Ghost, does not
exist outside the flow of information and home pages about the end times,
which in that Web master's view only serve to increase the tricks of Satan.
This site, in fact, is listed among the end times sites, along with Catholic
and Marian sites, Jewish and Protestant sites, and New Age and syncretic
sites.

The calls for strict boundaries do not end once we venture into the Web, but those who make those calls find themselves unable to support them. Indeed, along with others, they find themselves undermining them.

Winking Jesus and Irony on the Web

The Greek Orthodox Church has officially declared as a miracle the reported winking and weeping of a fresco of Christ in the Church of the Nativity in Bethlehem, regarded by tradition as the birthplace of Christ. Local Roman Catholic leaders are being more cautious, and say that they are investigating the events, first noted six weeks ago. Local tourism may benefit greatly from the reported miracle. The faltering peace accord and renewed violence between Israeli and Palestinian troops have forced the closure of hotels and the virtual abandonment of what should be the town's tourist zenith. Now, since the report of the miracle, numbers of visitors to the town are on the rise again. Witnesses of the miracle are not restricted to Christians. First reports of the occurrence were made by a Muslim cleaner, and other Muslims have reported seeing the image of Christ blink. Christian groups are divided on the events. Longstanding rivalries between Greek Orthodox and Christian priests have flared up. Greek Orthodox Archbishop's representative Fr. Anastasios has said that "it is a message for people to come back to God . . . Jesus is crying because the world is not going well . . . On the other hand a Franciscan Father, Michele, said "Can it be that they saw Jesus crying at the exact spot that they sell candles¿'[97]

This report, dated 29 November 1996, taken from an English Catholic site, was distributed by the largest news agencies on earth, and found its way into newsrooms around the planet. For example, Reuters reported that "Greek Cypriot pilgrims in the church on Thursday fell to their knees and wept before the painting after saying Jesus had winked at them."[98]

We have already encountered another case of a winking image: the winking Madonna, in 1991, in Boston, in the videotape of the procession of the Madonna del Soccorso, organized by the Sciacca Society. But as early as 1918 in Limpias, Spain, or in 1948 at Castel San Giorgio, Italy, similar phenomena were recorded.

It should come as no surprise that the field of miracles should reiterate and—still today—feature phenomena that boast a tradition and a power—

the attraction of moving images—that sink deep roots into the history of the various forms of popular Christianity. Once again, however, passage into the Web shifts all the traditional configurations and boundaries, paradoxically modifying the significance at the very moment in which it reinforces that significance and confers upon it new and extraordinary possibilities of actualization. In fact, on the Web an almost automatic quality of irony operates on all information and reports, delegitimizing the separateness of the sacred, its very sense of otherness with respect to the profane, inserting it into a welter of movements, shifts, and transfigurations that prevents all definitive qualification, any "eternal" sense.

Let us take as an emblematic example an image of a winking Jesus at the Web site called *The Miraculous Winking Jesus.*[99] Here the surfer is asked to stare at a drawing of the face of Jesus and notice whether it winks. If it does, the surfer will click on the legend: "Jesus winked at me." Otherwise the surfer will click on another legend: "Jesus did not wink at me." The ironic observation of the Franciscan monk concerning the winking Jesus of Bethlehem is no different from the irony to be found in the winking Jesus on the Internet. But the fact that some should be exalted and profoundly moved by seeing a winking fresco and that others should find the same thing laughable can be explained, outside the Web, as something that derives from the rivalry, for instance, between Catholics and Greek-Orthodox groups: in short, it can be traced back to broader contexts of diversification, with an individual episode of diversity taken as an indicator and a consequence of that diversification. Instead, this possibility of referring back to more general contexts, and from those contexts on back to yet others and yet others still, making it possible to work on the basis of common attributions of meanings, is not necessarily present on the Web, or may have to follow entirely new paths. *The Winking Jesus* cannot be placed in a context of recognizable accessibility, such as to easily reveal regularity and correspondence. The sum of several thousand visitors cannot be articulated in reference groups, and not merely because of their objective invisibility, but also because movements on the Web do not necessarily correspond to full-fledged subjectivities. The fragmentation of humanity at large and the splintering of identities on the Web renders highly problematic all logic of typification. It is possible, obviously, to identify a few trends and directions, as in this article that appeared on the Web site of the *Sydney Morning Herald*, which distinguished among "believers appalled by the blasphemy; people who can't tell if it's serious or not (sadly, this group is well represented); disbelievers who roar with laughter; and, perhaps most interestingly, believers who find themselves having a good old chuckle as well."[100]

In the Web site's guest book we find the accounts of people who actually express joy for the miracle which took place, in some cases announcing that this has changed their lives. But they could be falsifications, undertaken by correspondents or even by the Web master himself. No one can provide us with any guarantee that the dozens and dozens of messages from Web surfers published on the site are "real," that is to say, that each of them comes from a different surfer; nor, even if it had been possible to prove that, is there any guarantee that the messages correspond to real emotions, or that they are not themselves a game. What normally takes place in everyday life offline, that is, the placement of what a person says within the historical, social, institutional, psychological, and cultural context in which he or she says it, is not possible online, in a situation that may be entirely common and everyday, such as that of *The Winking Jesus*.

In reality, in a case such as this, we clearly see what is generally hidden in the shadows of the Web: that quite often the provisional context that is created around a Web page is not alone enough to tell us whether that which is stated is true or false, authentic or counterfeit.

I was looking for salvation on the internet this morning when I came across your site. I looked at the picture and prayed: "Jesus, if you are true, give me a sign." Sure enough, he gives me a little wink. Praise Jesus!!!

You might go to HELL for this BLASPHEMY! I am quite appalled at you Satan-worshipers!!!!!!!!!

When Jesus winked at me I felt inner peace that I had never felt before. I felt that my prayers came true. I prayed for this moment forever and now it has come. Praise the Lord. I believe. I feel alive!!!!!

I downloaded the image and discovered that this is a hoax. I am very offended. May god damn you to hell, Webmaster, in all of his glory.

Okay, the picture winked at me, but how do I know that it isn't computer generated to do so?

I noticed the wink twice . . . I'm smart enough to know that Computers
can do anything and a timer is probably set up to cause the eye to
wink. . . . I don't need a picture to wink at me to know that JESUS is
around and Loves me and everyone else as well. I do NOT approve of
some of the language on the page. IF these people are truly trying to live
in the image of JESUS then they had better work on their language.

Funny, Funny . . . it is a miracle, he he he he he he!!!!!!!!

Jesus winked at me! It was amazing this shows that he is alive and is
watching over us!

I did see Jesus wink at me. It may be a programmed thing, but it lifted
my spirits. I am a strong believer in Christ and his mysterious workings.

He did wink at me. Is this some kind of prank? Please don't play games
with faith.

You satanic motherfuckers. you will burn in the eternal flames of hell
for reaping such blasphemy.[101]

Given the impossibility of ascertaining the authenticity of these messages, what the visitor may ultimately begin to experience is a sort of unintentional staging, that is, an internal portrayal, while reading, of one's
own possible personal states of mind, which may swing among the various positions expressed or may focus decisively upon certain or even one
of those states of mind, or even express discomfort or embarrassment for
all of them. The surfer, in a certain sense, will find himself undergoing an
experience similar to that of someone reading a novel, aware of the fact
that everything she is reading is fiction, and feeling at the same time that it
is truer than the nonfictional reality, in that the novel opens a space for the
movement of internal emotional figures for the reader herself, organizing
a projection of her own inner ghosts or phantoms.

The imponderability of the winking Jesus in terms of reality external
to the Web does not mean that it is not real. On the contrary, it is a particularly apt representation of the way the Web works, in the sense that
it casts light on the condition of singularity of the surfer, who is in turn
articulated into personal fragments of desire, will, and expectation which
cannot always be reconciled one with another; indeed, they are relatively

autonomous because of the potential actualizations that the Web allows to the polymorphic virtuality of humanity. Once again, the winking Jesus explicitly makes manifest what other visionary sites keep vague or push to the background: that the significance and the meaning of a visionary Web site (and this general statement could be extended to other subjects) does not derive so much from the site itself, much less from the reality of the events external to the Web to which it refers, but particularly from the approach of the surfer, which is in turn determined by the "compelling vacuum," by the internal economy of desires and expectations, by the confluence of cultural, intellectual, and religious biography with the contingent conditions of the navigation that the surfer is currently undertaking through the Internet, a navigation whose actualizing course, directions, and halts are never the same in any given instance.

One of the pages of the winking Jesus, which appears if you click on a message bar saying "Jesus did not wink at me!" informs the visitor "Sorry. Some are fortunate enough to witness this miracle, others will have to return with hope and faith that they will see Jesus wink: GOD BLESS YOU! . . . To learn more about apparitions, visit Catholic Apparitions of Jesus and Mary."

This site, blasphemous for some and salvation-giving to others, pleasantly ironic or in horribly poor taste, leads its visitors, at the end, toward the general network of the sites of Marian apparitions. The transition from the facetious to the serious, from the blasphemous to the devout—or from the serious to serious, etc.—cannot be perceived save in the perceptions and attitudes of individuals. In the larger visionary network, *The Winking Jesus* is, in the final analysis, just one of the links through which the general flow of information passes, actualizing the virtual, or virtualizing the provisional devotional solution of the individual movement via the computer. And it has every right to be a link in the larger visionary network, contributing to its affirmations and negations, admittedly through an emphasis upon the mechanism of irony.

In fact, the reasons why it is rejected by some as blasphemous make it possible to go on to establish solidarity with an entirely different sort of site, to belong to other territories, in other words to open the network of visionary Catholicism to other networks. Once, as I browsed around *TWJ*, I found a link to a personal home page that denounced the winking Jesus as nothing more than a graphic animation, not a miracle at all.[102] The anonymous Web master added, moreover, that he had preferred to report the site without providing a link to enter it, because he found the comments published in it to be especially offensive, for two critical reasons: they were sacrilegious to a Christian conscience and they were homophobic. The strangeness of this second statement led me to continue to explore the home page, clicking on other links, in order to determine the religious or ideological basis for the Web site. It didn't take long to get to another archipelago, which featured among other things the site *Was Jesus Gay?*[103] Now the Web master's sources were reasonably clear to me, as was the question that then arose: was *The Winking Jesus* truly blasphemous to him, and if so, why? And by what criteria was *TWJ* deserving of condemnation, if the condemner then suggested linking to *Was Jesus Gay?* And we thus ask what is blasphemy on the Web? And what is truth?

The links between sites of this sort and Marian sites, whatever the intentions of the Web masters, encourage the dimension of irony, seen as detachment, awareness of contingent factors, the relativizing of identities, an understanding of the continually fluid nature of differences, all of which are effects of virtualization. This is a dimension that is continually overlapping territory for visionary sites and for visionary worshipers in general.

There is, first of all, a direct form of irony, which is that found in the ironic reproposal of sites that had been constructed for entirely different purposes. I have already mentioned in this context the site *Campaign for Net Frivolity,*[104] which made fun, among other sites, of the *Messages from Heaven* of Father Andrew, "The Trumpeter," mentioned in the second chapter.

More subtle, however, but also more significant, is the irony found in a few curious sites devoted to Jesus, which enjoy a certain popularity among Web surfers.

The *Jesus Homepage*[105] is a Web site that opens with a first-person statement: "My name is Jesus Christ. Welcome to My homepage! I work as the messiah for a major world religion—it's called *Christianity.* However, when I'm not at work I like to 'surf the net.' So I've finally made Myself a Web page. And I've got *e-mail* now, too! If you've been here before, be sure to check out *what's new.*"

It is important to be aware that the underlined words are links. If you open the first one, you will see a list of official Christian or devout Web sites present on the Web. In other words, the relatively lighthearted irony of this Web site does nothing to keep it from linking to a series of absolutely orthodox Web sites, such as the Vatican Web site, an online Bible Web site, another Revelation Web site, and a Shroud of Turin Web site.

Other links within the Web site are dedicated to "My Photo Album," which includes famous canvases and frescoes depicting Jesus; "Personal Information," with a map of Palestine and information about Jesus's "hobbies": carpentry, fishing, catering for weddings, lectures; "My Wacky Links," in which there is a little byplay with photomontages of Jesus and Elvis Presley, or jokes about the possible similarities between Jesus and Windows 95, and more.

In a review in an online magazine, *Netizen,* Jon Katz states, among other things, that "the Jesus Homepage is neither timid nor overdone. It's funny without being offensive; good-humored, but not pointlessly blasphemous. It makes the reader think about religion, dogma, art, ritual, history, and imagery. It takes nothing away from worship, nor from Jesus Christ; in fact, it makes both Christ and worship more approachable, less forbidding. The imagining of Jesus on the Web is a great creative stroke, the Web's own equivalent of spirituality."[106]

Obviously, these points of view are not shared by one and all, because many of the messages present in the site's mailbox are harsh accusations of blasphemy and defamation. But on the Web no point of view can exclude other points of view. It is significant that the Web master of *The Jesus Homepage* chose to use a pseudonym, Solomon Tunt, "considering some of the unpleasant e-mail messages that I have received." The same thing is true of the Web master of another Jesus Web page with a less subtly ironic approach, who received death threats.

In contrast, there was no external problem, but rather an unlooked-for source of revenue, for *The NunBun* Web site,[107] a very popular site that documents a "miracle." Here's the story: on 15 October 1996, in Nashville, Tennessee, an employee of the coffee shop Bongo Java was about to bite into a cinnamon bun when he noticed a curious and "astonishing" resemblance to the face of a world-famous nun, Mother Teresa of Calcutta. He immediately showed the bun to colleagues and customers, and everybody agreed that there was a remarkable resemblance. The bun was placed in a freezer and kept there for a week until another employee, Todd Truley, decided to buy it. The sharp-witted and fortunate Truley then joined forces with two other colleagues and produced a nine-minute documentary about the bun, entitled *A Music City Miracle*; the three coworkers began showing it at Bongo Java, and it became very popular. Ten days later a local newspaper, the *Tennessean*, published a front-page article about the "NunBun." Immediately thereafter, three local radio stations affiliated with Reuters interviewed the trio, and the case exploded: "In one day, we were interviewed by more than sixty American radio stations, half a dozen Canadian, the BBC, and did three radio spots for Australia."

Then they were contacted by American television talk shows, and then by newspapers, and radio and television broadcasters from around the world. Before long, the group was dealing with an unexpected and unpredictable national groundswell of curiosity. Right away, the phenomenon received coverage from forty-six magazines and newspapers, twelve television and radio networks. Twenty-six links hooked them up with other Internet sites. It became difficult, but highly profitable, to satisfy the demand for gadgets and souvenirs, which the group had already begun to produce: T-shirts, bookmarks, small holy images, coffee packets with the image of the "NunBun," and copies of the documentary. The Web site received a million hits in a few months, from people in eighty-two countries.

For any surfer who opens this site, it is possible among other things to receive online the image of the bun, and then to see it transformed—thanks to morphing software—into the true face of Mother Teresa. A series of punning references are found on each of the various pages. The first page begins with a phrase from the Gospel according to Saint John, 6:35, which refers to other miraculous baked goods in a very adroit manner: "I am the bread of life: he that cometh to me shall never hunger." On another page, we find "The Immaculate Confection," alongside a photograph of the confection itself, that is, the bun. Then there is "The bunediction," with the legend "the Nun that appeared in a Bun." The group of partners, who declare on each page that 10 percent of all income will be donated to charity, write:

> The bun is not a hoax. It was truly discovered by a Bongo Java employee who noticed the image in it. We never once imagined the capacity of media coverage we'd receive. We've all been working overtime trying to keep up with the demands of both the public and the press, trying to balance the humor and seriousness of the matter. When the local Nashville newspaper featured us in a cover story, we were ecstatic and really believed that it had gone as far as it would go. We never imagined in our wildest dreams this would reach the level it has and we never pursued it as such.

But the phenomenon came to a grinding halt when Mother Teresa in person wrote to the partners:

I am writing to ask you to stop selling merchandise bearing my
likeness. I have always refused permission for this use of my likeness
for commercial ventures. And, as we ourselves do not raise funds for
ourselves, I have also refused permission for the use of my name, image
or voice to raise funds for us or for any other cause. Therefore, I will not
be able to accept any funds from you earned from sales of merchandise
bearing my likeness. My legal counsel, Mr. Jim Towey, has written
asking you to stop, and now I am personally asking you to stop. I do
know that you have not done anything out of ill-will, and so trust that
you will understand and respect my wish.

However reluctantly, the NunBun company ceased selling some objects, but at the same time published the dozens of messages from people who wanted them to resume selling. "America is a land of free speech
and encourages resourcefulness and free enterprise," wrote one person.
"Maybe God does have a sense of humor, and is trying to teach us all a
little something about humility. The idea that God would allow a miracle
to take place on the face of a bun does show some humility on His part.
It also points out that we overlook miracles every day," wrote another.

This is not the first case in the Christian tradition of foodstuffs upon
which "true" miraculous images have been identified. To limit ourselves
to Catholicism, in the United States and in recent years, we might mention the face of Jesus on a tortilla in New Mexico,[108] which immediately
attracted eight thousand people, or the Jesus on the spaghetti dangling
from a fork in a billboard photo that astounded Joyce Simpson in Atlanta
immediately after she had asked for a celestial sign to help her decide
whether she should remain in the church choir or become a professional
singer.[109] And the use of sacred images to publicize a product was certainly
not an invention of the employees of the Bongo Java coffee shop.

But while offline there is a very clear distinction between those who see
an image on a piece of food and those who laugh about it, in their respec-
tive orders of cultural reference, on the Web things aren't so clear; indeed,
in the overlapping, the drift, and the confusion that appears between sites,
intentions, and devotions, there is produced an ironic relativization of everything, of devotional site and blasphemous sites, of fundamentalism
and its caricature.

If the coexistence of different attitudes is not necessarily visible outside the Web, and therefore the meaning of each phenomenon continues

to be characterized by its motivations, its end target users, its consequential practices and historic and social contexts of reception, on the other hand, within the Web, irony inevitably drifts over all the sites, none excepted, since the simultaneity and coexistence of sites that originate with ideological viewpoints and ideals that are radically distant outside the Web necessarily produce a mixture and blending of contradictory points of view that may however be perfectly reconciled into an often involuntary confusion.

Among the Web sites present in the list provided by the AltaVista search engine in response to the keywords "Virgin Mary," we can hardly help but notice the online newsletter of the Intersex Society of North America, from the summer of 1995, which headlines the first page with the question "Virgin Mary a hermaphrodite?" In this issue of the newsletter, a serious and earnestly reasoned argument is made that the strange results obtained from the DNA testing of the blood on the Marian statuette of Civitavecchia (it was the blood of a male human being, and many American newspapers therefore treated it as a hoax) can be easily explained if we admit that the Madonna was actually a pseudohermaphroditic male.[110] What is most important about this statement is not that it is reliable or that it is plausible, but rather that it is found side-by-side with all the other statements about the Virgin Mary. Outside the Web a statement of this sort would be, and in fact is, restricted to the most limited and specific circulation, or it would be framed and ridiculed in a slightly audacious article in a newsweekly, treated as a curiosity or a piece of social commentary. On the Web, however, it stands alongside all the other statements with the same legitimate status and right to speak and form part of the circuits of relevant information. In fact, in this way it rearticulates the field of meanings, rendering them more relative, not only with respect to itself but also in relation to all the other possible conflicting statements: on the Web sects are not pitted against churches, basement minorities are not matched against auditorium majorities; instead, sites are set alongside other sites, links are set next to other links, in a totally horizontal context.

On the Internet, the problem of boundaries is not restricted to the relationship between one religion and another, between Catholicism and Protestantism, or even to the relationship between Christianity and the New Age. The crossing of boundaries, the overlapping, the formulation of virtual dimensions all affect the very determination and definition of religion, which can no longer be distinguished with any precision from a caricature of religion, nor from a potential erotic subversion of religion.

The question of gays in the Christian and Catholic world stops being a fairly restricted and limited pastoral or theological problem, and can become one of the problematic nodes of the virtualization of Christianity; and not so much because of the substantial numbers of gay Christians, as for the numerous routes that lead to the links in question, for the confusion of the types of discourse, and for the overlapping of the flows of communication which mix Christianity and sex, miracles and tricks, sincere statements and fraudulent declarations, explicit fictions and authentic faiths.

In the final analysis, it is still the surfer, alone in front of a computer screen, who must recompose the nodes into an order—though that order may constitute a form of disorder for others—derived from that surfer's personal intertwining of fragments of desire and expectation, personal life history and pure happenstance, into the framework of actualization that he or she, in that moment and in that place, is operating. An actualization that is always provisional and temporary, since behind any movement related to it lies the interminable references of the virtualization, understood as "the very process of humanity's 'becoming other,'" or to put it more explicitly, the "change of identity."[111]

These processes, in reality, were hardly invented on the Internet. We know perfectly well that syncretism, hybrids, and inversions are dominant forms in the so-called postmodern era, when "the pure products go crazy."[112] Gillo Dorfles has written a book about "loss of interval," that is, the loss of the possibility of distinguishing among the perceptions, consumptions, and information flows that submerge us, with a resulting decline in the capacity to articulate distinctions.[113] In James Clifford's words, "difference is encountered in the adjoining neighborhood, the familiar turns up at the ends of the earth. . . . Everywhere in the world distinctions are being destroyed and created."[114]

The image of a completely standardized world, while it is not necessarily false, is certainly incomplete, since the uniformity of styles, tastes, and customs is just one of the processes at work; alongside it is a proliferation of local distinctions and diversifications, provisional but inextinguishable. But that is another story.

Advertising, among other things, has accustomed us to a continuous overlapping and intermingling of styles, ideologies, values, images, and symbols. We are no longer surprised at seeing the images and symbols of the radical politics of the sixties and seventies used to advertise this or that product. When a picture of Gandhi was used in an advertising campaign for Macintosh computers, the Indian writer Salman Rushdie made an attempt to criticize it. The image of the soccer player Ronaldo imitating the statue of Christ above Rio de Janeiro triggered a few mild objections, and there was even less uproar over the advertising for the movie *The People vs. Larry Flynt*, which wallpapered the walls of the cities and the covers of the newsweeklies with a photograph of the main character, a publisher of porn magazines, crucified on a woman's crotch as if it were a cross. A greater controversy arose over an almost perfect imitation of the crucifixion of Jesus portrayed in a photograph of the rock singer Terence Trent D'Arby; and in fact the photograph was rejected by many Italian and European publications.[115] There were also some protests over the runway presentation of the fashion designer Alexsandro Palombo, entitled "Pax Christi Cocktail," in which a model dressed as the Madonna did a striptease, displaying on one naked breast a painted image of Padre Pio, and wore a rosary as a necklace.[116] And even greater indignation was caused by the work of art done by Chris Ofili, mentioned above, and by the one presented to the Museum of New Zealand Te Papa Tongarewa, consisting of a statuette of the Madonna inserted into a prophylactic, by the English artist Tania Kovats.[117] Naturally, it is almost impossible to avoid the puns about the apparition of the Madonna and performances by Madonna, who in her turn has made a standard element of her publicity campaigns the overlap of her image with that of the Virgin Mary.[118]

But on the Internet, overlapping ceases to be a resource for advertising appeal, an intentional form of expression on the part of a provocative artist, or an unintentional effect of the proliferation of information, that is to say, a loss of interval. It is the very movement underlying the language of the hypertext, the process of virtualization and actualization of the events on the Web, the irregular framework within which the individual inputs are ordered.

In the world of visionary Catholicism this has the paradoxical consequence of creating an indefinability of field, an uncertainty about what falls within it and what does not, to the degree that boundaries and territories can no longer be reconstructed in accordance with spatial metaphor of certainty in the center and riskiness on the outskirts, since both center and outskirts change radically according to the point of view: in other words, they do not exist. You don't know whether it will be in the award given to a devotional site whose link appears there, or in the link closest to the parish Web site—remember the examples cited above—that the gates of erotic or pornographic hell may swing open. In the same list of links, you may find a devotional site on apparitions and another site that savagely attacks that same site, accusing it of satanic influence. It is on the face of Jesus as photographed by Sister Anna Ali at the express behest of the divine that you will find the features of Jesus-Sananda and other "Masters" of *SpiritWeb*; or on the face of Melchizedek in the same site, you will see once again the face of Jesus, the icon that opens the site of Vassula Ryden.[119]

A sort of blanket forms, pulled and tugged in all directions, which on the Web, magically, neither rips nor uncovers one part in order to cover up another; instead, it stretches and widens as needed, that is, in accordance with the point of view and the movement of the navigation. The uncertainty of definition and the vagueness of attribution are both in precise correspondence with the movement in relation to linked visions and miracles on the Web. Outside the normal institutions, the oversight and the discipline, where even ambivalent ecclesiastical affirmations—such as those concerning Medjugorje—obtain a reasonably regular definition and outline, the Web produces a framework of words and images in which it is no longer possible to be certain that truth is the opposite of untruth: everything is true to the degree that it is present.

More specifically, then, we should say that truth ceases to be a significant theme; it is marginalized, it gives way to the current, to that which halts at a certain conjuncture the interminable flow by affirming itself, an instant before another movement of virtualization and then of renewed actualization can reshift the center of the world. And the transition from the true to the current is not a minor shift, in the religious context.

The Shoals of Hierarchy and the New Leaders

In the face of the absolute liberty of both surfer and Web master, what options does an external hierarchy of meanings really have, a structuring of *auctoritates*, ideologies, values? Few, very few indeed, if we consider what effective limitations could be placed upon the explorations of the users. The attempts to control or influence entrusted to such automatic mechanisms as networks, Web rings, and approved site lists are partial and ineffective, and they fail if surfers don't adhere to them fully or avoid the use of the instrument of navigation in the true sense of the term. Aside from the automatic operation of a filter that disconnects the user when it encounters a forbidden site, suggestions or ratings of sites, and institutional seals of approval can work as long as the surfer accepts them and remains rigorously within the sites suggested, eschewing even those links that would appear to be comparable.

In Catholic ritual, outside the Internet, everything is reminiscent of hierarchy: the space of the church, divided between officiants and worshipers, the role of priests in the ceremonies, the central role of the word of the master, and much more. There is nothing that does not clearly inform us that the church is a religious structure founded upon the principle of authority.

Inside the Internet this architecture disappears, and indeed it cannot exist. The Web site of the Vatican occupies the same level as the Web site of the humblest worshipful Web master in the furthest corner of the earth: the Vatican Web site boasts no special real estate, no special time advantage, no authority of purpose that gives it a special ranking. Both sites are subject to the arbitrary whim of the mouse, one and the other take equal part in the construction of the hypertextualization of Web surfing.

For that matter, there is practically no way of checking the origins of the sites, whose names give few hints of their derivation: *The Fatima Network* is a site in multiple languages on the Portuguese apparitions of 1917;[120] full of "virtual" initiatives, it seems to express an official point of view. It is a little more difficult to discover, however, that it is maintained by Father Nicholas Gruner, a Canadian priest and the founder of *Our Lady's Apostolate,* against which the Vatican has repeatedly issued formal warnings. *Missionary Servant of Holy Love* is a site in four languages that describes the visions of a certain Maureen Sweeney, in Ohio.[121] The text points out that Sweeney is under the spiritual supervision of Father Frank Kenney, and we can read the favorable observations of another priest, Albert J. Herbert, S.M. There is no way of gathering, unless you are very lucky and you manage to find another apparitions Web site, *Major Apparitions of Jesus and Mary,*[122] that the diocese of Cleveland, which has jurisdictional authority, has warned the faithful not once but twice, in 1980 and 1990, against the activities of the Sweeney group. But a local warning no longer has much power in the global nonlocation, where there are neither authorities nor hierarchies. And the last site mentioned, which distinguishes between apparitions that have been approved or have not been approved, based on information gathered from the various dioceses with jurisdiction, is not really all that different, for instance, from the site of the fourteen-year-old Brian Alves, *Apparitions and Eucharistic Miracles,* which declares itself to be faithful to the pope and to the magisterium of the church, but then goes on to recommend, among the apparitions inserted in the list, the repeatedly condemned Bayside, and claims that the visions of Father Gobbi have been approved, when in fact they most certainly have not been.

It may be easy to unmask, from a viewpoint of orthodoxy, a Web site that announces the election of a new pope, Pius XIII, and accuses the current pope and his predecessors of being traitors to the church. But the site is called *His Holiness Pope Pius XIII,* and it might be easy to open it before realizing that for a devout and orthodox Catholic, it is not a Web site that should be bookmarked.[123]

It is a little less easy to understand immediately, as you enter the Web site *The Church of Mary Queen of Heaven,*[124] that it is not as devoted as it might seem simply because it has links to truly devout sites. If the Web surfer does not become suspicious immediately—and why should she, if she navigates habitually among the visionary oddities of the Web?—when she reads about an apparition of the Madonna upon a potato to Sister Covington, or about Sister Mary Victoria and her chorus of castrati, or when she reads an interview with the Virgin Mary about her image on the plateglass windows of Clearwater, she must be very lucky and just happen upon a site, run by David Van Meter, which warns her against *The Church*: "Warning: this is an anti-Catholic site."[125]

And then it is always very difficult to distinguish between official sites and unauthorized sites that treat the same subjects. The hypertext form makes it impossible to be sure whether the endorsement, or perhaps we should say, the absence of the endorsement "this is the official site of . . ." will be noticed by a surfer, in part because it may be a fairly rare thing, in the great sea of unofficial sites. There are several hundred sites dedicated to Medjugorje, scattered around the world: an incessant flow of words that often refer one to another, confirming each other but also contradicting each other, each with the claim of telling the truth about Medjugorje. There is an official site, then there are the sites that are acknowledged by the official site, and others still that claim legitimacy through an interview with the visionary, an article by a famous "Mariologist," a photograph of the pope, and so on. It is not possible to orient oneself or choose among all these sites. Everything is mixed up and blended together according to the preferences or interests of the surfer and the power of attraction of the Web page.

In fact, the graphic style replaces the liturgical style and is designed to catch the eye. The previously mentioned Catholic Network Banner Exchange of the Italian site *Miriam* encourages the construction of more attractive banners: "Special care should be devoted to find the right shades of color. It has been shown that the use of bright reds and yellows improves visibility and attracts more attention. The text is important too, however: we recommend using a few sentences, concise and complete. If you can, use animated banners."[126]

The work being done on the Web is striving to achieve a pastoral portrayal, a theatrical production of devotional pedagogy. It would be easy to hark back to the antecedents of the pedagogy of the religious orders in the immediate aftermath of the Counter-Reformation, during the Baroque period, with special reference to the Jesuits in the Kingdom of Naples[127] or to the policies of evangelization in the New World, based on the cult of images.[128] But there is a considerable distinction between the two forms of pedagogical production: nowadays, there is an absence of hierarchic control. The Inquisition, the institutional structure, illiteracy, and economic and military power worked together to constitute a total asymmetry in pastoral relations in the immediate wake of the Counter-Reformation. On the Internet, however, all of these factors are absent, and the only force at play is the logic of the market. That which is most attractive, best produced, most colorful, in other words, whatever sells best, enjoys the greatest success.

Nowadays the Catholic hierarchy is having a certain amount of difficulty in controlling the enormous proliferation of apparitions and mystical phenomena, and even more problems with taking the positions that in the sixties had worked so well to suppress the ecstatic possibilities of the Catholic world. We have seen this in the case of Medjugorje, where the clearly negative attitude of the diocese, balanced with the ambiguity of the Vatican, created without doubt a degree of discomfort among the worshipers. It can be seen in the rather ambivalent presentations of the third secret of Fatima in the year 2000: the presentation by Cardinal Sodano was more popular and in keeping with the expectations of the worshipers; the presentation by Cardinal Ratzinger a few weeks later was more measured and intellectual.

But this difficulty, or perhaps intentional ambiguity, translates on the Web into a redistribution of power and sacral legitimation in favor of new subjects, new leaders, who take control of spaces, and to the detriment not only of the hierarchy, but also of the traditional charismatics, whether they are seers or mystics. Among the new leaders, we can list

— the dozens and dozens of Web masters who put together Web pages about apparitions and miracles;

— the operators of portals that provide a selected universe of information and surfing possibilities, from which the devotional surfer can set out;

— the organizers and/or moderators of mailing lists, that is, groups of worshipers who correspond by e-mail, which connects thousands of subscribers around the world;

— the organizers of newsgroups, that is, discussion groups who post on the Web, with electronic "bulletin boards," messages about Marian apparitions or other Catholic subjects, which can be read by anyone from anywhere on earth;

— the activators of chat rooms or chat lines, i.e., sites through which it is possible to discuss on the Web in "real time" the devotional subjects indicated, even from very distant locations;

— the organizers of Web rings, that is, rings of sites linked and reachable automatically from one devotional site to another;

— the spreaders of the messages of seers via the Web;

— the developers of online archives;

— the organizers of online meetings, videoconference meetings, and other sorts of meetings.

By indirect effect of the invitations of the Vatican Council II to provide active spaces for the laity, there were already lay figures outside the Web, worshipers who were neither institutional agents nor representatives of the hierarchy, who were working to spread reports and messages related to Marian apparitions or other visionary phenomena. But even before the Council, a visionary event would use noninstitutional figures to reinforce itself. For instance, concerning the apparitions of Ezkioga in the thirties, in the Basque Country, William Christian emphasizes the importance of the "hyper-informed believers" who "play a crucial role in standardizing visions": "The scribes, interpreters, teachers, newspaper reporters and discerners were an interface to the written and photographic culture necessary to spread the vision messages and maintain the flow of everyday believers."[129]

But on the Web what changes is the autonomy of operation of the new subjects. A localized visionary event falls under the control of the local authorities, both religious and civil. Whereas the network of visionary events online cannot be subjected to any form of control.

Moreover, the scale of the phenomena that the new leaders are capable of producing is immense in comparison with the traditional forms of control and diffusion of news. One afternoon, when I went back to my car in the parking lot of the University of Salerno, I found tucked under my windshield wiper a little flyer promoting the visions of Michelina Izzo, from Poggiomarino (in the province of Naples), who sees and speaks with "Most Holy Trinity and the Celestial Throngs." When I looked around, I saw identical flyers on the windshields of all the cars in the parking lot. Here we see the difference between this sort of undertaking outside the Web and within the Web: Michelina Izzo may have reached the drivers in this and as many other parking lots as her supporters managed to leaflet, whether that be two, four, or forty parking lots, in two, four, or forty days. In contrast, Joseph Hunt, a self-proclaimed "Internet Advocate for Roman Catholic Visionaries," a diffuser of Marian messages through the Internet, reaches on behalf of twelve North American visionaries, no different really than Michelina Izzo, seventy-five countries, on the continents of "Australia, Asia, Europe, North and South America," with a click of the mouse.[130] Not unlike a theatrical agent, Hunt gathers locally and launches universally the visionary phenomena of John Leary, from New York State; Carol Ameche and Patricia Mundorf from Arizona; Patricia Soto, Sadie Jaramillo, and Harriet Hammons from California; Jack Marie Smith and Virginia Pelly from Pennsylvania; Denis Curtin and Joseph Della Puca from Connecticut; Teresa Whitt from Texas; and Josyp Terelya from Canada. Moreover, Joe Hunt asks that the reports he sends out be translated into local languages. If the number of people reading his online texts can be extrapolated from the number of correspondents sending him e-mail, it is so vast that Hunt writes in his collective messages, "I cannot possibly answer you all individually, you who write from Australia, Asia, Europe, North and South America."

Another sign of the redistribution of social power and legitimacy is provided by the multiplication of Web pages on apparitions and on prophetic phenomena developed by the young and the very young, who are, it is well known, very skillful in the connections of the corpus callosum.

Brian Alves is the American fourteen-year-old mentioned above who developed a Web page of Marian apparitions and eucharistic miracles.[131] When his site had been up for only a year he wrote, "Many many many people email me asking questions, asking prayers, asking help, and many just giving me thanks for making this. . . . I have made many many many friends in a period of only about 1 year . . . my website has been on the internet for only about 1 year and I have contacts all over the world now, even some visionaries, and friends who know visionaries."[132]

The example of this very young Web master can serve to indicate the dimension of the entry on the scene of these new subjects. Alves wrote, "I was hesitant to write about myself because I was afraid people wouldn't ask me questions anymore because they see that I'm only 14, and think 'Oh, he's only a kid, he doesn't know the answer to my question' Well, that's false!!! I am VERY knowledgeable about the apparitions of Our Blessed Lady; so please, don't be afraid to ask me questions!!!"[133]

Ben Nivison, on the other hand, is sixteen, and he is the Web master of *End Times,* a Web site about prophecies of the imminent "tribulations" that will herald the impending "Second Coming of Christ."[134]

Michael Lambert is twenty-five and he is an American Marine stationed in Japan; he is the Web master of one of the many prophetic sites on the imminent Warning that heaven is about to send, just prior to the return to earth of Jesus.[135]

Brian Alves's request to receive questions about apparitions and related phenomena is not uncommon. Indeed, another sign of the marginalization of the hierarchical structures is found in the fact that the Web pages on apparitions present themselves as authoritative sources of information, while their Web masters proclaim themselves to be authorities on religious subjects, conferring upon themselves legitimate rights to pronounce their opinions on questions of faith.

A female example: Rosemarie, American, twenty-five years old, married, childless, offers a site, *Maria Rosa Mystica,* whose objective is to offer teachings to others about "Some things which I have learned about Catholicism during an in-depth, personal study of the Faith over the past seven years. . . . It took years of personal study—including accredited correspondence courses, reading numerous theology texts, etc.—to learn these awesome truths, especially the truth of Grace. So now I want to share what I have learned with others (hopefully) for their benefit (especially those unable to dedicate years to an in-depth study of theology!)."[136]

These new leadership figures become organizers of new Marian devotional and community routes, with an influence, a penetration, a visibility, and a relevance that are entirely unprecedented, a possibility of spiritual orientation and a power of creating new hierarchies, online, to which the traditional Catholic priestly hierarchy is not always able to respond. There is often no institutional structure behind them: neither parish priests nor parishes, neither associations nor prayer groups. Save for a few cases, they work entirely independently, cutting right through the well-structured world of Catholic organizations and outdoing them easily in terms of visibility on the Internet.

The success of these new noninstitutional authorities is also partly determined by the fact that they radically embody the individualistic logic of the Web, which rewards the self-referential solitude of the surfer. Even though these individuals may set themselves up as legitimate authorities, everything about them reveals constantly that they are no different from other surfers, that is, they remain alone in the face of the Web. A passage from an e-mail that "john smith," the Web master of the Italian-language Web site *Profezie per il Terzo Millennio* (literally Prophecies for the Third Millennium, or PTM) sent to the mailing list *Messaggi Celesti* (Celestial Messages), addressing its Web masters, clearly shows the indifference— neither conflict nor submission—of the new leaders toward the traditional hierarchy, as well as the portrayal that they offer of the typical condition of cybersurfers, that is, of those who are the centers of orientation of their own worlds:

> Unfortunately the problem is that visionaries are a continual mystery, and the possibility of falling into error in the field of private revelations is already high for the Church—which as we all know has expertise, experience, and considerable resources to investigate individual cases— so how much greater it must be for us! And then it is truly difficult to read carefully all of the tens of thousands of messages from the many visionaries, or self-proclaimed visionaries, from around the world. I myself on PTM have recently eliminated a number of visionaries that I had long considered reliable, discarding messages that I had worked for weeks at a time to translate; and maybe just because out of the hundreds and hundreds of messages I had found a detail that had eluded my notice until now, but which proved that the visionary was not reliable after all. Unfortunately, it is a risk that we must run, as we all know, and on this point you are perfectly right; as we also know that we must always be ready to discard even substantial parts of our work if it proves necessary, because of the responsibility that we have toward our readers. Consider that when I decided to remove Veronica Lueken, in practical terms I eliminate about a fifth of the entire section devoted to eschatological prophecies.[137]

We hardly need mention that the apparitions of Veronica Lueken had long been condemned by the ecclesiastical authorities and that it was not until the year 2000 that "john smith" eliminated from his pages the messages about them.

Corresponding to this diffusion of personal self-legitimation, institutional authority is often called into doubt. There is muttering on the Web, or in some cases open proclamations, that the two successive bishops in the diocese of Mostar who have condemned Medjugorje should convert to different views; that the bishop who condemned Garabandal will receive inspiration from the Lord to change his beliefs; that the bishop of Naju, Korea, who has condemned Julia Kim's exudations of blood, simply failed to understand that the phenomenon is God-given, and so on.

The Web sites that mention the decisions of bishops within whose territorial jurisdictions cases of apparitions might fall are extremely rare, just a few in comparison with the hundreds of sites that ignore them. And in many specific cases, the sites level criticism and accusations against bishops who have expressed negative views, as in this letter to *Marian Discussion:* "You will find apparition sites disapproved by Bishops who have not even followed Canon Law and done a proper investigation. Would you want to be thrown in jail because a judge thought you looked like a thief without even a trial? Bruce."[138]

On the Web, there is no authority at the altar, as there is in church, answering the questions of all the faithful, nor is there any authority who ends a discussion with his official observations. Surfers weigh in as they think best, discussing whatever anyone else discusses, without the slightest possibility of establishing who has the better institutional justification for doing so. When a priest or a theologian has his say, he is just one among many. Even when someone makes reference to an authority who is recognized outside the Web, she is making use of only one of the possible foundations for authority, which however can immediately be debunked or dismissed or denied by someone else.

In the mailing lists, there are quite often statements of criticism, doubt, and sometimes even disgust expressed toward priests and even bishops, in relation to the subjects of faith and specific behavior.

When Cardinal Keeler called for an end to the meetings of the prayer group of Gianna Talone because of an apocalyptic prophecy of the visionary, in September 2000, Cristina wrote to *Profezie On Line:* "I believe profoundly that the messages of Emmitsburg are true, because when a bishop calls an end to them in this way, it is precisely because of the eschatological accuracy that they display, and that's not all. As was the case in Dozulè, unfortunately, many priests and bishops become jealous of the visionaries who receive the messages, thinking to themselves: 'Why does God or the Madonna give these messages to these human beings who are not even consecrated, while to Us, who are Consecrated to Christ, they refuse to reveal themselves?' "[139]

When Father Emanuel Burgos, in an e-mail, manifested his doubts about the authenticity of the locutions of Rita Ring, stating that in his view these were personal meditations of one woman, not messages from Jesus, the responses were immediate and annoyed. Among them, Jim: "What sort of limits are being put on Our Lord by judging His response to Rita's prayer as being a mere figment [sic] of her imagination. . . . Is it because it hasn't happened to you? Is that a proper criteria? It hasn't happened to me, either. But I have no problem accepting that it happens to others. . . . These love letters from Christ are not for Rita. They are for you. They are for each of us who read them. They are for each of us individually. Try letting him speak to you through them."[140]

In reality, priests rarely contribute to the mailing lists on apparitions, especially the American ones: the devotional interactivity of the Web is a sphere presently controlled chiefly by those who have no legitimate sacred standing in the offline world, and which does not offer the customary format of a vertical and asymmetrical apostleship. Here, the ecclesiastics are just a few among the many, enjoying no special standing. Often, in fact, they have an inferior status. Peggy noted, "I know that in one Marian Apparition Mary said that many Priests & Religious were on the road to Perdition & taking many souls with them."[141]

And Jessie agreed: "Remember, our Mother has even said the red caps [cardinals] some of them no longer believe . . . and that the smoke of satan has entered the Church."[142]

The pope alone is exempt from criticism; indeed, at times he is considered the sole careful listener to charismatic voices: "Sadly, the 'messages' of persons with extraordinary charisma and their testimonials are taken into serious consideration only by Pope John Paul II, who is also a great charismatic, and by a small minority of Bishops, Theologians, and Priests."[143]

Or emphasis is placed upon a request by the pope to recognize a certain apparition, and the subsequent rejection of that request: "Pope JOHN PAUL II has asked repeatedly for the recognition of Dozulè, but the Bishop has always rejected that request. Thereby going against the will of the pope."[144]

Without Cardinal Points

> Messages of love given by Divine Wisdom to a soul, that they may reach the souls of all men. The person who receives the messages remains anonymous by divine will, but we can assure you that not a word is published without the supervision and authorization of the priest who accompanies that person in his spiritual voyage. We have been undertaking a collection of the messages for 1992 to 1998 at the following address: *Messaggi Gesù*. Moreover, at the earliest, we shall also send a number of translated messages.
>
> Attention, this site is updated continuously. The messages are updated to the first of August 2000 and the site has been online since 15 October 1998.[145]

This untitled home page, present among the links to *Profezia On Line*, is rather emblematic of the absence of control over the information that circulates on the Web concerning visionary phenomena. In this case, the anonymity and delocalization are explicit, but they remain implicit in the background, even when identity and location are stated, inasmuch as the names of people and places are entirely negligible, superfluous, and even pointless elements—in some cases, fictitious, moreover—in a flow where it is impossible to establish points of reference or any verification of accuracy or authenticity.

The metaphor used in connection with the new communications technologies, especially apt for the Internet, is that of a "new oral tradition"—with, paradoxically, the written word as its chief vehicle: "Nowadays," says Ernst Jünger, "with new communications technologies, with the spread of videowriting, multidimensionality, and the possibility of creating hypertexts, the traditional, fixed form of writing is becoming newly fluid, mobile, and transformable, as in the oral tradition."[146]

But this oral tradition is entirely devoid of the instruments of organization and structuring typical of the cultural forms of orality. In oral cultures—or in societies that operate on an oral basis—the formalization of orality and the sharing of a relatively homogeneous symbolic universe allow the formation of connective tissues, which may be quite rigid, preventing dispersion and drift, potential threats to a universe of communi-

cations that are entirely entrusted to the spoken word, without any surviving traces in written form. What Peter Bogatyrëv and Roman Jakobson
called the "preventive censorship of the community"[147] ensures that an
oral creation that establishes itself within a community develops already
within the ideological possibilities of the community itself. Moreover, the
presence of institutional or informal *auctoritates* ensures that the interpretation of the symbolic contents does not go beyond a given horizon
of compatibility and social organization. From this point of view, a territory of oral communication, concerning for instance the announcement
of a Marian apparition, has well-organized and functional restrictions. In
my research on the apparitions of Oliveto Citra, it appeared evident right
from the beginning that the words exchanged between visionaries, leaders, worshipers, and onlookers—which at the beginning had a dominant
role over written communications—followed specific restrictions, caused
by the intercession of local powers, between those who had legitimate
grounds to speak and those who did not, between those who had the authority to confer the word and its meaning to all the others, and all the
others who could only struggle to obtain it. This scenario of negotiation in
the new horizon of meanings that opened out with the children's visions
could be organized in virtue of an existing shared symbolic or religious
tradition, an already functional distribution of powers, a geocultural localization of the actions organized around the phenomenon. If there had
been no determined cultural localization—in the society and the culture
of Oliveto Citra—either the phenomenon would not have taken place or
it would have been scattered into trickles of multiple, noncommunicative
enunciations. Only the presence of shared localized traditions, or at least
of recognized *auctoritates* that could indicate the correct interpretation of
the facts that were taking place, could allow a shared and common production of truth and reality.

The "oral tradition" on the Internet, instead, is unique, not only lacking
in auctoritas and genuine tradition of any sort, but also distinguished by
a weak social and cultural context.

Let's consider an example. John Doe talks to a worshiper offline about
a new apparition. Without even being fully aware of what he is doing, the
worshiper will not merely listen to John Doe's ideas and presentation. He
will bring into his evaluation, whether unconsciously or simply through
ingrained habit, considerations of John Doe's way of speaking, language,
dialect, accents, and syntactical and thematic organization. He will also
immediately notice John Doe's clothing, his way of presenting himself

in public, as well as his age and his gender. And before that, there was already a judgment on his social standing: a priest and a taxi driver in this context are not equivalent. Another important factor contributing to the final judgment will be the time and place in which they speak. If he listens to John Doe in a coffee shop, at the ball field, or on the beach, distancing mechanisms will come into play that derive from the inappropriateness of those occasions for a very serious discussion. If, instead, he listens in a church group or in his parish church, it will become harder for him to dismiss what he has heard with a witty comment. But what if John Doe doesn't say these things, but writes them instead? Here too a worshipful reader will be very aware of the context in which he reads them: it's one thing to read them in a weekly entertainment column, and another to read them in a semiofficial magazine like Italy's *Famiglia Cristiana* or in *L'Osservatore Romano*.

On the Internet everything, or nearly everything, disappears. That which operated outside the Internet in terms of evaluation, that is, an attention to cultural hierarchies, social legitimations, the criteria of common sense, works badly if at all on the Internet. Offline, a worshiper moves within the context of limitations established by conventions, customs, the distribution of social powers, which allowed her to orient herself through vertical paths running from that which is more socially relevant and that which is less. Online, what strikes her immediately is the totally horizontal structure of the interventions.

If she devotes herself to thorough research into the subject, she may have a clearer and better organized view of things after a couple of weeks of hard work. But if her objective is simply to gather a quick, "official" overview on a certain phenomenon, she will be quite frustrated, since she will not be able to rely upon those mechanisms that would have assisted her in finding an orientation among the various opinions and arguments, according to a culturally and institutionally hierarchical point of view.

Outside the Web, the criterion is to recognize the sources, distinguish among derivations, identify and circumscribe the contexts, articulate the sequences in keeping with relationships of authoritative/not authoritative or orthodox/heterodox. Inside the Web, on the other hand, the relationships of inclusion/exclusion respond to other logical approaches, more mechanical in nature; the religious symbols are grouped not in relation to the groups that embody them or the contexts that express them, but rather in relation to the dynamics of affiliation by links, keywords, and search engines. The offline logic is based on textuality: the text is identified, its context and boundaries are established, its derivations are reconstructed. The mechanism of the Web, instead, is one of a fluctuating intertextuality that is difficult to order; the references are much more immediate, through similarities and standardization, or better yet, through formal identities. Certainly the origins of the sites, their denominations—when they are evident—offer a relatively accessible means of evaluation. But for a surfer it is not always easy to know in advance which sites are most authoritative on this or that subject.

Search engines are being developed that will be capable of selecting, upon request, the most authoritative Web sites on a given topic and avoiding the less reliable ones. This will make it possible to use the Web in a more "ecological" way, though also in a less libertarian way, but it is exceedingly unlikely that the characteristic horizontality of the Web will ever be eliminated entirely. What promises to be most effective are the so-called "bots," that is, special software that promises to allow Web surfers a more individualized orientation.[148]

In short, what can be found nowadays in the Marian visionary universe on the Web is a gigantic and disorderly "oral" flow of supposed and alleged Marian messages: thousands of messages, linked to hundreds of cases around the world, distributed over the course of many weeks or years. These chattering Madonnas intertwine their words in an incredible manner, confirming and reinforcing one another, or even undercutting, debunking one another, contradicting freely in an uncontrollable verbal production that cross-references in terms of the formal relationships of the words used, and certainly not because of hierarchic recognitions. In this way, the overall effect is disarming even to the worshipers themselves, who have no ultimate points of reference.

In the mailing lists we frequently see one or another correspondent weighing in with complaints of confusion on a certain topic. We have seen it in connection with the subject of the Apocalypse. But equally common are expressions of varying degrees of reassurance:

> As Pat and others in this thread pointed out, the actual answer to the confusion felt by the person asking for help, is that Our Blessed Mother in fact does not contradict herself, but merely gives different messages in different places. . . . Stephen.[149]

> Each seer is given one piece of the puzzle. That helps in limiting the potential for sins of pride if one human doesn't know everything.

Therefore, the messages to each seer have a different perspective
because their mission (i.e. focus of messages to disemminate) is
different. . . . Bruce.[150]

These reassuring responses only temporarily ward off the sense of discomfort that continues to crop up here and there. Looking at the "whole
picture," as Jacci suggested above, is practically impossible with an instrument that multiplies information exponentially. Outside the Web, localized apparitions are relatively easy to keep track of, for worshipers. The
messages, though they may be frequent, coming daily and even multiplied through various visionaries—as was true in the case I studied at
Oliveto Citra—never reach numbers that are truly unmanageable. Moreover, the messages of the various visionaries refer to one another in accordance with strategies of affirmation of leadership that indirectly create
a consensus-based coordination of meaning. In the third place, the fact
that the events are contextualized in a given geocultural territory allows
levels of consistency and logical and symbolic correspondence that are
sufficient to keep from creating problems of interpretation. Finally, there
is an institutional hierarchy functioning locally, and it is possible to avail
oneself of it if necessary.

But when one, two, three, a hundred, or five hundred apparitions are
launched on the World Wide Web, adding their own flow of information
to the thousands and thousands of other flows, the river that is created is
truly uncontrollable and incomprehensible.

In order to keep pace with this overwhelming clutter of information, in the mailing lists and on the Web sites there are people who
offer instruments of orientation—the "discernment" described above—
correspondents of the mailing lists who quote sacred texts, documents
from the Vatican, from the popes, who identify relationships between a
given message from a given apparition and the messages from the apparitions approved by the church, especially the apparition of Fatima, or
relations with the most famous and widely quoted apparitions, or again
with a given speech by the pope or a specific phrase attributed to a certain mystic, or a saint, and so on. All the same, these interpretations in
turn trigger responses that tend to be discordant, rather than in agreement, creating new effects of disorientation. In particular, on Medjugorje, genuine verbal brawls break out, sometimes continuing for days
at a time.

Another element complicates the already difficult "whole picture."

Often different sites offer different information about the same events or declarations or messages. And that is when a round of e-mails begins to circulate, asking or offering explanations, refutations, and confirmations.

One significant example involves the statements about Medjugorje and the pope attributed to Father Malachy Martin, a priest who is famous in the United States for his sharply conservative views. This case is a good example of the risks of devotional Web surfing, because of the difficulties in identifying attitudes and affiliations, as well as genuine errors, which are not easy to blame on anyone in particular.

We reprint below an exchange of messages in *Marian Prophecy & Current Events Discussion List,* from late September 1998:

> Dear Pat, In trying to access Fr. Martin's website, I was taken to something totally irrelevant. If you will try to access it for yourself, you will be taken to some WindsurfingBrazil site. Could you have copied the wrong address? Ann.

> The other person is correct, accessing the web site brings you to a web page on wind-surfing. Hope someone discovers the answer to the puzzle . . . Don.

> Don't know why you are having problems. I clicked on the given site and went right to his web site. Maybe someone else can figure this out, I sure can't. . . . Love ya! Pat N.

> I wouldn't waste my time looking at this website. I've checked it out today and found a lot of erroneous information regarding Medjugorje. . . . Pam.

> There seem to be two Websites for M Martin which seem to differ somewhat on Medjugorje. They are in conflict with each other. So check out both before you make a decision. B.K.

Navigational errors or counterfeits of official Web sites? The doubt persisted for some time in the exchanges, often prompting arguments and brusque dismissals. In another mailing list, *Messages from Heaven,* Yancy, in a message entitled "wolf or sheep?" criticized a certain ambiguity in the image of Malachy Martin as presented on the Web sites:

As I look around various web sites concerning catholicism and current church issues and even on apparitions, I have seen the name Malachai Martin or "Father" Martin refered to several times. From what I've seen so far he is either a modern prophet with valid warnings for the faithfull or he is a trouble maker taking part in Medj. bashing and weakening faithful resolve. I've seen him presented as a respected figure whose endorsement is intended to lend credibility to some conservative catholic causes, and I've read of him as being a defrocked, sensationalist taking his message to some of the same venues that one finds defenders of Bigfoot, UFO's and other trendy conspiracies. . . . Yancy.[151]

The case of Malachy Martin expresses very well the state of confusion in which it is possible to find oneself with the proliferation of messages and information. It is not as if Father Martin were a minor figure, and it were possible to misunderstand his "true" thought. On the contrary, he is a very popular figure in the world of American Catholicism, given his frequent participation in talk shows and other television programs, his books and articles, and even his Web sites on the Internet. And yet that does nothing to reduce the number of misunderstandings, in fact it increases them, because the proliferation of information about him, once it has been refracted through the thousands of trickles of every Web master or correspondent who chooses to write about him, including Malachy himself (or the Malachy's themselves), builds up into an unstoppable flood. The identity, the authority of the texts, the specific targeting of the messages, all of these things have vanished in the devout Internet.

One correspondent takes a lesson from Father Malachy's misunderstandings: "Just proves that you can't trust everything you read on the internet!"[152]

But what can you trust and what can't you trust? Another surfer suggests that you can trust the authentic sources of understanding: "It is obviously confusing (you're not the only one confused!) and counterproductive to your formulation of your faith. Go to the more trusted sources: the Bible; the Vatican web site; EWTN web site; and books that have been 'approved.' "[153]

We should note that, on the one hand, there is no longer any reference to any filters based on communities of faith, parishes, associations, or spiritual leaders, priests, confessors, parish priests; and, on the other hand, alongside the Bible and the Vatican Web site we find the Web site of the Catholic television network EWTN, which has been cited on other occasions as a point of reference for knowledge and clarification when disputes or disagreements have arisen in the exchanges of correspondence. EWTN is run by Mother Angelica, a nun who is known for her undisciplined positions with respect to the religious hierarchy: she publicly expressed her critical views of a directive on liturgy issued by Cardinal Mahony of Los Angeles; then she retracted her criticism when the Vatican weighed in. Precisely for these reasons, as others have pointed out, not even EWTN can be considered an absolute authority: "Another example of disagreement is that between Cardinal Mahoney [*sic*] and Mother Angelica. Aren't they both supposed to be in the service of God? Why then do they disagree? How do you know who is right?" [154]

When not even the ecclesiastical authorities are exempt from doubt, the authentic sources of understanding dwindle down to the conscience of each individual, assisted, obviously, by the Holy Ghost: "In other words the real entity that helps us discern is the 'Holy spirit.' . . . Mike." [155]

To Darlene, who asked how and when the ordinary person could understand that Jesus was about to return to earth, Craig replied, "How will we perceive that HE is Jesus? Simple, through 'discernment' by the Holy Spirit, by way of prayer to God. Jesus speaks to you princebly through your soul not through what you see, hear, think, feel, and smell. All these sensation are 'self' and it is easy to be mislead if you depend only on these gifts from God. He gave you a much better way to understand His Word. The intimacies of our souls are spoken through us and understood only within by an enlightened state of grace. Pray! Pray! Pray!" [156]

Even if the invitation to individual discernment in effect is borrowing a characteristic of Protestantism, what counts is that it corresponds perfectly to the logic of the Internet, where the fragmentation of groups is only a screen, behind which is expressed the centrality of the individual surfer.

The devotional mailing lists, chat lines, and newsgroups function in a certain sense as compasses in the larger sea of navigation. But, generally speaking, freedom of debate within these contexts is quite ample, even in the moderated lists, where a moderator reads every message that circulates, and, in exceptional cases of evident violation of the ground rules of the list, erases some of them. He is not the leader of the discussion; he is only in charge of ensuring that the ground rules are respected, and his intervention is based on "netiquette," not content. "I think the idea behind this discussion group is 'not' to have a leader but to 'discuss' topics,"

Richard reminds a correspondent who is annoyed at the space given to messages on the apocalyptic future, and the lack of a theological supervision of the messages.[157]

In the unmoderated lists, there is no limit, indeed the correspondents make it a point of honor not to set limits even for those members guilty of infractions of netiquette. For instance, from the *Marian Prophecy & Current Events Discussions List*:

> As one of the "old-timers" of this List . . . I say and even shout: "FREEDOM OF SPEECH IS NOT DEAD ON THIS LIST"!!! Hey, I use my delete button a LOT, but see, this is my decision! No-one makes this decision "for me" like on some other lists! . . . Pat.[158]

> Amen, Pat. I don't always agree with what folks discuss, and their opinions, but I do agree there needs to be a forum where they can discuss their true feelings. And yes, I use my "delete" button quite often when I'm not interested in reading about a certain "thread." Democracy in action—right on! Yours, in Christ and Mother Mary, pat bell/gator.[159]

Discussion groups, therefore, cannot provide any stable orientations, because on the contrary they register the fragmentation of the ideological, doctrinal, and personal positions that make up the online visionary world.

The lack of orientation becomes still more evident if we consider that the Web is also a formidable research tool for many surfers seeking Marian devotion: "Thanks. By the way, I've learned more about what's current in the 'Catholic Community' on line than through our local Churches. Great job!" wrote a worshiper in the guestbook of the site *A Catholic Online*.

On the Web, people ask for help, advice, URLs, bibliographies, and so on with messages that are launched like bottles in the sea, but it is almost certain that a response will come, often an overwhelming excess of response. Anne is converting to Catholicism and asks for assistance with prayer and encouragement, especially for the difficulties that she will encounter with the Marian dogmas, like so many Protestants who convert to Catholicism. In just twenty hours, Anne receives 158 messages in her e-mail inbox.[160] We can safely assume that, if we could read them all, we would be unlikely to find a single, uniform point of view concerning Marian dogmas.

Personal Home Pages

I walk into a bookstore that specializes in religious subjects. I wander over
to the section on Marian titles and books on apparitions; I glance at the
titles and I scan the new publications. Essays on theology, sociology, and
spirituality, hagiographic works, accounts of personal experiences, jour-
nalistic reporting. The repertory of the various forms of written communication that I can find there is limited and predictable. Should I be interested in knowing more, for the purposes of my research, about people
who have had or are having experiences of faith on the sites of apparitions, I can do a few things besides reading their published accounts or
seeing documentaries on the subject. I can go to the place, I can interview
people, and I can hear eyewitness accounts. Then I can gather stories of
the lives of the worshipers, through the various methods available, and I
can thereby reasonably hope to discover the reasons and meanings of this
particular experience of faith.

This is a typical working approach, which occupies me and those who
are studying this field. It reflects the organizational customs and schemes
of the world, and it provides the practical context both for those who study
the experiences of faith in apparitions, and for those who live them themselves. That means that both worshipers and scholars operate within the
context of the same cultural environments and take for granted, accepting
them implicitly, the same assortments of practices: writing, oral histories,
official documentation, eyewitness accounts.

Let's see, instead, what happens if the worshiper or the scholar tries to
perform the same activities on the Web.

31 October 1998: an exploration of the Italian sites about Medjugorje.
The search engine is Lycos, the keyword is "Medjugorje." There are hits
for numerous sites, displayed ten to a page. I skip the first, more traditional one, and I go to the second one, *Persona's Home Page,*[161] whose name
arouses my curiosity. I become still more curious when, having opened
the site, I find a picture of Liv Ullmann in Ingmar Bergman's film *Persona,*
with a link to a text about the movie. I return to the main page, after reading the note: "This site is registered in the List of Catholic Sites in Italy,
with the supervision of Francesco Diani," and then I go to consult the map
of links for the site, created by Paolo Ruata; I find that is organized with the
following links: "Bergman," "Bookmark," which recommends a number
of sites, including one that features an online book about the Internet,
"L'Osservatore Romano," "Inter" (which is dedicated to the soccer team

of Ronaldo and Vieri), "Medjugorje," "Opera" (which basically promotes the browser of that name, not as well known as its huge rivals, Microsoft Internet Explorer and Netscape), "Special" (which opens a Web site about the parish church of San Lorenzo in Casette, in the province of Massa Carrara), and finally, "E-mail."

Here I am, faced with a communications structure about Medjugorje that I could never have found in a specialty bookstore or in a church or in the Bosnian sanctuary of the Queen of Peace. I was seeking Medjugorje and I found many other things that have no relation to that place.

So I go back to the general "Medjugorje" list that I started from. This time I click my mouse on the fifth site, "Welcome to the home page of Massimo Conti." The *Massimo Conti* Web page[162] opens with a list of fourteen "useful phrases," such as: "Examine all things and keep what is good" (Saint Paul), "Soft water hollows out hard rock" (Ovid), "Vanity of vanities, all is vanity" (Ecclesiastes), "Carpe diem (Seize the Day)" (Horace). Further down, "Notes on Catechism," with links to "Jesus, the Son of God," "Answers to the Jehovah's Witnesses," "the Shroud of Turin," and "Genealogy of Jesus." Then, prayer links: "Simple Prayer—Saint Francis of Assisi," "The Credo," "Prayer of the Candle," "The Best of Yourself—Mother Teresa of Calcutta," and finally, a "Prayer Before Going to Sleep—My Great-Great-Grandfather Giuseppe." And then there are links to "folk wisdom," including "Proverbs of My Grandmother Lina." Then there is a link to "Satire and Jokes," another link called "Music, Maestro," with the Ave Maria, John Lennon, Bob Dylan, and USA for Africa/We Are the World. The link "Virtual Pilgrimages" provides tours of Lourdes, Fatima, Medjugorje, Padre Pio, and Mother Teresa of Calcutta. Before the conclusion, that is, the link "the catechist answers: send me your messages, your questions, your doubts about your faith, etc., and I will try to answer you," there is another link called "my links," which contains, among other things: The Holy Bible, the Center for Studies on Homeopathic Medicine, the "Collection of Scientific Publications of Prof. Luigi Di Bella," the "Di Bella Case: Facts and Opinions," the Italian WWF, Maharishi Ayurveda, and lastly "My Home Town: Arezzo and the Encouragement of Tourism in Arezzo." The site, set up in 1997, received in a little more than two months 1,491 hits, an average of 24 visits a day. Just to get a sample, I open "Satire and Jokes," and there are jokes of all sorts, largely untranslatable. Then I open Maharishi Ayurveda, a site in English which describes the products from this commercial and philosophical Indian enterprise, which offers "the promise of a vibrant body, a peaceful mind, a heart filled with joy, and long life . . . what more could one ask? Well, here is the path that leads you there." [163]

Certainly, in the face of this highly fragmented supply of links—which began with a search for Medjugorje, one should remember—it becomes clear that this is the obvious consequence of searching by keyword, which offers quantitative advantages, but fails to provide any selectivity. Perhaps I would obtain the same type of confusion if I were to do a search through a bibliography using a keyword. It would then be my responsibility to choose from among the various responses after obtaining the master list. In other words, a database is an enormous but very crude pool of information; the data that it provides are heterogeneous, and it is the intelligence of the user that renders those data homogeneous.

In reality, the database of any given context—books, newspapers, statistical data, or what have you—already contains an intrinsic limitation, constituted by the fact that it is a repository of those given objects, whether in paper form or numerical or some other form. But when the database is no longer a bibliography, a documentary archive, or a collection of data, but rather the whole of the immense flow of digital communications on the Web to which all the users contribute, then you will encounter two unexpected and unprecedented effects: an overlapping, between the objects of knowledge and the subjects, between the topics and persons; and, in part as a consequence and in part independently, a fragmentation and remixing of the topics and themes.

Certainly, in order to prevent these effects, one may decide to avoid personal Web pages and limit oneself exclusively to sites that feature information about a given subject, in our case, Marian devotion. But, even if that were always possible, we would be eliminating the stimulating and distinctive opportunity evoked by Lévy: "Each individual, each organization is encouraged, not only to add to the store [the Web] but to provide other cybernauts with a view of the whole, *a subjective structure*" (my italics). [164]

And so, if we choose, as would seem "natural," to remain in the personal Web pages in order to gain the point of view of a specific Web master on the subject of devotion, we will find wholly unexpected leads.

These Marian Web pages, as we now clearly understand, are not exclusively Marian; they cover dozens of other subjects, and among those other subjects Marian subjects fit in, they are transformed, they disappear, and they reappear. In fact, the Web masters of personal Web pages do more than just present the subjects of their Web pages; they also present themselves through their sites.

We are faced with an inversion of the habits of knowledge: there is not an object (scientific, aesthetic, or religious) in whose name the researcher (whether scientific, artistic, or religious) is summoned and authorized, as its "delegate," to occupy the stage, and with a clear limitation to the context of the topic itself; instead there is a communicating subject which, by utilizing arguments, assembling objects, and designating thematic routes, presents itself.

In normal social life, the potential chaos of the representations of the world is put under control, ordered, and classified according to segments, broken down into various levels of being and knowledge. The word becomes legitimate only within a given correlative order: science, art, religion, ethics, everyday life, common sense, and so on. The order is under the control of political, religious, and economic institutions, it is expressed with codes, norms, and then with infrastructures. Finally, even human beings themselves, who are also the actors of the social whole, are placed within an order and classified along with the rest. They act and they speak—they are legitimized to do so—only within the classificatory contexts that envelop them, whether they are numerous or few in number, and on the occasions that each of them permits. Professions, classes, sectors, genders, ages: everything that we do and say corresponds to the numerous divisions in which we are inserted and it is in their names that we are legitimized to do and speak. Moreover, when we operate in virtue of a given division, we are no longer authorized to operate in virtue of others as well, except for exceptional and specific cases, or at the risk of stirring objections or disapproval or censure or, at the very least, baffled curiosity.

In particular, in terms of knowledge, the legitimacy to speak is limited to the context of the object about which we can speak. For example, the anthropology of Marian apparitions does not authorize me to speak about the fact that I might be a fan of a soccer team or about my holidays at the sea or in the mountains or about the Web browser that I use or the music that I listen to.

But online there is not a similar structure of partitions. On the Web there is no previously structured cultural "institute" (Egyptology, mathematics, cellular biology, the Madonna) with its various experts, its libraries, its journals, its channels, and its forms of communication; instead, there is a multitude of cybersurfers, who are hardly organized at all, each of them choosing this, that, or the other thing, putting together things and sending them out to the people of the Internet and taking in turn from them. Now, Egyptologists do talk about Egypt on the Web, but so do thousands and thousands of nonacademic lay people, who choose to post Web pages about the pharaohs, next to Web pages about some other subject. With respect to the criteria, the models, the social customs in relation to communications, authorization to speak, there seems a clear risk of disorder—or new order—and it is difficult to make out its outlines, if outlines there are.

I go to the *List of Catholic Web Sites in Italy*. I nose around a little in the list of personal Web pages, and the abbreviation "CED" catches my eye, so I open *CED Center Electronics Di Pasquale. Company Founded in 1950*, the Web site for an audio-video technical service center, where I read this short autobiographical essay, which has nothing to do with the general subject of the Web site:

> The life that I was leading failed to satisfy my aspirations; I was always on the move, always searching for something. Everyday I became more restless, every day I felt a greater sense of emptiness. Like leaves tossed on the wind, I watched as my hopes fluttered away and vanished. Like breakers on the rocks, my plans crashed and ebbed. So much sadness, such darkness. Now my days are full. I have given a meaning to my life, a value to everything I do. I was wandering in the darkness, but no longer. I have found Jesus Christ, and he is my light, he is the way, he is Peace, Truth, and Life.[165]

I continue my navigation through the archipelago of Marian devotion. This time I stop at the *TSSite*, an American Web page with links to two "services": one is an electronics repair service run by the Web master Greg, the other provides information about canoeing.[166] Then there is a link to Internet games, and finally there is a series of links to religious subjects, such as the statue of the Madonna that wept blood; Julia Kim, the Korean visionary; a Mexican "miracle of the sun"; a "Madonna in the Clouds," and so on.

Massimo Conti, Paolo Ruata, Di Pasquale, Greg, and the dozens of other examples that I have examined here, the thousands of creators of personal Web pages on Marian subjects do not limit themselves to talking about the Virgin Mary or even about their personal relationships with the Madonna. They mix documentation about Medjugorje with information about Bergman and canoeing; they treat on the same level—rightly or wrongly, depending on the point of view—the "Woman Dressed in Sunlight" and Maharishi Ayurveda.

In reality, they are presenting on the Web peculiar juxtapositions that have no correspondence to any given cultural order, or any systematic and shared region of knowledge and reality; rather they fit with a private, personal order, obtained biographically and therefore through chance, at least up to the point of entering the Web—I mean to say that they could change their order, and in fact often do, the next day. They are presenting the topics dear to their hearts and so, in this way, they are presenting themselves in a new, original form of autobiography, in which the story line is no longer central, and in which the narrative is no longer limited to a single medium, the written or oral form. An autobiography made up of hypermedia hypertexts, composed of lists and organized in the form of archives, around one's favorite themes, juxtaposed in accordance with one's own approaches, in the form of links and banners, texts and music, photographs and guest books; images more than stories, bric-a-brac more than a linear succession of elements, timelessness more than a temporal flow.

But we shouldn't think that this phenomenon translates into a sort of recovery of the totality of the human experience, into a "humanization" of science. For a surfer, to enter into an autobiography of this sort, where obviously there is no respect for the linear text, or time's arrow, means being able to exit it at any point, without even noticing that he has done so, slipping back into the open sea of the Web and losing both the sense of biographical compactness and the chosen thematic direction.

Let's take an American personal home page. Judith Gormley, from Woodlynne, New Jersey, has put together a Web page which can be reached by surfing through the vast visionary archipelagoes; it is called *Little Flower's Web Page*: "This web page is dedicated to the Blessed Virgin Mary. You will find other pages that I feel relate not only to the Blessed Mother but to those who, like myself, consider her the link to our Lord. Could there be any stronger link than a mother to her son? I hope to provide links to religious webpages (primarily Catholic). This is my first venture into webpages—so please be patient."[167]

The site is a vast collection of links to Catholic Web sites of the Madonna, various saints, prayers, and devotions. But, at a certain point, as we run through the various links provided, we come to this: "JUST CLICK HERE! My husband's WebPage at GeoCities. My husband's WebPage (AGAIN) on Angelfire. Another favor—this time for a young man who keeps my computer from doing those crazy things we don't want them to do. The only reason I list my husband's webpages is because he helps me with this nonsense. He told me 'No link to my pages—no help on your page.' Sooooooo, please visit his webpages, sign his guest book and make him happy."

And so we open the Web pages of her husband, Dennis Gormley, on Geocities and Angelfire. We find two pages about the police department of Camden, New Jersey, where Dennis is a policeman, with a number of recommended links about the police, criminal investigations, and forensic technologies, and another set of subjects, aside from "my wife's Web site," a link to a horse-racing site and another site with *Con te partirò* sung by Andrea Bocelli, "the tenor of the 90's."

In short, from the Madonna to the police and criminal investigations and horse racing and from there, depending on your tastes, on to yet other subjects, with a generalized dispersion of the individuality that was originally supposed to be represented, and a fragmentation and overlap of the themes through which someone had intended to present their individual personality.

If you take as a whole the devout communication present on the Web, especially the Marian subset of that communication—including the personal Web pages—what emerges is an inconfigurable flow of messages that submerges and fragments everything that passes through it: subjects and themes. The distinctive features, which represent arguments or human beings, are so interconnected and intermingled that all possibilities of precise delimitation—of themes or persons—are undercut, with the general de- or pluri-identification.

On the Web, every element of an autobiography obtained through hypertextual juxtapositions harks back, not only to the rest of the hypertext, as was the intention of the autobiographer, but also to the rest of the Web, or perhaps we should say, to the array of paths through the Web that are available to the surfer who happened upon the autobiography. And between the two intentions, what prevails is the second one, or we should say, the second ones, since each surfer will have her own array. The unitary nature of a classical biography, that is, a biography that works by narration, is fragmented not only by the hypertextual dimension, but also by the forms of the new juxtapositions that the various surfers will each produce. In the end, there remains nothing or almost nothing that can evoke the biological, psychological, and sociological point of reference constituted by the person about whom the hypertext was intended to "speak."

Each surfer is confronted with hypertextual fragments. What scrolls past him, in the search for "apparitions" on personal Web sites, is always a reference to something else, a text that refers to other texts, which in their turn reflect yet other texts, all entirely devoid of any context other than the general context of the Web, which is to say no context at all.

At the physical site of an apparition, it is possible to glimpse at once the general features of the institution, the symbolism, and the people; it is possible to identify the general structures of the ecclesiastical institution within the context of the specific dialogue with the charism that has been produced in that place; that symbolism is interpreted into action as the actualization of the general symbolic schemes of visionary Catholicism; you will meet and you will become acquainted with—and even talk with—people who are concrete creators and consumers of these general and abstract models. It is precisely in the ongoing lives of the worshipers that it becomes possible to glimpse the features of mediation between biographical experiences and the collective themes and forms of symbolism, that is, between the people who feel, say, and do, and the general institutions within which their experiences become possible.

The Internet, on the other hand, produces a sort of abyss between institution and life, since neither of the two is capable of recontextualizing itself while including the other, which is the sort of thing that does happen offline, where an institution takes concrete form in human beings, whose life experiences, in turn, become possible only within a larger institutional context. At a physical site of an apparition, the visionary context is established by the institutions that make it possible and by the concrete experiences that implement it. In a virtual location, a homogeneous context of the institution could survive only if it comprised strictly and exclusively institutional elements, excluding all biographical features. Inversely, a unified biographical context could survive only if it were rigorously linked to its own biographical features, ruling out all possibilities of flight into thematic and institutional elements that can open the floodgates of dispersion. This is because there is no physical location in which the macro is reproduced in the micro, the global in the local, the institutional in the personal.

In a virtual place, what counts is a temporary micro that manages to echo, with thousands of subtle facets, the entire patrimony of virtualizations and actualizations. The worshipful surfer will find herself, involuntarily, obliged to decontextualize and recontextualize everything that comes within reach, extracting everything from the context in which it was produced or into which it was inserted, connecting it to other things, other relatively provisional contexts, and to virtually all other things. Even when the surfer preserves the contextualizations offered by the site, she does nothing other than to use her own power of recontextualizing according to the possibilities at her disposal, which only coincidentally correspond to the configuration of the site itself.

And so the personal Web sites that deal with visionary phenomena (among other things) implement twice the operation of de-recontextualization: the first time, through the juxtapositions created by the Web master among themes belonging to various contexts, each implicitly decontextualizing the other; the second time by an analogous and even more powerful operation on the part of the surfer.

Let it be clear that specific contexts exist on the Web, within the general context of digital communications. I myself, in my research, have gone in search of specific sites that fit into the context of devotional, Marian, and visionary sites. I have looked for them using keywords of the same kind. The sites that I found were linked, except for specific situations, with other sites of the same sort. Then there was a more general Catholic context which was presented to me very clearly. But the point is that this specific context—Catholic, Marian, visionary—is by and large the product of movements of hardware and software, search engines, and keywords. It is mechanical. It is organized in virtue of homogeneous technological movements, to which need not be added, in order for them to function, any common cultural system.

In recent years, there has been a reaction against the theses that described electronic communications as devoid of social signals capable of defining the context of communications itself. In Italy, for instance, Giuseppe Mantovani claims that these theses are naïve or obsolete, inasmuch as the context of the communications does not consist "merely of exchanges of information between people who are present in a single physical environment, but is rather structured by the cognitive and cultural resources that allow people to agree with one another, at least by and large, concerning the significance that they bestow upon the situations that they are experiencing and the meaning that they attribute to the information that they are exchanging."[168]

In particular, in communications on the Internet, according to Mantovani, as soon as "the discourse shifts away from the most superficial sort of conversational banalities" to topics that have to do with the expertise of the correspondents—be they psychiatrists or Tibetan monks, electronics gurus or jazz saxophonists—or to topics "that establish the personal and social identities of the interlocutors," then it becomes impossible to pretend or to trick people. There emerges the context of shared attributions of meaning to things, a preexisting context or a context that has developed within the ongoing communication, and that is when identities emerge.

But on personal Web pages with Marian devotional links, this is exactly what cannot emerge. If the sites were devoted solely to the Madonna and if those sites were put together only by theologians, bishops, priests, and lay scholars of "Mariology," that is, by "experts," then there is little doubt that this would be the case. But that is not how things work. All the worshipers speak about the Madonna with self-conferred confidence and authority, mixing that topic with an entirely different series of topics. In a situation of this sort, it is not possible to fool oneself about the existence of a unifying context for the significance—based on authority or expertise or a relationship between the role and the discourse. The phenomenon is precisely that of a discourse of Mariology merged with "the most superficial sort of conversational banalities," which it is, actually, only from the point of view of a grim and critically demanding Web surfer: that is, from the point of view of the Web master. In fact, that which at first glance might seem frivolous and superficial is his own life—or perhaps we should say, the portrayal (sincere? fictional?) of his life.

And so, is Medjugorje the context of significance amid the topics of apparitions, or is it Medjugorje and a popular soccer team in the private experience of Paolo Ruata? Who or what authorizes the selection of one context or another, if not the interests, the expectations, and the preferences of the individual surfer? Do there exist stable contexts, then, independent of the actions of the surfer in question? And what constraining force can those contexts exert?

In reality the contexts proliferate and are fragmented endlessly in the individualized dust cloud that is the Web; no one is able to win out over others, precisely because of the absence of those legitimizing structures of institutional jurisdictions that exist offline.

In a certain sense, the Web imitates life, because like life it resists any static institutional definitions, enclosed fields in which only the normative grass grows; instead it shifts incessantly, overflowing and remixing. Like life, it inserts faith into an overall experience, in which there is also space for your favorite soccer team and your interest in canoeing and for much more, with hierarchies that are never definitive. And it makes this operation plausible and legitimate, despite the operation of any institution that separates things, rendering them hierarchical in a definitive form.

But at the same time the Web can marginalize life, because it simulates life, it replaces it, it is a surrogate for life.

Or it can expand and broaden life, with its new virtual dimension. But what happens to life when it discovers and immerges itself in a new, unexpected, and unexplored region?

It may happen, as Sherry Turkle suggests, that this provides a great opportunity for self-awareness and reflection.[169] But this is not an ironbound rule.

It may happen that one is overwhelmed. But not always.

And in the final analysis, that question is not the subject of this book.

Virtual Communities

Being born in a traditional location (a site) means entering into a world where there is already a religion composed of rituals, beliefs, myths, habits, and devotions, thoroughly interrelated with the rest of the social reality. It means submitting to, more than choosing, this *religio*, this community, which in turn, expects from birth forward that the new subject will adhere, and that all this will take place without the subject having to do anything other than simply live in that place.

Entering into the Web, on the other hand, is the result of an impulse on the part of the surfer, driven either by curiosity or by a specific search for information or images (a "compelling vacuum"). The surfer sets out in search of information. With respect to the original and total inclusion from birth onward in a geographic and cultural site, travel through the Web is a series of actualizations of temporally limited virtual sites, even when it has to do with Web communities. Membership in a virtual community (whether it is a newsgroup, a mailing list, or a chat) is always dependent upon a voluntary option on the part of the surfer who belongs to that community, and only as long as that surfer belongs to that community. To pass from a geographic and cultural community—which is always there, and whether those who are physical members (more than symbolic members) like it or not, they are locked into its existential totality—to a virtual community—which exists only when the surfer "opens" the site in question, and which disappears when the surfer "closes" it, at his discretion, means passing from the solidity of collective institutions (themselves, it must be admitted, "invented" and produced, but with a far different relationship with the time and use of common energies) to the lightness of individual states of mind, from the resistance and inertia of "history" to the fragility and inconsistency of happenstance and random chance. It means transferring the "objectivity" of the things of the world that is outside me to the subjectivity of my persona, my screen, the corpus callosum that connects my mind and the hardware. It means entrusting to the individual an almost absolute power to enter or exit any group or any community. Certainly, offline as well, an individual has this power. But at what price can she exercise the power? Painful good-byes, long voyages, emigration, tragic separations from one's native community. Online, all that is required is a click.

And yet the communities of Marian worshipers on the Web portray themselves as solid universes:

> I love this site [*Marian Discussion*]. I go nowhere else. we speak our
> minds, instruct, laugh and pray together. . . . Jessie.[170]

> I feel that this Catholicity Marian crosstalk is in itself a community
> of believers from which we all can gather strength and contribute to
> one another's growth in our love of Jesus and His mother. . . .
> Bunny.[171]

> Good Morning My Sweet Ones!! If anyone would care to join me, I am
> offering up my day, my work, my driving, my suffering . . . but most
> of all . . . the JOY in my heart . . . for all the intentions of my Brothers
> and Sisters at Crosstalk to the lovely Blessed Mother. May The Joy of His
> Gentleness Embrace Us All Today. Adrienne.[172]

A response to this last message came, the same day:

> Yes. . . . I shall join you in the JOY in your heart. I feel good about all of
> us. We are a family who is learning to Love. In the Two Hearts, Laura.

Even if this family meets mystically in common prayer—and this is not far from the idea of the church as a unity of triumphant, suffering, living levels—in concrete experience it is above all in the privacy of the computer of each of them, that is, in a certain sense, within each of the members of that family or in the corpus callosum linking that member with the computer. The Web links personal computers, but it is not capable of providing external rituals, or procedures of visible community self-recognition, recognizable, and above all, independent of the continual reconfirmation of community that every action of each member—actualization—puts into play. The experience of feeling oneself to be a member of the discussion group family is entirely solipsistic, private, if not ghostly.

For that matter, entering a virtual community while sitting at your desk, at home, may correspond with your exiting your own local physical community. Not in the sense that one thing causes the other, since there is no question of so mechanical a relationship, but rather in the sense that one will inevitably influence the other, since it can justify it, attenuate it, and so on. In the most explicit cases, the success of the first type of community can accompany the failure and collapse of the second type of community, which is to say, it can lead to a self-isolation in terms of one's own social milieu, which can in turn be caused precisely by the contrast that is perceived between a positive aspect of the former and a negative aspect of the latter.

Here is an exchange of correspondence from the *Marian Discussion* group concerning experiences and impressions of the presence of evil:

> I . . . feel a "sense of evil" and the more I pray, the more I feel it. My husband, wanted to take me out on the town a few weeks ago, He took me downtown to this bar that you had to go underground to get in. A real trendy place. I had such a sense of evil that I was almost sick. I didn't say anything to my husband because he is already sick of me talking but it's nice to know that someone else feels this too. Your Christian Sister, Adrienne.

> Dear Adrienne, I agree with you. I think we, as the remnant (which I truly believe we are), are attacked continually. And as we pray, more and more, good and evil become more clear—more black and white. People begin to think we are 'crazy.' Remember that being despised by the world for the name of Jesus is a tremendous grace. When I go to get togethers with my in-laws, I have to excuse myself continually, because I do not condone the conversations (they must think I have a bladder problem). However, I have found that I can retreat into my soul and pray for them while I am with them. Remember always, as Our Mother tells us: "Pray, pray, pray." . . . Terry.[173]

Dear Adrienne . . . Sometimes I'll go places or walk past people (or even drive by them) and get a strong sense of evil around the area. One time I went into a store at a shopping mall where I had not been in a long time. When I went in the discomfort was so great it was like I was being forced out of the store or removed from the store. . . . Diane.[174]

I am very relieved that others of you can feel the evil around us. Some of those i have told about this think i am paranoid. Peace, Sue.[175]

Thanks to this list, many of us have found the spiritual support from our friends that we lacked in our "physical" surroundings. I know that my time in front of my computer now is spent with people who share many of my views, challenge me in my Faith, and teach me how to be a better Catholic. . . . Tom.[176]

Certainly, these feelings towards one's own environment, the people one is close to, one's own physical world, may derive from personal experiences, long-standing problems, or even conditions of paranoia, as the criticism leveled at Sue implied, and not caused by the Web at all. But here we are not looking for causes; rather we are observing that the success of virtual communities and the crisis of offline social communities, including religious communities, are interrelated phenomena, though in multiform and complex ways.

Dear Pat, This is why this group is so wonderful. We just have to ask for prayers and all are ready to help us. The Gospel today is all about that to love our neighbors from afar not just the ones we know round us. . . . Rita.

Here the "afar" is the virtual group of correspondents, the "neighbors" are the relatives and friends of one's own social setting. The very evangelical Christian precept to "love thy neighbor" has been successfully twisted to fit this new form of community affiliation.

But moving away from your neighbors also means losing or decisively undermining the power of the cultural instruments with which we recognize others and their ideas, with which we judge the affiliation or lack thereof to a shared ideological universe. A chat line or a mailing list that is too generic fails to permit easy recognition of not only identities, but even of the cultural and ideological horizons of the participants. Over time, it is always possible to establish recognition, but at the beginning especially, one hovers in an atmosphere of uncertainty, even if the mailing list is organized around powerful shared interests, as is the case, for instance, with Marian or devotional mailing lists. In fact, there is not always an entirely precise ideological or cultural discriminating factor. In *Marian Discussion*, for example, ideological positions can be quite distant one from another, at times even clashing violently, so that one or another of the correspondents either leaves or is asked to do so. At other times, you may notice the coexistence of radically differing religious orientations, as if the participants had decided simply to ignore one another. For example, you may find an exasperated, practically cartoonish and unwittingly ironic devotionalism, as in the following fragment of a message:

> Every house should have Holy Water, Blessed Salt, and Blessed Oil, Sacramentals, Sacramentals, Sacramentals. . . . The evil one hates blessed salt! It stays longer than holy water and you can put it everywhere!!!! A little dab of blessed salt makes every meal better! Blessed Oil is usually olive oil but other vegetable oils will do as well. Here are the reasons for the Water, Salt, and Oil. Holy Water is the symbol of life and our baptism. Blessed Salt is the symbol of perseverance. Blessed Oil is the symbol of healing. Father John Scanlin would make a special trip to the salt isle everytime he went to the grocery store. Yep, he would bless all of the salt! Salt last a long time as well. . . . Paul.[177]

Alongside viewpoints of this sort, however, in the same mailing list we find others that are more educated, refined, and open-minded:

> As DOCTOR-St Theresa of Liseux said "God's will for each of us is as different as the difference in our faces." -So as catholics we do not have to believe in the same prophecies or practice the same spirituality. These things are like the different melodies we sing in chanting the creed. You might like gregorian—i might like mozart or comtemprory christian; the melody dosent matter as long as we hold to the same creed. . . . Anthony.[178]

Keep in mind that participating in discussion groups and mailing lists is often anything but a part-time job or a minor commitment. The quantity of correspondence that can be exchanged is overwhelming. I have direct experience of this phenomenon. Despite the fact that I have contacted numerous mailing lists, I was able to subscribe to only five, and those were not at the same time. In fact, even though I did not actively write letters, unlike most people, when I was doing my research I would receive an average of fifty letters a day, and at especially busy times, 100–150 a day. All I had to do was go four or five days without checking my e-mail, and the computer would be overwhelmed with two or three hundred messages. Jill, in *Marian Discussion*,[179] wrote that her server had been down for two days, and that now she has six hundred letters to answer (or perhaps just to read?). Sarah Burnett in *Catholicity* complains that because of her laziness, she now has 3,800 unread messages and that she feels frustrated and tempted to delete them all.[180] Joe Moorman works at home for part of the week: on those days he sits at his computer and checks his e-mail inbox, where he sometimes finds as many as eight thousand unopened or unerased messages, among which he can choose by name or topic.[181] Joseph and Maria Collura tell us that they subscribe to fifteen different mailing lists.[182] In *Profezia On Line* Mario Gregorio tells us that he is busy reading messages in almost five hundred lists. In *Piccolo Gregge*, Luciano answers as follows to Mauro who, in July, expressed concern over the fact that the number of messages had dropped from twenty or thirty a day to two or three a day:

> Let me try to explain it to you. I am a subscriber to dozens of ML and these days, from the 240 e-mails a day that I used to receive, I am down to less than half that. The reasons are pretty evident, people are on holiday or else they aren't in the house in front of their computer, they are out and about. For that matter, most of the members are very young, and they are either finishing their school exams or else they are out of school and they are away.[183]

"I have to ask though, how much time some of you spend at the computer a day to post and respond to so many messages," asks Ann of the others. "Where do you find the time?" And someone replies, "It's called 'sleep deprivation' ;-)"[184]

These virtual Marian communities, which as you can see, take up time—even if there are those who recommend using the "delete" key for messages of no particular interest—are very demanding communities as well in terms of the depiction of the emotions involved. In that connection, it is not easy to feel certain that the depiction actually corresponds to real emotions. This is a problematic element of virtual communities; one is tempted to say that this is a weakness of those communities. It may well be that an "I love you" is real, that "I wept when I read your message" actually does correspond to tears on the face of the person who wrote the message; but certainly there is no instrument on the Web that allows us to have that certainty.

Now, it is not that outside the Web "I love you" and "I hate you" are not representations, that speaking face-to-face is somehow more "sincere" than writing online. But outside the Web there are institutional cultural models, which certainly do nothing to make life particularly sincere, but which do lay out the rules of appropriateness for the various representations, making it so that they are considered adequate for the "expression" of feelings. The manifestation of condolences, the expression of joy, the interplay of reserve and expansiveness all correspond to very specific cultural canons, which vary from group to group and make social life a venue in which we recognize each other sufficiently adequately to coproduce on a continual basis the collective representation of the feelings, the idea of people that we have, of their emotions and their duties, to be clear and sincere: in short, the implicit anthropology, whereby feelings and emotions come to life. Communities are built and continually reinforced by respect for the norms of social representation, which may include, for instance, etiquette, sharing, compassion, and detachment. Feelings and emotions are, in a certain sense, the product of these norms, or at least they can live only in the cradle of these norms. In other words, the social dimension of those norms is upstream from the individual development of feelings; in effect, it produces them, it determines them, or at least it conditions them.

But what happens in the communities of the Web? The frequent gathering of numerous people who, mutually, on the outside, ensure the form of representation, is impossible inside the Web: the community is always a voluntary individual option, in the sense that it exists, for me, only as long as I choose to form part of it. But it is especially the complex framework of the numerous media of representation present outside the Web, based on the presence/absence of bodies—writing, images, voices, times, settings, places—that is reduced here to a single medium, that represented by messages sent by modem. It is in this medium that the expression of my feelings and my ideas must be concentrated, and it is there that I must perceive the feelings and ideas of others, in effect almost exclusively through the use of words. There are unwritten rules of netiquette, but they have to do with a basic level of courtesy and manners; they cannot go so far as to model the complex forms of relationships and expressions. Those are generally left up to the effects, which may be haphazard, of the integration of machines and users, and tend to leave something to desire in terms of models of expectations upon which most human relationships are based, at least offline.

And so, in a certain sense, writing and reading on the screen of your computer—nothing more than that—and yet at the same time being profoundly caught up in a network of shared emotions, excitement, expectations, and hopes constitute a singular experience of inventing an external world that is entirely internal to the computer screen, and yet at the same time also internal to the self,[185] the self that is the agent of those external movements that could not exist without your hands on the keyboard and your head in the software and the desires. A self, for that matter, that is destructured by the phantom game for which you wind up becoming a theater.

In order to assure that not everything depends upon words, online exchanges have been endowed with a graphic lexicon of little signs, which are meant to add power to the depiction of the writer's emotions. These lexicons include dozens of terms. The most common signs are the smiley-face, :-), and the frowny-face, :-(. In chats, then, these signs are replaced by little icons, the so-called emoticons. Another way of depicting emotions is to use all capital letters. Being familiar with these resources is important if you wish to correspond properly:

Dear Group Members: Earlier today or maybe yesterday, I wrote two posts. It was brought to my attention that writing in full caps is a sign of anger or yelling. I apologize for this as it was not my intent to yell or show anger. It was merely my inexperience at computer talk and my sin of laziness. I hope I didn't offend anyone and if I did I'm truly sorry. Please forgive my inexperience. I will try to do my best and show proper behavior in my future posts. Thank you for understanding. A newcomer, Val.[186]

Some correspondents use other graphic resources to convey standard feelings. For instance, here is how Joe wished a happy birthday to Patrice in the mailing list Catholicity:

"HHHHHhhaaaaaaaaaaaapppppppyyyyyyyyy biiirrrrrrrrrrrrrrrthhhh
hddddaaaaayyyyy toooooooooooooooo youuuuuuuuuuuuuu.
"HHHHHhhaaaaaaaaaaaapppppppyyyyyyyyy biiirrrrrrrrrrrrrrrthhhh
hddddaaaaayyyyy tooooooooooooooooooooooooooo youuuuuuuu
uuuuu.
"HHHHhaaaaaaaaaapppppppppppyyyyyyyyyy
Biiiiiiiiiiiiiiiiiirrrrrrrrrrrrrrrrrrrttttttttthhhhhhhddddddddaaaaaaaaa
ayyyyyyyyyy
Deaaaaarrrrrrrrrrrrr Paaaaaaaattttttttttrrrrrriiiiiiiiiiiii, iiiiiiiiiiiiiiiic
ccceeeeeee
"HHHHHhhaaaaaaaaaaaapppppppyyyyyyyyy biiirrrrrrrrrrrrrrrthhhh
hddddaaaaayyyyy toooooooooooooooo youuuuuuuuuuuuuu.
(verse TWOOOOOO)
"MMMMmmmmaaaaaaayyyyyyyyyy the Dearrrrrrrr Loooooooorrrrrd-
ddd
Bleeeeeeeeessssssssss Youuuuuuuuuuuuuuuuuuuu.
"MMMMmmmmaaaaaaayyyyyyyyyy the Dearrrrrrrr Loooooooorrrrrd-
ddd
Bleeeeeeeeessssssssss Youuuuuuuuuuuuuuuuuuuu.
"MMMMmmmmaaaaaaayyyyyyyyyy the Dearrrrrrrr Loooooooooo
rrrrrddd
blllllllleeeeeeeeessssssss Patttttrrrrrrrrrrrriiiiiiiiiiiiiiiiiii, iiiiiiiiiii
iccccccccceee
Mayyyyyyyyyyyy theeee Deeeeeeeaaaaaaarrrrrrr Looooooorrrrrrr
rrrrrddd
Bleeeeeeeeeeeeeeessssssssssssssssss Yoooooooouuuuuuuuuuuuuj'
May God bless you with a day filled with smiles.
Joe M.[187]

But can the virtual community provide a form for conveying feelings
only with these means? Doesn't the risk of misunderstanding lie just
around the corner? Berretti and Zambardino have this to say:

The problem is the misunderstanding of the "tones" of the words. On
the monitor appear a series of words, which are read in the mind as if
they had been "pronounced." In everyday language, we normally say:
"Tom told me that . . . ," but in reality Tom wrote me that. . . . And yet
this imaginary tone of voice cannot escape the process of being read
on a monitor and goes on to form the perceived telematic personality

of an individual. "G. is very aggressive," "P. is quite destructive": then you happen to share a cup of tea with G. and you will find that he never looks anyone in the eye and speaks in a tiny timid voice. It was his written persona that was aggressive.[188]

Vincent Kaufman has written a very good book about the correspondence of great authors, and he admits in his introduction that he was never sure if he was dealing "with someone who was living or with someone who was writing."[189] But the worth and the roles of Kafka, Proust, Baudelaire, Flaubert, and other authors are, for us readers, entirely confined to their writings. To know things about Rilke or Mallarmé, apart from their writing, makes sense only within the context of understanding their writing. And so a question about the dichotomy between life and writing, as far as these writers are concerned, provides only a further confirmation of exclusive interest in the writing, at least for us as readers. But for a community that lives only through individual choice and through the medium of writing, and yet which does not recognize its members only as a community of writers, but rather of people who have lives outside of the writing they do, this alternative takes on a very different meaning. Let us not forget that the Web is a great jungle gym for the interplay of identity, fiction, concealment, and masquerading, carried on, to a greater or lesser degree, consciously.

And yet the correspondents seem to have no doubt that Pat, Joe, and Joseph are living persons, that they are more than just "someone who writes." This is unquestionably a product of constant participation in correspondence groups, which leads one to become accustomed to certain personalities through the repetition of elements of individual recognition, so that only rarely does the suspicion arise that it is not possible to penetrate behind the construction and manipulation of an electronic mask, as in this case: "We may have your e-mail address, but that doesn't tell us who you are," as Theresa wrote.[190]

But the decisive element for conferring certainty upon the identification of writing and real life is, in a circular manner, precisely the vast array of written depictions of feelings, emotions, and impulses, within an atmosphere of very intense love. Already the Jesus and the Madonna in the messages that circulate cry, suffer, and are generally quite emotional. The requests attributed to them for prayer, fasting, and conversion are always set within dramatic contexts, full of pain and suffering, with only distant promises of joy and salvation. Consequently, in relation to this style of communication established for relationships between heaven and earth, we quite often see the same style used in the messages among worshipers. And so we have worshipers who weep as they pray and worshipers who are deeply moved when they read about those who weep. Tears fill their eyes as they read about the tears that filled other eyes. Words that touch their hearts, and hearts that dictate words. All of these exaggerated depictions of love and emotion are part of an attempt to construct a strong, intense "theater," that will leave no doubts about its "sincerity." To that, a celestial sanction is sometimes added, when the emotions are no longer seen as mere human expressions, but rather as mysterious divine signs. For example, in the face of an overabundance of these forms of expression, there begins to arise a fear of negative, diabolical reactions. And so, when a Croatian named Petar finds himself weeping as he recites the rosary without being able to explain the reason, Mike, an American, points out that if there was no conscious reason for him to cry, then it was probably the Holy Ghost who was causing his emotion, in order to attract his attention to his sins and to open his heart to God. But if that is true, then he would have to expect a "counter-attack" that will attempt to distract his attention.[191]

Heightened tempers and nerves rubbed raw—that is, a vivid depiction of the same—often lead to the exact opposite of expressions of affection, that is, to harsh conflict; groups and grouplets tend to form, admonishing one another in turn, criticizing, accusing, engaging in verbal aggression, until finally someone gives up and vanishes from the list. This is "physiological" to the Web, characterized by "flame wars":

> The greatest degree of communications, the "world at your doorstep," produces the greatest degree of fragmentation. It is as if in the vast expanse of a jungle the tribes were to split up into ever-smaller clans. And so the Real Time Tribes create social interaction, communities, and communications only at the price of the emergence of small and exceedingly small clans which tend to be quite isolated. The Great Space seems to need to recreate claustrophobic cells.[192]

As we have seen, in the Marian lists conflict arises most frequently about the most famous, most venerated, but also the most widely demonized contemporary apparition: Medjugorje. From time to time, like flame springing up suddenly from slumbering ashes with a gust of wind, this conflict-ridden debate, never wholly settled, flares up suddenly, and in the course of a few days violently immolates all of the participants with its violence.

> I think your reply to my reply about your comments was one of the most vicious attacks on me personally I have come across . . . Joyce.[193]

> Again, John, you demonstrate why you are a complete idiot. . . . If you try to use my email to sell me something, I'll hunt you down and parody you. This is your first and last warning! Karl.[194]

> I must admit I have never heard so many insulting words for many a years for my beliefs. The fact that they are coming from so called Catholics is mind boggling.[195]

> I consider the tone of Mr Ford's comments to be more than a little hysterical in his defence of these critics of Medjugorje. My comment is that Satan chooses who Satan chooses to do his work and perhaps there are some people who really need to examine their own ideas very carefully before they expose themselves in such an open way. . . . Margaret.[196]

The weakness of these communities, however devoted they may be to the continuous expression of feelings, both in the form of bonding and affection and in the form of conflict, lies in the fact that they cannot engage anyone to the point that they are not free to disappear suddenly and without any explicit reason, without a trace. There are those who leave angrily or in disappointment, there are also those who are invited to leave. But the largest number of those who leave do so suddenly and without any advance notice. And this is certainly an aspect that calls into question the supposed equivalence between writing and life that is touted in virtual Marian communities. Even the formula for resigning from a mailing list of this sort is emblematic. In order to "leave," a member must write in the body of an e-mail message the word "unsubscribe," and then they are gone, vanishing into the void, without explanations, without a trace. You can spend time exchanging regards and proclaiming affection with your correspondents and then, suddenly, you can vanish with a simple "unsubscribe." Certainly, this is not how everyone leaves. There are some who offer this reason or that, but technically, and therefore, institutionally, you can leave without a word. And, for that matter, you can enter without any real obstacles. Some mailing lists say that acceptance is at the moderator's discretion, but usually all that is required is a generic declaration that a new subscriber will accept the mailing list's netiquette. For other mailing lists, the same simple formula, "subscribe," suffices.

As we saw in the message of *Piccolo Gregge* quoted above, it is possible to shift from twenty or thirty messages daily to two or three messages without any of the "missing" being obliged to say anything to justify their disappearance. And this, mysteriously, can happen even in periods that are distant from the holidays. Philip, from Australia, wrote on 11 November to *Marian Discussion* wondering, "Hi list, where is everyone? It's not vacation time in U.S. is it? I've hardly seen a message over the past few days. Is America still on line? We down here in Australia are waiting to hear from you all. In Jesus and Mary, Philip."[197]

For a few days, almost no messages at all had arrived in Phil's computer in-box, down in Australia. In response to his inquiries, the answers finally began to trickle in, first one, then another; someone says that she chose to remain silent in order to allow the disputes that had raged over the previous days to settle down; someone else jokes about the tornado that touched down in his neighborhood, someone else mentions other reasons. But that is how it is: the community of *Marian Discussion*, which is admittedly one of the liveliest and the most popular, can experience sudden slowdowns, to the point of almost vanishing, since it is the product of individual choice. When the individuals fall silent, the community, lacking anything other than the sum of the individual members, falls silent.

As in other types of online communities, which often organize offline meetings, in Marian communities as well an effort may be made to strengthen the ties outside the Web. But in part because of the distances separating the correspondents, and in part because of a certain lack of interest in physical encounters, it is mostly online that the correspondents who worship the Virgin Mary attempt to reinforce their ties and create solid communities, with instruments directly linked to their shared Catholic faith.

One way of testing the strength and cohesiveness of the community is to exchange news and information. We have already seen how the newly converted Anne obtained 158 responses in just twenty hours for her request for information that might be helpful on her new religious path. Susan, who recently subscribed to the *Marian Discussion* mailing list, asked for help in learning more about the Madonna: "Can any one help me out? I have need to read, I would like to learn some prayers etc."[198] Others ask for more specific information: "Can the green scapular—asks Wendee—work for people who are not sick and who do believe?"[199]; "Can somebody explain me what is SPEAKING IN TONGUES????" asks another.[200]

There are also correspondents who suffer from physical or psychic illnesses and who exchange e-mails in an attempt to establish a small community of sufferers:

> hi please pray for me. i suffer from clinical depression . . . i am so sick that i want this nuclear war to come soon so i can die and be with God. all theses messages, this world in itself is so very depressing.[201]

> I, too, suffer from clinical depression; plus meniere's disease, migraines, and a few other complaints that seem small in comparison. . . . If you want, why not keep in touch? We can commiserate and help each other? I got a PTM job today, but if you can hang on a few hours, I can answer your email. So many times, when I've felt so low, I wished I had someone I could email, when I was at my lowest. Would you consent? And you could email *me* also, if you would like. Like a mini-support group.[202]

But aside from e-mail exchanges of this sort, which are not very frequent, and which sooner or later drop away into private exchanges, concealed from all the others, one of the most effective ways of creating a community is in any case that of referring to devotions, and especially to prayers for this or that specific purpose. Not a day passes in the storm of correspondence without someone asking for prayers on behalf of their own sicknesses or the sicknesses of relatives, for family crises, lost jobs, tests or exams that are about to be taken. Every so often a correspondent asks for everyone to pray together for a shared objective. For instance, Laura Zink asked everyone to dedicate shared prayers for the victims of natural calamities around the world.[203] On more than one occasion, Laura Zink had also proposed simultaneous prayers around the world, to be done online: discussions had then followed concerning the schedule that would allow everyone to participate, depending on time zones, with considerations of who would have to wake up at night and who would have to interrupt their work during the day.

The community also forms around devotional objects. Fergal O'Neill, from Ireland, is twenty-seven years old, and for twenty years now he has been wearing the "miraculous medal" of Saint Catherine Labouré. Now he has obtained three hundred medals, and he wants to distribute them free of charge to anyone who requests one.[204] Three days later he reports that he was been overwhelmed with requests from the United States, England, Italy, Colombia, the Philippines, Japan, Russia, Alaska [*sic*], and Canada. He adds that he will personally pay for shipping for anyone who cannot afford it. Kellie Detrick, who had not read Fergal's original message, knows nothing about these miraculous medals and asks for more information, but in the meanwhile wants Fergal to send her ten medals, and asks how much she will have to pay.[205] In the meanwhile, Fergal, thrilled by this success, has gone even further. He now reports that he has decided to offer a gift to the Lord on the occasion of the new millennium: a 10 megabyte Web page, with a sacramental image of Jesus:

> It is for me a place of "Virtual" Perpetual Adoration. You are welcome to this page in order to spend a prayer in contemplation of this great mystery. I get great peace knowing that I have a place to go if I wish to gaze on an image of the Blessed Sacrament. My main mission on this page is to get 1,000,000 prayers offered to the heart of Jesus, again as a small gift for such a Incomprehensible Mystery. Please tell as many people as you can to visit my page at http://www.iol.ie/ fergalmj. Remember say a small prayer for any intention and visit as often as you like. Please help me attain this goal as it would be one big consolation to a HEART that receives such little love. Peace, Fergal O'Neill Dublin, Ireland.[206]

This example of O'Neill speaks eloquently of the extremely ductile and unstable methods by which virtual communities form around the subject of Marian devotion, where—as we can clearly see from the case under examination—the virtual and online dimension of the devotion aims implicitly to replace the devotion that focuses on a physical community and the physically concrete sacrament of the Eucharist.

At this point, it will come as no surprise that in all the months during which I followed English-language discussion groups and Marian mailing lists—several thousand messages in all—only rarely did I find any reference to parish life, to the private dimension of liturgical celebration, to the sharing of religious practices in a local community. There are a few references, here and there, surfacing in biographical references, which sometimes discuss these subjects in harsh, critical terms.

Here too the case of the Internet has not been an asteroid that plunged to earth, overturning a previously static and traditional situation. Modernity had already greatly weakened affiliations with religious communities. Social mobility had also produced a corresponding religious and devotional mobility. The believer was no longer tied to the place set aside for the expression of her faith; instead she had a chance to choose, to move. "Studies of religious practices in urban settings clearly show that the faithful tend to break down less by place of residence and more in terms of personal preference," says Salvatore Abbruzzese.[207]

And the reasons for the choices have to do with different pastoral and liturgical styles, in a context where personal choice on the one hand and religious mobility on the other hand are crucial. It comes as no surprise then that the parish church and community should encounter difficulties, as the site of an administrative division of worshipers, in specific contrast with the availability of personal choice, which tends to reject the forms of traditional institutions, and to move toward emotional forms of legitimizing faith, or toward devotional clusters that emphasize the sense of membership, the "creation of community," as in the post—Vatican Council movements.[208]

The Internet extends and radicalizes these processes, since not only does it affirm the freedom of choice of the individual, it makes it permanent: the Web surfer never gives up his freedom of choice in a definitive community commitment to reciprocal recognition, whether it is to a group, a movement, or an association. Every time that he goes online, he confirms the community; in other words, each time, he has an option not to confirm the commitment that he has entered into. And so it can be hypothesized as a devotional double world: the world of choices that in some sense bind and constrain, though never in a definitive manner, offline, and the choices whereby capriciously and pleasantly it is possible to vary, repeatedly, even during the course of a single browse and even simultaneously, opening up numerous sites and interacting with numerous virtual realities. By reading the mail, you can see that for a good number of correspondents, offline liturgical participation fails to provide the same pleasure as virtual participation. In other words, for the latter, the Web is an occasion through which the expression of faith becomes primarily a private electronic exercise, in which others are sought out and found in unions that are at once mystical and electronic, amounting to the same thing in the final analysis: the mystic body is the virtual body on the Web.

But both of them, in the end, are elaborations of private emotions, of impulses that are both personal and indecipherable.

Such a radical inward passage is not devoid of consequences in the field of Catholic religion, public religion, ceremonial religion, with the mystical body represented physically by the faithful in the church, since the drastic dematerialization of religion experienced in a community context, replaced by the electronic movement of actualizations and virtualizations, winds up creating a crisis in the very notion, or, if you like, presence, of God.

In communities where everything is reabsorbed into the perimeter of the debate, to which each contributes with statements and by reading the responses to the statements; in which the existence of the Madonna is continually confirmed by the echo of her voice in the sites of apparitions, by the telematic voice of her visionaries and locutionists, and directly by her herself in the online messages; in which the devotional practice is reaffirmed by rosaries, scapulars, crowns, and little outfits; in which the mystery of faith dissipates with the hundreds of new revelations, in which visionaries are told everything about the destiny of mankind, and everything is verified and tested, what disappears is precisely God, that is, God the "object." It almost seems, from the point of view of virtual Marian communities, as if God belongs to a time gone by, in which reality consisted of "subjects" and "objects," things that existed independently of persons and persons who acted on things. And that nowadays, when that which is, is that which has been actualized, God has disappeared because he is a virtual entity that can never be actualized. In a mechanism of production of things, in which the subject that produces those things no longer counts, what counts instead is the automatic procedure of technology, no longer the productive intention but rather the network of virtualities, whose flow from time to time is condensed into actualizations that, as soon as they come into being, are repositioned as new virtualities. As a Subject of the highest degree, can God therefore expect to decide, manifest, conceal, that is, maintain his own autonomous subjective dimension of doing, of acting? When doing is not acting but rather an automatic and fortuitous movement?

Igino Domanin and Stefano Porro, among the few Catholic scholars who have examined the problem, in the concluding remarks in their book *Il Web sia con voi* seem to sense the challenge, but they do not fear it; indeed, they seem to hint at a new theological structure engendered by the Web:

The religious experience that is produced in the cosmos of the Web cannot be understood unless one overcomes a strictly anthropocentric viewpoint. God, the creator of humanity ex nihilo, determining the essence of the human race in the breath of the eternal moment, is replaced by a faith in a more enigmatic and suffering God, a God that manifests himself in the uncertain signs of chance.[209]

This is a sign of how the Internet creates formidable challenges to Catholicism, and not only to visionary Catholicism. But it is the latter, in its turn, in a singular but evident manner, that winds up working on the Web to place God himself in parentheses, reabsorbed in the incessant involutions of the technological circuits that take on the entire role of creating, without demanding or allowing human intention, much less divine intention. The diffuse visions, invisible to most people and yet perceived as more certain than that which the eyes perceive in the normality of everyday existence, pushed their way onto the Web, which is likewise invisible to everyone and yet certain, with the certainty of the everyday surfing that people allow themselves, producing this paradox of the certainty of the virtual, of the Web, of apparitions, and of the obsolescence of God, a pretechnological artifact of a naïvely anthropocentric world, now dissolved in a general swarm of singular and syncretic human-machine "marginal centralities."

To my brothers and sisters in Christ, Spread throughout the world (wide web). Especially in CATHOLICITY Greetings. . . . One of my problems is that I want to know it all. I want to read everything that catches my eye. And the internet is like a black hole, it sucks you into it's little world. Anyone who loves to read and has been in the EWTN library knows what I mean. There are also so many discussion groups and sooooo many people to converse with. . . . It's amazing how we can all communicate with each other over long distances. We type a messege and everyone gets it. This Techknowlegy . . . is sort of a physical earthly representation of Prayer. Mary gets all our prayer requests through the mainserver (JESUS) and than she looks at them (she has eternity to do so) and than talks to her son about them. I don't know how tech. works but I know it does, just like prayer. I don't know if I explained my self correctly but modern communications can help explain (in a limited sence) to Heavenly communication with God and the saints. With the Internet we have access to the whole world (those with a computer).

With Prayer we have access to the universe (people of all times and places). The UCS (universal communication System) is activated by anyone who has the heart modum to get on-line with God (by prayer), Mary, and the Saints. In his service, Mark S. Wilson.[210]

NOTES

Introduction

1. *Messages from On High,* Message 614, 27 August 1998; http://mfoh.com.

2. D. Van Meter, "There Walks a Lady We All Know," Introduction to the Web site http://members.aol.com/UticaCW//Mar-lady.html.

3. Paul Virilio, *The Information Bomb,* translated by Chris Turner (New York: Verso, 2000), 14–16.

4. C. Formenti, *Incantati dalla rete: Immaginari, utopie e conflitti nell'epoca di Internet* (Milan: Cortina, 2000).

5. "The 'prophets' of the Internet are visionaries, at least in the Anglo-Saxon sense of the word. Vint Cerf, one of the creators of the Internet, in discussing the development of his creation, said: 'I no longer simply believe in miracles, I rely on them.' " P. Casati, "Oltre Internet: Economia di una visione," *Aut-Aut* 289–90 (January–April 1999): 167.

6. "Pew Values Update: American Social Beliefs 1997–1987 [*sic*]; Individualism Still Strong"; http://www.people-press.org/valuetop.htm. Cf. M. O'Keefe, "America's Belief in Miracles Growing," *Oregonian,* 25 December 1998.

7. Comitato Italiano per il Controllo delle Affermazioni sul Paranormale, or the Italian Committee for the Investigation of Claims of the Paranormal.

8. Committee for the Scientific Investigation of Claims of the Paranormal.

9. A. Hoplight Tapia, "Y2K: Apocalyptic Opportunism," *Enculturation* 3, no. 1 (Spring 2000), available online: www.uta.edu./huma/enculturation/3_1/hoplight.html.

10. In *Marian Prophecy & Current Events Discussion List*, message 6 October 1998.

11. Ibid., message 1 October 1998.

12. See http://members.xoom.com/sjs/mary, messages 15 and 24 October 1998.

13. "[The beast] causeth all, both small and great, rich and poor, free and bond, to receive a mark in their right hand, or in their foreheads" (Revelation 13:16), King James Version).

14. P. Filo della Torre, "Con un chip nel braccio nasce il cyborg-professore," *La Repubblica*, 27 August 1998.

15. "Un microchip per leggere nel pensiero," *La Repubblica*, 29 August 2000. But scientific research into man/machine hybrids, for the most part for therapeutic purposes, is quite widespread. See Formenti, *Incantati dalla rete*, 142n3.

16. S. Rodotà, "Il secolo del Grande Fratello," *La Repubblica*, 20 January 1999.

17. See daily press for 4 July 2001.

18. The Italian political party Rifondazione Comunista (Communist Refoundation) expressed this concern; see daily press for 27 February 1999.

19. All sites of nineteenth-century apparitions—*Trans.*

20. See in general, concerning the relationship between the "naturalization" of technology and the loss of awareness, G. Longo, "Faccia e interfaccia," *Aut-Aut* 289–90 (January–April 1999).

21. L. Bianchi and L. Dogo, *Medjugorje (Testimonianze 1981–85)* (Gera Lario, 1985), 63.

22. *Medjugorje*, photocopy of pamphlet 4 of the prayer group Regina Pacis, Turin, p. 2.

23. E. Sala and P. Mantero, *Il miracolo di Medjugorje* (Rome: Edizioni Mediterranee, 1986), 101 and 148.

24. Marc Augé, *The War of Dreams: Studies in Ethno Fiction* (London: Pluto Press, 1999), 24.

25. John Davis, editor of *Wild Earth*, quoted in Formenti, *Incantati dalla rete*, 225.

26. http://puthenthope.tripod.com/Apparition.html.

27. G. Bettetini and F. Colombo, *Le nuove tecnologie della comunicazione* (Milan: Bompiani, 1994), 76–77.

28. http://www.garabandal.org/story.shtml.

29. See note 5, above.

30. R. Lellouche, "Théorie de l'écran," in the online magazine *Traverses* 2; http://www.cnac-gp.fr/traverses.

31. Concerning this pair of terms, of crucial importance to my analysis, see "Virtual Voyages," in chapter 4 below.

32. *"Dice che hanno visto la Madonna": Un caso di apparizioni in Campania* (Bologna: Il Mulino, 1990).

33. After ibid., *Il Cielo in Terra: Costruzioni simboliche di un'apparizione mariana* (Bologna: Il Mulino, 1992). Published in the United States with the title *Apparitions of the Madonna at Oliveto Citra*, translated by William Christian, Jr. (University Park: Pennsylvania State University Press, 1988).

Chapter 1

1. http://web.frontier.net/Apparitions/hillside.html.

2. W. A. Christian, Jr., "Religious Apparitions and the Cold War in Southern Europe," in *Religion, Power and Protest in Local Communities: The Northern Shore of the Mediterranean*, ed. Eric Wolf (Berlin: Mouton, 1984), 239–66.

3. Included in these statistics, aside from "apparitions" proper, are also those collateral phenomena attributed by worshipers to the presence of the Madonna: miraculous discoveries of images, lacrimations or the exudation of blood from devotional images, the animation of images, and then, in the area of interior and exterior auditory perceptions, locutions and messages. In any case, among these data, the percentage of apparitions in the narrowest sense is very high, roughly 79 percent. Among the cases included, moreover, there are also a few examples from Orthodox or Protestant areas; they are included in this list inasmuch as they can be considered to be part of a phenomenon of crossing religious boundaries, since they attracted interest as well in the Catholic community.

4. This figure is widely attributed to Father René Laurentin, but I have found no specific mention of it in any of the publications of the abbot.

5. *Enciclopedia delle religioni*, supplements to "Famiglia Cristiana," entry "Cristianesimo," undated, 83.

6. S. Picciaredda, "I confini dell'Impero," *Limes: Rivista Italiana di Geopolitica* 1 (2000): 18.

7. B. Billet, R. Laurentin, et al., *Vraies et fausses apparitions dans l'Église* (Paris: Edition P. Lethielleux, 1973).

8. G. Hierzenberger and O. Nedomansky, *Tutte le apparizioni della Madonna in 2000 anni di storia* (Casale Monferrato: Piemme, 1996).

9. http://web.frontier.net/Apparitions/.

10. http://members.aol.com/bjw1106/marian12.htm.

11. http://www.udayton.edu/mary/resources/aprtable.html.

12. http://members.aol.com/UticaCW/Mar-vis.html.

13. http://www.geocities.com/Athens/Atrium/2358/pmt_c3-2.htm.

14. R. Laurentin, *Le apparizioni della Vergine si moltiplicano* (Casale Monferrato: Piemme, 1989), 27.

15. "La mariologia tra il passato e il futuro: L'impulso della 'Redemptoris Mater,'" editorial in *La Civiltà Cattolica* 3310 (1988): 315.

16. W. Beinert, *Il culto di Maria oggi* (Rome: Edizioni Paoline, 1985), 13.

17. E. Fouilloux, "Le due vie della pietà cattolica nel XX secolo," in G. Alberigo and A. Riccardi, *Chiesa e papato nel mondo contemporaneo* (Bari: Laterza, 1990), 324.

18. William A. Christian, Jr., *Visionaries: The Spanish Republic and the Reign of Christ* (Berkeley: University of California Press, 1996), 8.

19. E. Pace, "Le possibili basi del fondamentalismo cattolico contemporaneo," in *Ai quattro angoli del fondamentalismo*, ed. R. Giammanco (Florence: La Nuova Italia, 1993), 357.

20. J. P. Willaime, "Le pentecôtisme: Contours et paradoxes d'un protestantisme émotionnel," *Archives des Sciences Sociales des Religions* 105 (February/March 1999): 24.

21. Quoted in R. Cannelli, "Chiese evangeliche o chiese americane? Il caso del Guatemala," *Limes: Rivista Italiana di Geopolitica* 1 (2000): 70.

22. Pace, "Le possibili," 369.

23. L. Catucci, "Genesi e fasi di sviluppo del movimento pentecostale: La situazione italiana," in F. Ferrarotti, G. De Lutiis, M. I. Macioti, and L. Catucci, *Studi sulla produzione sociale del sacro: Forme del sacro in un'epoca di crisi,* vol. 1 (Naples: Liguori, 1978), 298.

24. Ibid., 293.

25. Ibid., 312.

26. http://members.aol.com/bjw1106/marian10.htm. Bax dates the episode back to 1979 and attributes it to Father Branko: M. Bax, "The Madonna of Medjugorje: Religious Rivalry and the Formation of a Devotional Movement in Yugoslavia," *Anthropological Quarterly* 2 (April 1990): 65–66.

27. E. Gale, "Virgin Mary Takes Center Stage," *Detroit News,* 26 December 1998, 38.

28. See R. Giammanco, *L'immaginario al potere: Religione, media e politica nell'America reaganiana* (Rome: Antonio Pellicani, 1990), and especially, 303.

29. Ibid., 135–36.

30. Ibid., 135.

31. Pace, "Le possibili," 366.

32. T. W. Roberts, "Le destre religiose si coalizzano," *Jesus* 11 (November 1997); English version in *First Things* 43 (May 1994): 15–22.

33. Apolito, *"Dice che . . . ,"* 15.

34. Ibid.

35. S. M. Meo, "Fame di soprannaturale," *Jesus* 8 (March 1986): 25.

36. G. Caprile, "Circa i fatti di Medjugorje," *La Civiltà Cattolica* 3238 (1985): 363.

37. L. Rastello, "La Vergine strategica: Medjugorje come fulcro del nazionalismo croato," *Limes: Rivista Italiana di Geopolitica* 1 (2000): 136.

38. An example: 27 October 1987, in the *Corriere della Sera.*

39. The bishop of Mostar, Ratko Peric, has pointed out more than once that at Medjugorje there is no sanctuary; there is only a simple parish church dedicated to Saint James. But if the church of the apparitions is not a sanctuary in institutional terms, it is, de facto, for millions of pilgrims.

40. L. Rastello, "La Vergine strategica," 136.

41. D. Van Meter, "There Walks a Lady We All Know," Introduction to the Web site http://members.aol.com/UticaCW//Mar-lady.html.

42. J. Nickell, *Looking for a Miracle* (Amherst, NY: Prometheus Books, 1993), 188.

43. *Medjugorje Press Bulletin* 93 (17 June 1998): 1.

44. V. Messori, and J. Ratzinger, *Rapporto sulla Fede* (Cinisello Balsamo [Milan]: Edizioni Paoline, 1985), 113.

45. Laurentin, *Le apparizioni,* 59.

46. http://www.grancruzada.org/Imprima.htm.

47. E-mail quoted in Van Meter, "There Walks a Lady."

48. "Our Lady of Marmora": http://members.tripod.com/~marmora/visionaries.html.

49. Van Meter, "There Walks a Lady."

50. Rastello, "La Vergine strategica," 127.

51. On these aspects and in general on the Medjugorje case, see M. Bax, *Medjugorje: Religions, Politics, and Violence in Rural Bosnia* (Amsterdam: VU Uitgeverij, 1995).

52. Concerning Spain, see W. A. Christian, Jr., "Religious Apparitions and the Cold War in Southern Europe," in M. Hanagan, L. Page Moch, and W. TeBrake, eds., *Challenging Authority: The Historical Study of Contentious Politics* (Minneapolis: University of Minnesota Press, 1998), 111.

53. See the daily newspapers for 1 March 1988.

54. Laurentin, *Le apparizioni*, 198.

55. Pastoral Marian Organizations in the United States: http://www.dayton.edu/mary/pastoral.html.

56. http://www.catholicity.com/Cathedral/Medjugorje/default.html (and) http://walden.mo.net/~bagpiper/.

57. http://pages.prodigy.net/rhiner/index.html.

58. *Marian Prophecy & Current Events Discussion List*, message 2 January 1999.

59. http://web.frontier.net/Apparitions/scottsdale.html.

60. http://web.frontier.net/Apparitions/ruiz.html.

61. L. Bianchi and L. Dogo, *Medjugorje (Testimonianze 1981–85)* (Gera Lario, 1985), 49.

62. "A aparicâo em Belo Horizonte": http//www.geocities.com/Athens/Aegean/3074/sp1.htm.

63. "The Miracle Page," link to "Signs of the Holy Mother": http//www.mcn.org/1/Miracles/HolyMo2.html.

64. Quoted in R. Laurentin, "È stata la Vergine di Medjugorje che mi ha salvato," *Il segno del soprannaturale* 100 (August 1996): 32. [My translation. —*Trans.*]

65. Concerning these aspects, see C. Gallini, "La soglia del dolore dai racconti di guarigione di Lourdes," *Etnoantropologia* 2 (1993) 8–31; and J. Roma, "La mistica popular com a superació del sufriment i la por," lecture at the conference "Les Apariciónes Marianes," in Reus, Spain, 15–17 October 1992.

66. *Marian Discussion*, digest 7, 15 June 1998.

67. E. Barry, "The strange case of Audrey Santo," *Worcester Phoenix*, 26 December 1997/2 January 1998.

68. *Marian Discussion*, digest 28, 1 July 1998.

69. http://members.aol.com/bjw1106/marian14.htm.

70. http://www.jesustree.com/.

71. This case is described with interviews and eyewitness accounts in: http://members.xoo.com/sjs/mary0084.htm.

72. W. Christian, Jr., "Believers and Seers: The Expansion of an International Visionary Culture," in D. Albera, A. Block, and C. Bromberger, eds., *L'anthropologie de la Méditerranée/Anthropology of the Mediterranean* (Paris: Maisonneuve et Larose/Maison méditerranéenne des sciences de l'homme, 2001), 411.

73. *Marian Discussion*, digest 27, 30 June 1998.

74. http://web.tiscalinet.it/apparizione_cristo/storia.htm.

75. *Marian Discussion*, digest 295, 17 October 1998.

76. *Marian Prophecy,* message 23 October 1998.

77. To offer just one example: *Bad Lieutenant,* by Abel Ferrara (1992).

78. To offer just one example: *Box of Moonlight,* by Tom DiCillo (1996).

79. C. Ostwalt, "Vision of the End: Secular Apocalypse in Recent Hollywood Film," *Journal of Religion and Film* 2, no. 1 (April 1998).

80. *Marian Discussion,* digest 47, 14 July 1998.

81. *Marian Prophecy,* message 10 October 1998.

82. Message from Diane Ele in *Messages from Heaven,* digest 456, 29 January 1999.

83. Ibid., digest 297, 18 October 1998.

84. *Forum Yellowstone,* 28 April 1998.

85. Reported by Joyce Lang in *Marian Prophecy,* message 6 October 1998.

86. Ibid.

87. P. Mantero, *La Madonna di Medjugorje* (Milan: SugarCo, 1987), 48–49.

88. From the English translation, at http://members.tripod.com/~chonak/documents/m19870725_zanic.html.

89. From a letter to Mr. Boutet, 2 October 1997, at http://members.tripod.com/~chonak/documents/m19971002peric.html.

90. http://www.tlig.org/index.html.

91. Ibid.

92. *Il segno del soprannaturale* 100 (August 1996).

93. http://pages.prodigy.com/AmbassadorofGod/.

94. http://www.geocities.com/Athens/Agora/8571/index.html.

95. http://www.apparitions.org/sanbruno.html.

96. "The Kindness Society": http://www.kindness.org/requests.shtml.

97. http://web.frontier.net/Apparitions/sanbruno.html.

98. "Apparitions of the Blessed Virgin—1996 Developments": http://members.aol.com/bjw1106/marian96.htm.

99. As is pointed out by the correspondences of the mailing list *Messaggi Celesti* in this period.

100. http://www.tlig.org/it.html. [My translation. —*Trans.*]

101. http://webcon.com/enddays/mjeven.html.

102. ̦polito, "*Dice che . . . ,*" 148.

103. Personal e-mail from Ginny Lopez, the distributor of the messages of Al Scott on the Internet.

104. http://www.conyers.org/humanity/s8.htm.

105. http://www.tlig.org/index.html. [My translation. —*Trans.*]

106. R. Laurentin, "Apparizioni in USA: Gianna evangelizzazione e carità," *Il segno del soprannaturale* 100 (August 1996): 24.

107. Ibid.

108. Personal e-mail from Ginny Lopez, the distributor of the messages of Al Scott on the Internet.

109. "E ora la Madonna vuole che mi sposi," *La Repubblica* (28 April 1993).

110. http://www.culturewars.com/medj.htm.

111. Lucy Rooney and Robert Faricy, *Medjugorje Journal* (Chicago: Franciscan Herald Press, 1988), 75.

112. Ibid.

113. *Il segno del soprannaturale* 100 (August 1996).

114. http://www.geocities.com/Athens/Forum/6832/ind.

115. http://www.geocities.com/Athens/Forum/letterit.htm.

116. www.geocities.com/Athens/Agora/4190/.

117. Christian, "Believers and Seers," 409.

118. Apolito, *"Dice che . . . ,"* 17.

119. Ibid.

120. http://www.top.net/cathcom/mmrintro.htm.

121. http://www.shepherds-of-christ.org/.

122. Christian, "Believers and Seers," 411.

123. http://www.post1.com/home/avemaria/index.htm.

124. http://www.frontiernet.net/~vyyper/guardian.html.

125. C. Ameche and H. Hammons, *Do Whatever Love Requires* (Santa Barbara: Queenship, 1997).

126. *Apparition List,* message from Elizabeth Ann Stevens, 16 May 1995.

127. *Marian Prophecy . . . ,* message from Michael Coppi, 23 October 1998.

128. This case is reported with interviews and eyewitness accounts at http://members.xoo.com/sjs/mary0084.htm.

129. http://members.aol.com/bjw1106/marian98.htm.

130. http://members.aol.com/pelemeje/index.html.

131. http://members.aol.com/bjw1106/marian98.htm.

132. A. Desiderio, *Un cavallo di Troia americano, Limes: Rivista Italiana di Geopolitica;* available at http://members.xoom.it/IctrlU/limes2.htm.

133. G. Maritati, "Le nuove tecnologie, l'uomo, la religione," *Vita Pastorale* 6 (June 1998). See also the concerns of the pope in M. Muolo, "Formazione, accumulare non basta," *Avvenire,* 27 October 1998.

134. See sources in nn. 7–13 above.

Chapter 2

1. *Gaudium et spes,* sec. 37.

2. P. Bourdieu, *La parola e il potere* (Napoli: Guida, 1988), 15; English edition, Pierre Bourdieu, *Language and Symbolic Power,* translated by Gino Raymond and Matthew Adamson (Cambridge, Mass.: Harvard University Press, 1991).

3. For example, by Pope John Paul II, quoted in M. Politi, "L'Apocalisse secondo Wojtyla," *La Republica,* 23 April 1998.

4. Victor Witter Turner and Edith Turner, *Image and Pilgrimage in Christian Culture: Anthropological Perspectives* (New York: Columbia University Press, 1978), 149.

5. Lucy Rooney and Robert Faricy, *Medjugorje Journal* (Chicago: Franciscan Herald Press, 1988), 57–58. English edition: Robert L. Faricy and Lucy Rooney, *A Medjugorje Retreat* (New York: Alba House, 1989.)

6. R. Laurentin and L. Rupcíc, *La Vergine appare a Medjugorje: Un messaggio urgente dato al mondo in un paese marxista* (Brescia: Queriniana, 1984), 158. In English: René Laurentin and Rupcíc Ljudevit, *Is the Virgin Mary appearing at Medjugorje?: An Urgent Message for the World Given in a Marxist Country,* translated by Francis Martin (Washington, DC: Word Among Us Press, c1984).

7. Quoted in K. Juarez, *La Madonna di Medjugorje: Perché è vera perché appare* (Milan: Editoriale Albero, 1987), 21.

8. E. Sala and P. Mantero, *Il miracolo di Medjugorje* (Rome: Edizioni Mediterranee, 1986), 139.

9. Concerning these aspects, see D. Wojcik, *The End of the World as We Know It: Faith, Fatalism, and Apocalypse in America* (New York: New York University Press, 1997).

10. Ibid.

11. Quoted in *Skeptic News,* available online: http://www.skeptic.com/990111.html.

12. R. Giammanco, *L'immaginario al potere: Religione, media e politica nell'America reaganiana* (Rome: Antonio Pellicani, 1990), 90.

13. *New York Times,* 23 October 1984.

14. [My translation. —*Trans.*]

15. J. L. Sheler, "Dark Prophecies," *U.S. News* online: http://www.usnews.com/usnews/issue/971215/15prop.htm.

16. M. W. Cuneo, "The Vengeful Virgin: Case Studies in Contemporary American Catholic Apocalypticism," in *Millennium, Messiahs, and Mayhem,* edited by T. Robbins and S. Palmer (New York: Routledge, 1997). Edition consulted online at http://www.scitec.auckland.ac.nz/~kinf/Preprints/book/rebirth/comment/virg.htm.

17. Donna Haraway places at the focal point of her "Cyborg Manifesto" the ironic figure of the cyborg, "a hybrid of machine and organism, a creature of social reality as well as a creature of fiction." Donna Jeanne Haraway, *Simians, Cyborgs, and Women: The Reinvention of Nature* (New York: Routledge, 1991), 149.

18. P. Casati, "Oltre Internet: Economia di una visione," *Aut-Aut* 289–90 (January–April 1999): 177.

19. *La Republica,* 24 February 1996.

20. "The Three Days of Darkness: The Great Chastisement?": http://www.nd.edu/~mary/dark.html.

21. From Anita Sullivan to *Apparition List,* 31 December 1996.

22. Ibid.

23. *Marian Discussion,* digest 24, 29 June 1998.

24. Ibid., digest 20, 27 June 1998.

25. "What Has Just Happened? It's Called The Warning": http://geocities.com/Athens/Academy/7041/main.html.

26. *Messages from Heaven;* http://catalog.com/endtimes/.

27. http://www.thoughtport.com/CNF/victims/messages51398/.shtml.

28. http://www.netside.com/~lcoble/welcome.html.

29. Cfr. A. Hoplight Tapia, "Y2K: Apocalyptic Opportunism," *Enculturation* 3, no. 1 (Spring 2000), available online: (www.uta.edu./huma/enculturation/3_1/hoplight.html.

30. Wojcik, *The End of the World.*

31. *Marian Discussion,* digest 1115, 8 June 1998.

32. Ibid., digest 17, 24 June 1998.

33. *Marian Prophecy & Current Events Discussion List,* message 25 October 1998.

34. *Marian Discussion,* digest 25, 30 June 1998.

35. Ibid., digest 26, 30 June 1998.

36. Ibid., digest 27, 30 June 1998.

37. Ibid.

38. Ibid., digest 1114, 7 June 1998.

39. Ibid., digest 64, 22 July 1998.

40. *Marian Prophecy,* message 4 November 1998.

41. P. Apolito, *Apparitions of the Madonna at Oliveto Citra,* translated by William Christian, Jr. (University Park: Pennsylvania State University Press, 1988).

42. D. Gasking, "Mathematics and the World," in *Logic and Language,* 1st and 2nd ser., edited by Andrew Flew (New York: Anchor, Doubleday, 1965), 432.

43. *Eyedoctor's Site: The Warning:* http://www.se.mediaone.net/~hereiam/warning.html.

44. *Marian Discussion,* digest 220, 15 October 1998.

45. *Marian Prophecy,* message 15 October 1998.

46. Ibid.

47. *Messages from Heaven,* digest 293, 15 October 1998.

48. Message from Louise Starr Tomkiel, 1 October 1999, quoted in an e-mail from Daniela to *Messaggi Celesti* on 9 September 2000.

49. As is promised by the visionary Maureen Hughes from Malta: http://www.maltanet workresources.com/oasis/maureenhughes.html.

Chapter 3

1. See C. Ginzburg, "Idoli e immagini: Un passo di Origene e la sua fortuna," in *Occhiacci di legno: Nove riflessioni sulla distanza* (Milan: Feltrinelli, 1998), 118–35.

2. Victor Witter Turner and Edith Turner, *Image and Pilgrimage in Christian Culture: Anthropological Perspectives* (New York: Columbia University Press, 1978), 82.

3. D. Wojcik, "Polaroids from Heaven": Photography, Folk Religion, and the Miraculous Image Tradition at a Marian Apparition Site," *Journal of American Folklore* 109, no. 432 (1996): 140.

4. Ibid., 137.

5. C. Gallini, "Fotografie di fantasmi," *Campo* 14–15 (1983): 30.

6. See C. Gallini, *La sonnambula meravigliosa: Magnetismo e ipnotismo nell'Ottocento italiano* (Milan: Feltrinelli, 1983).

7. F. Faeta, *Strategie dell'occhio: Etnografia, antropologia, media* (Milan: Franco Angeli, 1995), 28.

8. W. Christian, Jr., "L'oeil de l'esprit: Les visionnaires basques en transe, 1931," *Terrain* 30 (March 1998): 10.

9. J. Eisenbud, "Paranormal Photography," in *Handbook of Parapsychology,* edited by B. B. Wolman (New York: Van Nostrand Reinhold, 1977), 414–16.

10. Wojcik, "Polaroids from Heaven," 135. The study mentioned is B. Allen, "The 'Image of Glass': Technology, Tradition, and the Emergence of Folklore," *Western Folklore* (1982): 85–103.

11. S. Marquez García, "Mary 'appears' near Elian," *Miami Herald,* 26 March 2000.

12. http://home.earthlink.net/~edgekay/jc/b1.html.

13. http://www.eclipse.it/Medjugorje/0.Italiano/VoltoSanto.html.

14. F. Romano, *Madonne che piangono: Visioni e miracoli di fine millennio* (Rome: Meltemi, 1997), 91; see Pino Casagrande, *Veggente-profeta e fotografo dell'invisibile?,* edited by P. Mantero (Udine: Il Segno, 1993).

15. "Catholic Apparitions of Jesus in Africa to Sr. Anna Ali" (25 April 1995): http://www.apparitions.org/Ali.homepage.html.

16. J. A. S. Collin de Plancy, *Dizionario delle reliquie e delle immagini miracolose* (Rome: Newton Compton, 1982), 215–18. In English: J. A. S. Collin de Plancy, *Dictionary of demonology,* edited and translated by Wade Baskin (New York: Philosophical Library, 1965.)

17. http://www.qbc.clic.net/~adurand/jesus.html.

18. The quotes are taken from the printed brochure of the sanctuary, and reappear with a few minor changes in the introduction to the Bayside Web page dedicated to the "miraculous photographs."

19. In fact, protests from local residents obliged the worshipers to move, in 1975, from Bayside to Flushing Meadows-Corona Park, but people continue to refer to the pilgrims as "Baysiders," i.e., worshipers from Bayside.

20. Wojcik, "Polaroids from Heaven," 134.

21. Ibid.

22. Ibid., 135.

23. Ibid., 132.

24. From the *Los Angeles Times,* 16 February 1997, quoted at http://www.ufomind.com/area51/list/1997/feb/a16–003.shtml.

25. *Messages from Heaven,* digest 293, 15 October 1998.

26. http://198.62.75.1/apparitions/http%3a/pr00038.htm.

27. http://www.conyers.org/forum/forum1.htm.

28. Wojcik, "Polaroids from Heaven," 142.

29. P. Virilio, *La macchina che vede* (Milan: SugarCo, 1989). In English: Paul Virilio, *The Vision Machine* (Bloomington: Indiana University Press, 1994).

30. Ibid., 47.

31. http://www.se.mediaone.net/~hereiam/mars1.html.

32. http://mcs.drexel.edu/~gcmastra/strange2.html.

33. U. Galimberti, *Psiche e techne* (Milan: Feltrinelli, 2000); and A. Gorz, *Miseria del presente, ricchezza del possibile* (Rome: Manifestolibri, 1998).

34. P. Apolito, *Apparitions of the Madonna at Oliveto Citra*, translated by William Christian, Jr. (University Park: Pennsylvania State University Press, 1988), 238.

35. N.a., *La Madonna a Medjugorje* (Citadella: Bertoncello Artigrafiche, 1985), 141.

36. R. Laurentin and L. Rupcíc, *La Vergine appare a Medjugorje: Un messaggio urgente dato al mondo in un paese marxista* (Brescia: Queriniana, 1984), 64–65.

37. C. Malanga and R. Pinotti, *I fenomeni B.V.M.: Le manifestazioni mariane in una nuova luce* (Milan: Mondadori, 1990), 275.

38. http://www.geocities.com/Heartland/Ranch/5691/fatimaf4i.html.

39. http://members.aol.com/servantson/Frame4.html.

40. I am indebted in this part of my essay to the discussion that I was able to hold, in Bassano Romano in September 2000, during the proceedings of the summer session of the Associazione Internazionale Ernesto De Martino, organized by Clara Gallini, with the participation of Clara Gallini, William Christian, Jr., Marlene Albert-Llorca, Nicola Gasbarro, Francesco Faeta, Vincenzo Padiglione, and others, all of whom I would like to thank, obviously without in any way implicating any of them in any analytical shortcomings of which I may be guilty.

41. C. Gallini, "Immagini da cerimonia: Album e videocassette da matrimonio," *Belfagor* 43, fasc. 6, 690.

42. G. Filoramo, *Le vie del sacro* (Turin: Einaudi, 1994), 28.

43. http://community-4.webt.net/JCOTO7MaryImage/index.html.

44. V. Zucconi, "Aspettando Dio in TV," *La Republica*, 26 March 1998.

45. R. Laurentin, *Le apparizioni della Vergine si moltiplicano* (Casale Monferrato: Piemme, 1989), 190.

46. J. Bubalo, "Mille incontri con la Madonna" (Padova: Edizioni Messaggero, 1985), 147; Janko Bubalo, *Ivanković, Vida, 1964—A Thousand Encounters with the Blessed Virgin Mary in Medjugorje: The Seer Vicka Speaks of Her Experiences* (Chicago: Friends of Medjugorje, c1987).

47. Laurentin and Rupcíc, *La Vergine appare a Medjugorje*, 67.

48. Ibid., 165.

49. P. Mantero, *La Madonna di Medjugorje* (Milan: SugarCo, 1987), 54.

50. Ibid., 92.

51. Ibid., 95.

52. http://www.geocities.com/Athens/Atrium/2358/ptm_stanley.htm.

53. Laurentin and Rupcíc, *La Vergine appare a Medjugorje*, 112.

54. http://members.tripod.com/~chonak/documents/m19971002peric.html.

55. U. Volli, *Il libro della comunicazione* (Milan: Il Saggiatore, 1994), 241.

56. Christopher describes this episode in *Marian Prophecy & Current Events Discussion List*, in a message 10 October 1998.

57. http://www.grancruzada.org/background.html.

58. "Signs of the Holy Mother": http://www.mcn.org/1/Miracles/HolyMo2.html.

59. http://www.conyers.org/Conyers Pilgrim's Forum.

60. Malanga and Pinotti, *I fenomeni B.V.M.*, 76.

61. http://www.geocities.com/Athens/Forum/2735/.

62. G. Beccaria, "Il fanatismo-killer incubo dell'Occidente," interview with Massimo Introvigne, in *La Stampa*, 24 December 1995.

63. *La Republica*, 28 March 1997.

64. M. Introvigne, *Il cappello del mago* (Milan: SugarCo, 1990), 118–19.

65. http://www.geocities.com/Heartland/Ranch/5691/Fatimaf2i.html.

66. K. Hayes, "40th Parallel: A Highly Charged Occult Ley Line?," *Despatch Magazine* (1992), a publication of the organization Endtimes Ministries Christian Resource Centre, now to be found on the Web site http://www.despatch.cth.com.au/Transcripts/ufo2_app5.html; this information was in turn published by the Italian magazines *Gente* and *Oggi* and is now present in many "miraculous" Web sites online.

67. V. Aversano, "La stella polare e la Madonna di Lourdes," *Avvenire, settimanale della Diocesi di Salerno*, 7 December 1991.

68. From the report by Ricardo Castañon, which was available at http://www.conyers.org/cast.htm before Nancy Fowler broke off her association with Our Loving Mother's Children. But documentation on the experiment can still be found at many Web sites, for instance at http://members.aol.com/bbu84/biblicalstupidity/science.htm.

69. http://www.conyers.org/tesor.htm, now in http://members.aol.com/bbu84/biblical stupidity/science.htm.

70. http://www.conyers.org/body.htm, now in http://members.aol.com/bbu84/biblical stupidity/science.htm.

71. E. Sala and P. Mantero, *Il miracolo di Medjugorje* (Rome: Edizioni Mediterranee, 1986), 71–73.

72. Ibid., 95.

73. Ibid., 71.

74. R. Laurentin, *Racconto e messaggio delle apparizioni di Medjugorje* (Brescia: Queriniana, 1987), 179.

75. Ibid.

76. Ibid.

77. Apolito, *Apparitions of the Madonna*, 74.

78. Ibid., 84–85.

79. H. Joyeux and R. Laurentin, *Études médicales et scientifiques sur les apparitions de Medjugorje* (Paris: OEIL, 1985).

80. Scientific dossier on Medjugorje, edited by L. Frigerio, L. Bianchi, and G. Mattalia, self-published, 1986.

81. *Press Bulletin* 90 (6 May 1998).

82. *Press Bulletin* 109 and 143.

83. M. Margnelli and G. Gagliardi, "Le apparizioni della Madonna da Lourdes a Medjugorje," *Riza Scienze*, monographic issue 16 (July 1987): 20.

84. Ibid., 93.

85. Ibid., 39.

86. P. A. Gramaglia, *Verso un "rilancio" mariano? Voci d'oltre terra* (Turin: Claudiana, 1983), 84n19.

87. Margnelli and Gagliardi, "Le apparizioni," 38.

88. M. Margnelli, *L'estasi* (Rome: Sensibili alle Foglie, 1996), 58.

89. Margnelli and Gagliardi, "Le apparizioni," 39.

90. See for instance G. Rouget, *Musica e trance* (Turin: Einaudi, 1986), 52. In English, Gilbert Rouget, *Music and Trance: A Theory of the Relations between Music and Possession* (Chicago: University of Chicago Press, 1985).

91. Quotations in Sala and Mantero, *Il miracolo di Medjugorje*, 112.

92. Margnelli and Gagliardi, "Le apparizioni," 93.

93. Quotations in Sala and Mantero, *Il miracolo di Medjugorje*, 123.

94. R. Fischer, "A Cartography of Ecstatic and Meditative States," *Science* 174 (1971): 874–904. The reference of the two Italian authors to this model is found in Margnelli and Gagliardi, "Le apparizioni," 17.

95. Gallini, *La sonnambula.*

96. C. Gallini, *Il miracolo e la sua prova: Un etnologo a Lourdes* (Naples: Liguori, 1998), 157.

97. http://www.conyers.org/humanity/s8.htm.

98. Ibid.

Chapter 4

1. G. Gilder, *Life after Television* (Knoxville: Whittle Direct Books, 1990), 17–18.

2. Ibid., 24.

3. Pierre Lévy, *Becoming Virtual: Reality in the Digital Age,* translated from the French by Robert Bononno (New York: Plenum Trade, 1998), 25.

4. Quoted in F. Colombo, *Confucio nel computer* (Milan: Rizzoli, 1998), 44.

5. Ibid., 46.

6. D. de Kerckhove, *Brainframes: Mente, tecnologia, mercato* (Bologna: Baskerville, 1993), 69, 178. [Excerpt is my translation. —*Trans.*]

7. Ibid., 178–79.

8. C. Formenti, *Incantati dalla rete: Immaginari, utopie e conflitti nell'epoca di Internet* (Milan: Cortina, 2000), 132–33.

9. *Corriere della Sera,* 12 July 2000.

10. A. Berretti and V. Zambardino, *Internet: Avviso ai naviganti* (Rome: Donzelli, 1995 and 1996), 97.

11. De Kerckhove, *Brainframes,* 143. [Excerpt is my translation. —*Trans.*]

12. M. Augé, *An Anthropology for Contemporaneous Worlds* (Stanford: Stanford University Press, 1999), 59.

13. Marc Augé, *The War of Dreams: Studies in Ethno Fiction* (London: Pluto Press, 1999), 7.

14. Augé, *An Anthropology,* 95.

15. Quoted in Marc Augé, *Non-Places: Introduction to an Anthropology of Supermodernity,* translated by John Howe (New York: Verso, 1995), 92.

16. Augé, *An Anthropology,* 95.

17. Toni Morrison, *Sula* (New York: Knopf, 1974), 118–19.

18. G. Gilder, *Conclusione: La vita dopo la televisione* (Rome: Castelvecchi, 1955); in English: George Gilder, *Life after Television* (New York: Norton, 1994). [My translation; excerpt appears only in Italian edition. —*Trans.*]

19. Colombo, *Confucio nel computer*, 124.

20. Ibid., 125.

21. Ibid., 46.

22. Ibid., 68.

23. *La Repubblica*, 9 September 1998. Similar advice was provided by the Italian Pediatriacs Association) following an investigation of the use of chat rooms by Italian children: see *Avvenire*, 14 November 2001.

24. W. Christian, Jr., *Person and God in a Spanish Valley* (New York: Seminar Press, 1972), 48, 181–82.

25. Victor Witter Turner and Edith Turner, *Image and Pilgrimage in Christian Culture: Anthropological Perspectives* (New York: Columbia University Press, 1978), 209.

26. C. Gallini, *Il miracolo e la sua prova: Un etnologo a Lourdes* (Naples: Liguori, 1998), 149.

27. Shrine of Saint Jude: http://www.ivic.net/~stjude/home23.html.

28. Concerning this famous case of statues weeping and moving, see W. Christian, Jr., *Moving Crucifixes in Modern Spain* (Princeton: Princeton University Press, 1992).

29. http://grancruzada.org.

30. http://web.frontier.net/Apparitions/sanbruno.html.

31. http://www.mcn.org/1/Miracles/HolyMo2.html.

32. http://www.mcn.org/1/Miracles/weeping.html.

33. http://www.stpaulus.it/madre/0198md/0198matb.htm.

34. For Lourdes, see Gallini, *Il miracolo e la sua prova*, 111.

35. Howard Rheingold, *The Virtual Community: Homesteading on the Electronic Frontier* (Cambridge, MA: MIT Press, 2000), 72.

36. Turner and Turner, *Image and Pilgrimage*, 278.

37. http://www.carpatho-rusyn.org/spirit/limanova.htm.

38. http://www2.siol.net/ext/kurescek/it/itstran.html.

39. Lévy, *Becoming Virtual*, 24–26.

40. Ibid., 74–75.

41. *Catholicity*, digest 217, 13 July 1998.

42. *Marian Discussion*, digest 44, 13 July 1998.

43. Lévy, *Becoming Virtual*, 63.

44. G. Balandier, *Il disordine: Elogio del movimento* (Bari: Dedalo, 1991).

45. Ibid., 205.

46. There are already portals that ask visitors to report links to sites that are now dead, and there has been more than one initiative to collect and archive the dead sites.

47. See K. Kelly, *Nuove regole per un mondo nuovo* (Florence: Ponte alle Grazie, 1999).

48. http://www.catholicgoldmine.com.

49. http://www.siticattolici.it/.

50. Brother John Raymond, *Catholics on the Internet* (Roseville, CA: Prima Lifestyles, 1997).

51. Thomas C. Fox., *Catholicism on the Web*, 1st ed. (New York: MIS Press, 1997).

52. Igino Domanin and Stefano Porro, *Il Web sia con voi* (Milan: Mondadori, 2001).

53. Uniform Resource Location.

54. Berretti and Zambardino, *Internet*, 34.

55. F. Carlini, *Lo stile del web* (Turin: Einaudi, 1999), 96.

56. The *Catholic Woman's* Web ring.

57. *Immaculata* Web ring.

58. *For the Love of the Blessed Virgin Mary* Web ring.

59. *CATH* Web ring.

60. http://www.geocities.com/Heartland/1373/.

61. http://web.arca.net/miriam/.

62. To be specific, HyperBanner Italia, Spanish Banner Intercambio de Enlaces, LinkExchange Member, SmartClicks: Target Advertising For Free, SmartAge.

63. http://www.geocities.com/TheTropics/7177/safe.htm.

64. Lévy, *Becoming Virtual*, 27.

65. Joyce Lang discusses this case in *Marian Prophecy & Current Events Discussion List*, in a message 10 January 1999.

66. See the account in http://web.frontier.net/Apparitions/vas_rome.html.

67. *Medjugorje* (Genoa) 49 (December 1995).

68. Both in *Il segno del soprannaturale* 106 (February 1997).

69. G. Filoramo, *Le vie del sacro* (Turin: Einaudi, 1994), 19.

70. O. Calabrese, *L'età neobarocca* (Bari: Laterza, 1991).

71. http://www.spiritual-wholeness.org/.

72. http://www.housetop.com/welcome1.htm.

73. http://easyweb.easynet.co.uk/answers.htm.

74. Ibid.

75. www.osho.org/products/insearch.htm.

76. P. D. Ouspensky, *In Search of the Miraculous* (London: Routledge & Kegan, 1950).

77. E. Milingo, *The World in Between* (Maryknoll, NY: Orbis 1984).

78. http://www.miracles-course.org/Miracles1c.html.

79. M. Introvigne, *Il cappello del mago* (Milan: SugarCo, 1990), 105.

80. http://www.dreamscape.com/morgana/.

81. http://www.meninblack.com/meninblackmag/Volume1/weeping.html.

82. http://www.serve.com/shadows/mystery.htm.

83. Letter to soc.culture.italian, 26 May 1998.

84. L. Berzano, "Le generazioni dei new agers," *Quaderni di sociologia* 19 (1999): 9.

85. http://www.akasha.de/miracles/.

86. http://www.mcn.org/1/Miracles/HolyMo2.html.

87. http://www.mcn.org/1/Miracles/weeping.html.

88. http://www.sirius.com/~monte/miracles.html and http://www.mcn.org/1/Miracles/Encounters2.html.

89. *Marian Discussion*, digest 1116, 9 June 1998.

90. http://www.spiritweb.org/.

91. http://www.angelfire.com/hi/nanc/iangels.html

92. Introvigne, *Il cappello del mago*, 123.

93. http://www.eclipse.it/Medjugorje/0_Italiano/VoltoSanto.html.

94. http://watch.pair.com/marian.html.

95. http://internet.com/~ripp/marian.htm.

96. http://internet.com/~ripp/thirtee.htm.

97. http://churchnet.ucsm.ac.uk/news/files/news55.htm.

98. http://www.christusrex.org/www1/news/11-96/es11-28-96.html.

99. http://www.winkingjesus.com.

100. http://www.smh.com.au/computers/archive/961217/columns/171296-columns 1.html.

101. http://www.winkingjesus.com.

102. http://www.geocities.com/NapaValley/6665/jesus.html.

103. http://www.angelfire.com/ct/gayjesus/.

104. http://www.thoughtport.com/CNF/victims/messag51398/.shtml.

105. http://members.aol.com/jesus316/index.htm.

106. http://www.hotwired.com/netizen/96/20/katz1a.html.

107. http://www.qecmedia.com/nunbun/index.html.

108. *Newsweek*, 14 August 1978.

109. *Chicago Tribune*, 23 May 1991.

110. http://www.isna.org/HWA/Summer95/Summer95.html.

111. Lévy, *Becoming Virtual*, 16 and 26.

112. To cite the title of the introduction to a famous book by the American anthropologist James Clifford, *The Predicament of Culture: Twentieth-Century Ethnography Literature, and Art* (Cambridge, MA: Harvard University Press, 1988).

113. G. Dorfles, *L'intervallo perduto* (Milan: Garzanti, 1980).

114. Clifford, *The Predicament of Culture*, 27 and 30.

115. M. Poggini, "Ecco la foto che ha scandalizzato l'Europa," *Sette giorni illustrati del "Corriere della Sera"* 21, 21 May 1988, 21.

116. L. Asnaghi, "E a Milano le pistole arrivano in passerella," *La Republica*, 13 January 1999.

117. "The Virgin Mary and Condom," 13 March 1998; http://www.nzine.co.nz/hot/virginmary.html; or http://dhushara.tripod.com/book/rebirth/comment/mad.htm.

118. To cite one example, consider this headline from *La Repubblica*, 12 January 1991: *Non è Madonna, sono solo visioni* (It's Not the Virgin Mary, They're Just Visions).

119. http://www.tlig.org/index.html.

120. http://www.fatima.org/core.html.

121. http://www.holylove.org/.

122. http://web.frontier.net/Apparitions/.

123. http://www.truecatholic.org/pope/.

124. http://www.erols.com/dmyles/.

125. http://members.aol.com/UticaCW/Mar-Review.html.

126. http://www.miriam.net/banner/faq_banner.htm.

127. C. Ginzburg, "Folklore, magia, religione," in *Storia d'Italia*, vol. 1, *I caratteri originari* (Turin: Einaudi, 1972), 646.

128. S. Gruzinski, *La guerra delle immagini* (Milan: SugarCo, 1991). In English: Serge Gruzinski, *Images at War: Mexico from Columbus to Blade Runner (1492–2019)*, translated by Heather MacLean (Durham, NC: Duke University Press, 2001).

129. W. Christian, Jr., "Believers and Seers: The Expansion of an International Visionary Culture," in D. Albera, A. Block, and C. Bromberger, eds., *Anthropology of the Mediterranean* (Paris: Maisonneuve et Larose/Maison méditerranéenne des sciences de l'homme, 2001), 408.

130. By means of his mailing-list address: njkoti@nji.com.

131. *Apparitions and Eucharistic Miracles:* http://198.62.75.1/www1/apparitions/.

132. Personal letter, 10 September 1998.

133. *Apparitions and Eucharistic Miracles:* http://198.62.75.1/www1/apparitions/.

134. http://www.geocities.com/CapitolHill/9272/endtime.html.

135. http://www.geocities.com/Athens/Academy/7041/main.html.

136. http://hometown.aol.com/spiritlife/index.htm.

137. In *Profezie On Line,* 10 September 2000.

138. *Marian Discussion,* digest 1, 10 June 1998.

139. *Profezie On Line,* message 12 September 2000.

140. *Apparition List,* 31 December 1996.

141. *Marian Discussion,* digest 35, 6 July 1998.

142. Ibid., digest 50, 16 July 1998.

143. "La Venuta intermedia di Gesù," curated by Father Angelo Maria da Loreto, at www.geocities.com/Athens/Atrium/2358/ptm_approf_rifless3.htm.

144. Cristina to *Profezie On Line* on 12 September 2000.

145. http://www.freeweb.org/religioni/messaggidivina sapien/homenet.html.

146. E. Jünger, *I prossimi titani: Conversazioni con Ernst Jünger,* edited by A. Gnoli and F. Volpi (Milan: Adelphi, 1997), 117.

147. P. Bogatyrëv and R. Jakobson, "Il folclore come forma di creazione autonoma," *Strumenti critici* 1, fasc. 3 (1967).

148. See P. Casati, "Oltre Internet: Economia di una visione," *Aut-Aut* 289–90 (January–April 1999): 179.

149. *Marian Discussion,* digest 1, 10 June 1998.

150. Ibid.

151. *Messages from Heaven,* digest 294, 16 October 1998.

152. Ibid., digest 297, 18 October 1998.

153. *Marian Discussion,* digest 1115, 8 June 1998.

154. Ibid., digest 1, 10 June 1998.

155. *Messages from Heaven,* digest 297, 18 October 1998.

156. Ibid., digest 279, 6 October 1998.

157. Ibid., digest 1116, 9 June 1998.

158. *Marian Prophecy,* message 22 October 1998.

159. Ibid., message 23 October 1998.

160. *Marian Discussion,* digest 2, 11 June 1998.

161. http://users.iol.it/mir.59/.

162. http://userspace.ats.it/free/maxconti/index.html.

163. http://www.all-veda.com/.

164. Lévy, *Becoming Virtual,* 61.

165. http://www.freeweb.org/freeweb/ceddipa /.

166. http://www.yesic.com/~mtota/index_b.html.

167. http://www.angelfire.com/nj/transnate/.

168. G. Mantovani, "Le mobili frontiere della realtà," in *La realtà del virtuale,* edited by J. Jacobelli (Rome-Bari: Laterza, 1998), 105–6.

169. S. Turkle, *La vita sullo schermo* (Milan: Apogeo, 1997). In English: Sherry Turkle, *Life on the Screen: Identity in the Age of the Internet* (New York: Simon & Schuster, c. 1995); see K. Hafner, "At Heart of Cyberstudy: The Human Essence," *New York Times,* 18 June 1998.

170. *Marian Discussion,* digest 59, 20 July 1998.

171. Ibid., digest 39, 10 July 1998.

172. Ibid., digest 63, 21 July 1998.

173. Ibid., digest 44, 13 July 1998.

174. Ibid., digest 46, 14 July 1998

175. Ibid., digest 45, 13 July 1998.

176. Ibid., digest 48, 14 July 1998.

177. Ibid., digest 46, 14 July 1998.

178. Ibid., digest 63, 21 July 1998.

179. Ibid., digest 224, 17 October 1998.

180. Ibid., digest 20, 12 June 1998.

181. Ibid., digest 91, 23 June 1998.

182. Ibid., digest 1113, 6 June 1998.

183. *Piccolo Gregge,* 9 July 1998.

184. *Catholicity,* digest nos. 89 and 90, 22 June 1998.

185. Colombo, *Confucio nel computer,* 117.

186. *Marian Discussion,* digest 64, 22 July 1998.

187. *Catholicity,* digest 107, 24 June 1998.

188. Berretti and Zambardino, *Internet,* 49.

189. V. Kaufman, *L'equivoco epistolare* (Parma: Pratiche, 1994), 7. [My translation. —*Trans.*]

190. *Catholicity,* digest 87, 22 June 1998.

191. *Marian Discussion*, digest 92, 30 July 1998.

192. Berretti and Zambardino, *Internet*, 47.

193. *Marian Prophecy*, message 12 November 1998.

194. Newsgroup: torfree.religion.discussion.alt.religion.apparitions, 24 February 1998.

195. *Marian Prophecy*, message 16 January 1999.

196. *Marian Discussion*, digest 59, 20 July 1998.

197. Ibid., digest 270, 11 November 1998.

198. Ibid., digest 260, 4 November 1998.

199. Ibid.

200. *Catholicity*, digest 16, 11 June 1998.

201. *Marian Prophecy*, message 8 October 1998.

202. Ibid., message 10 October 1998.

203. *Marian Discussion*, digest 56, 19 July 1998.

204. *Messages from Heaven*, digest 48, 14 July 1998.

205. Ibid., digest 53, 18 July 1998.

206. Ibid.

207. S. Abbruzzese, "Catholicisme et territoire: Pour une entrée en matière," *Archives des Sciences Sociales des Religions* 107 (July–September 1999): 7n8.

208. Ibid., entire issue. Cf. articles by Abbruzzese, Garelli, and Courcy. Cf. also P. Apolito, *La religione degli italiani* (Rome: Editori Riuniti, 2001).

209. Domanin and Porro, *Il Web sia con voi*, 101.

210. *Marian Discussion*, digest 39, 10 July 1998.

INDEX